ISAIAH

SCROLL OF A PROPHETIC HERITAGE

ISAIAH
SCROLL OF A
PROPHETIC HERITAGE

by

William L. Holladay

The Pilgrim Press
New York

Holladay, William Lee.
    Isaiah, scroll of a prophetic heritage.

    Bibliography: p. 239.
    Includes index.
    1. Bible.   O.T.   Isaiah—Criticism,
interpretation, etc.   I. Title.
BS1515.2.H59   1987   224'.106   86-25154
ISBN 0-8298-0658-X
The Pilgrim Press, 132 West 31 Street, New York, NY 10001

Contents

Foreword   vii

Orientation

I. *Four Centuries of a Prophetic Heritage*   3

The First Isaiah

II. *God is High and Holy, and Isaiah is his Prophet*   25
III. *The Breakdown of Community*   46
IV. *Nations on the March*   66
V. *Renewal After Disaster?*   91

"Second Isaiah"

VI. *A Return for Exiles*   117
VII. *The Folly of Idols, and the Call to Suffer*   139

"Third Isaiah"

VIII. *The Grandeur and Misery of those who Returned*   163

Other "Isaiahs"

IX. *Visions for a People Forgotten*   189

Summation

X. *Prophets for the Centuries*   215

Further Readings   239
Notes   242
Index of Passages   261

Foreword

THIS LITTLE BOOK is intended as a guide to the Old Testament book of Isaiah for people who have had no specialized training in biblical matters. It is conceived as a companion to my earlier study on Jeremiah,[1] but it is in no sense a sequel and may be read without any reference to that earlier work. Readers who wish to use both the Isaiah and Jeremiah studies, however, should be reminded that the story of Jeremiah (626-585 B.C.) comes chronologically between the events described in this book in Chapters II-V (742-701 B.C.) and in Chapters VI-VII (540 B.C.).

The two study guides may be companions, but it turns out that the nature of the book of Isaiah is different enough from the nature of the book of Jeremiah to demand a rather different approach. Though the book of Jeremiah offers its share of difficulties to the reader who wishes to read it from beginning to end, at least it offers the words and deeds of the one prophet Jeremiah. Furthermore, it offers enough biographical information to allow us to reconstruct a kind of story line, so that we come to know a rather remarkable person from ancient times about whom much is known.

Not so with the book of Isaiah. As we shall see in Chapter II, we are given very few biographical details at all about the prophet Isaiah. The man we meet is little more than a disembodied voice—an extraordinarily powerful and compelling voice, it is true, but simply a voice nonetheless. And the book of Isaiah further turns out on investigation to reveal a whole array of voices, more even than the two (the first Isaiah and "Second Isaiah") about whom scholars most often speak.

These two circumstances—our inability to find much more than a "voice" for the name Isaiah, and the multiplicity of voices within the book—make it necessary for this study guide to focus not on the nature of a *person*, as was the case with the study guide on Jeremiah, but rather on the nature of a *book* of 66 chapters. This focus of the present study may make it a bit less attractive at first glance than the Jeremiah study; after all, we would all rather get engrossed in a book about a *person* who risked his well-being and his career for the sake of godly proclamation than we would in a book about a *book*.

But I hope the reader will persevere. The word "scroll" in the subtitle may help a bit. "Scroll" suggests the Dead Sea Scrolls and the romance of archeology, and we shall be touching on that a bit. But "scroll" also suggests an ancient manuscript in the making, and this is important, too, reminding us that the book of Isaiah did not start out as 66 neatly printed chapters in the middle of our Bibles but rather took shape over a long period of time. The first item on our agenda, then, is to try to make clear how the whole array of 66 chapters came into being, so far as we can determine. Scholars have been working on problems like this for a long time, and people who like to read detective stories can share a bit in the detective work which scholars undertake when they try to unravel the complicated sequence of events of speaking and writing in ancient times which the book of Isaiah embodies.

Thus whenever groups undertake to examine the book of Isaiah with me, questions like the following seem to arise. Why do we have to wait until chapter 6 to learn of Isaiah's call rather than to find it in chapter 1, as we do with the calls of Jeremiah and Ezekiel and Hosea in those respective books? And why have the translators of the *New English Bible* placed 5:24-25 after 10:4? And above all, how can we make any coherent sense out of all the poems and narratives which come and go through the book of Isaiah without obvious rime or reason in their ordering? Readers of a biblical book need answers to these questions as well as to questions about the messages of the specific passages they read, and this need must be taken seriously. The present study is an attempt to fill that need.

So Chapter I offers a preliminary survey into the *structure*, the *ordering process*, of the book of Isaiah. Chapters II-V deal with the first Isaiah, Isaiah of Jerusalem, the original Isaiah, concentrating on four aspects of his message: (1) his high view of God, (2) his sense of the breakdown of the community of Israel, (3) his conviction of the meaning of the international events of his day, and (4) his expectation of what God could make of Israel after the dislocations of the disasters to which he pointed. Chapters VI and VII deal with the message of the so-called "Second Isaiah," whose words are to be found in chapters 40-55. Chapter VIII deals with the so-called "Third Isaiah," material in chapters 56-66—material which may, as a matter of fact, stem from several prophets rather than from a single one. Chapter IX deals with other later prophetic material which found its way into the Isaiah collection. And finally Chapter X tries to sort all this out in terms of the meaning the material had for later generations, particularly to the New Testament Christian community, and what the material might mean to us today.

Since we cannot depend upon a biography of Isaiah and his followers, much of our study will be concerned with various passages of prophetic utterance, verse by verse, as we try to grasp their meaning in the light of the historical circumstances and the theological hungers which stimulated them.

Now there may well be some readers, nurtured on particular traditions within the Jewish or Christian faiths, who are unhappy about or even hostile toward the idea of the multiple authorship of the book of Isaiah. Such traditions have sometimes even made their conviction about the single authorship of Isaiah a touchstone of their faith. Present-day Roman Catholics, accustomed to sharing in the biblical scholarship reflected in this book, may be surprised to learn that the Pontifical Commission on biblical matters in 1908 forbade the view that there was more than one Isaiah;[2] but the teaching of the Roman Catholic Church on this matter has changed,[3] and the teaching of other traditions has been changing too. I invite readers who are uneasy about this matter to learn about recent computer work which has been done on the text of the book of Isaiah (see Chapter I) and in general to keep an open mind.

I hope that readers will keep an open mind, too, on a related matter, and that is the degree to which Christians are justified in seeing in various passages of the book of Isaiah direct reference to Jesus Christ. Now of course Christians who so view the passages are doing precisely what the gospel writers themselves did: I count 28 quotations from or reminiscences of the book of Isaiah in the Gospel of Matthew—indeed they are doing precisely what Jesus himself is recorded as doing (see Luke 4:16-21). But this issue, too, may be more complicated than the reader at first recognizes, and I hope that the reader of this study will allow for the complications of the question to work on his or her awareness. There will be several occasions to deal with this matter in the course of this book, particularly in Chapters IV, V, VII, and X.

This caution leads to the question of the contrasting use which Jews and Christians have made of the book of Isaiah. There is no way I can be neutral on this matter: I am a Christian, and this study guide is written with the needs in mind of groups which take the New Testament as seriously as they do the Old. But in the summing up which I do, particularly in Chapter X, I have done my utmost to be fair to Jewish positions. I cannot expect Jewish readers to agree with my suggestions about the meaning the book of Isaiah has for Christian communities, but at the same time I hope I have not misunderstood Jewish perceptions.

All of us, Jews and Christians, are indebted to numberless copyists, translators, commentators, and scholars who have preserved the book of Isaiah for us and have brightened our understanding by their insight. I shall do my best to share with the reader the consensus of present-day scholarly work on the book of Isaiah, but of course not everything I offer will be acceptable to all scholars. Many matters about the book of Isaiah are in dispute, and some will perhaps still be in dispute until the last trumpet sounds. Because so many matters are uncertain, I have offered substantiation for my presentation, and documentation, at many points, through notes. These notes are gathered at the end of the book so that they need not distract the reader who prefers not to bother with them. But they are there for the curious reader who may wish to follow out some point in more detail. Indeed, a few notes may be helpful only to the occasional student who wishes to pursue some issue on the farther shores of scholarship (especially in the matter of commentaries on Isaiah written in earlier centuries, a topic explored in Chapter X). But, whether the reader bothers with the notes or not, he or she is invited to share the scholarly tolerance for uncertainty on many questions. I may say that only occasionally have I presented views of my own which differ from the consensus of scholars. The most important of these are the matter of "self-extended oracles" discussed in Chapters III and IV; my understanding of the new names in 9:6 of the marvelous king, discussed in Chapter V; and my suggestion of the authenticity of 24:1-3 to the first Isaiah, discussed in Chapter IX.

The book of Isaiah is too long to allow me to deal in this study with every passage, but I hope I have covered enough passages to allow the reader to get a grip on the subject. To help the reader, an index of scripture passages is offered at the end of the book.

I urge the reader to look up the references to passages in Isaiah or elsewhere which are under discussion, or at least a good number of them. Isaiah is the longest book in the Bible except for the Psalms, and it makes no sense for me to insert large blocks of the biblical text itself into a study guide like this. Although the explanations may make some sense without a Bible at hand, they obviously make more sense if the text which is being discussed is handy.

In the same fashion as was my practice in the study guide to Jeremiah, all references to a chapter (or to chapter and verse) in *Arabic* numerals, unaccompanied by any reference to a biblical book, are to be understood as referring to passages in the book of Isaiah. The only exception to this practice is to be found in an extended discussion of material from 2 Kings in Chapter IV, but the references are obvious at that point. Further, all verse numbers will be to the *English* versification rather than to the *Hebrew* one, where these differ. It should also be noted that "verse 5a" means "the first half of verse 5," and so "verse 5b" refers to the second half. I shall also use the abbreviation "vs." for "verse," and "vss." for "verses."

The basis for this study is the English of the *Revised Standard Version* unless otherwise indicated. But there will be occasional references to the renderings of the *Jerusalem Bible*, the *New English Bible*, the *New American Bible*, and the *New Jewish Version*,[4] where appropriate. And it should be clear that chapters designated by *Roman* numerals refer to chapters *within this present study guide*.

So, thanks once again to college students, seminary students, and above all to lay men and women in various churches in the Chicago area, in the Near East, and in New England who have constantly kept me on my toes regarding the book of Isaiah by their witness and their questions. And finally, thanks to the Rev. Mr. Norbert E. Johnson, of the First Covenant Church of Omaha, Nebraska, who asked me to write a book about Isaiah.

Orientation

CHAPTER I

Four Centuries of a
Prophetic Heritage

IN THE WILDERNESS near the northwest shore of the Dead Sea, in the spring of 1947, an Arab shepherd boy found some scrolls in a pottery jar in a cave. About a year later, one of these scrolls came into the hands of John Trever, at that time a young graduate student at the American School of Oriental Research[1] in Jerusalem. Despite the supply shortages and power failures of the 1948 Arab-Israeli war, he managed to make a series of color photographs of the scroll. It turned out to be a great scroll of the book of Isaiah, now one of the most famous of the Dead Sea Scrolls, a complete Hebrew text of all 66 chapters of the book of Isaiah in a scribal handwriting which, to Hebrew scholars, is wonderfully readable. The date the scroll was copied, scholars say, was about 100 B.C., or a few years after.[2] Readers who want to gain some idea of its appearance can see two color photographs of it in Volume 12 of *The Interpreter's Bible*,[3] pp. 632-633 (plates 8 and 9); the scroll itself is now on exhibit in the "Shrine of the Book," a museum devoted to the Dead Sea Scrolls in Jerusalem.

The excitement which this discovery caused in 1948 can be gauged by the fact that up to that time the earliest Hebrew manuscript of Isaiah known to the world was part of a manuscript of the prophets, dated to A.D. 895, in a synagogue in Cairo.[4] Now, suddenly, we had at hand a manuscript a thousand years older, a thousand years closer to Isaiah than anything we had seen before. Further research into the fragments of other Dead Sea Scrolls yielded a good dozen more portions of Isaiah manuscripts, some originating from at least the century before the great Isaiah

3

scroll.[5] It is plain that the book of Isaiah was the favorite prophetic book in the Dead Sea Scroll community, as it has been a favorite in many other Jewish and Christian communities before and since. The Dead Sea Scroll community also produced commentaries on passages from Isaiah. (For some of this material, see Chapter X.)

The great Isaiah scroll measures 24 feet in length—66 chapters is a long text, after all—covering 54 columns of writing. It must have been a tedious procedure for an ancient reader to turn the rollers of the scroll to find the passages he wanted, particularly without the benefit of any chapter and verse references (for these would be an innovation of much later times). When Jesus consulted the text of Isaiah at his synagogue in Nazareth (Luke 4:16-21), it was a *scroll* he consulted, rather than a "book" bound at the spine as the *Revised Standard Version* text would seem to suggest. The idea of binding leaves of text together for easier reading was evidently first worked out by Christians living at the end of the first century A.D.[6] It took time to find the spot one wanted. "He opened the book [understand "scroll"] and *found* the place where it was written. . ." (vs. 17).

We realize, then, that because of the make-up of today's printed Bibles it is much easier for a modern reader to find his or her way through the long book of Isaiah than it was for an ancient reader; but still, the modern reader encounters many barriers to smooth reading. Most of the passages of the book claim to be words from God, yet one finds the subject matter changing abruptly, not only from chapter to chapter, but even within a chapter; and sometimes one finds words from Isaiah to other persons, or of other persons to Isaiah, so that one asks again and again for some guidance in reading. What is this all about? What road-map can be devised by which to find one's way through this long book?

The first question we need to ask as we begin our inquiry is: How did the long text take shape which appears in the great Isaiah scroll? The evidence is quite convincing that the 66 chapters did not come into being overnight, but had a long history of being built up into their present form.

This is especially true of chapters 1-39, the first that greet the reader: these chapters seem even more "helter-skelter" than does the remainder of the book—in chapter 40 and beyond we find clearer sailing. So let us start with the first 39 chapters, where we meet our prophet Isaiah, a man who preached during the period 742-701 B.C. (1:1).

The first 12 chapters evidently form a unit in themselves. We can see that chapter 12 is a short chapter of thanksgiving to God, a chapter which rounds off what has come before, while chapter 13 begins with a new introduction (vs. 1) and offers the first of a long series of pronouncements about foreign nations, a series that continues through chapter 23. We can make a list of the foreign nations referred to in chapters 13-23.

13:1-22   — Babylon;
14:1-23   — mostly about a fallen king of Babylon;
14:24-27   — Assyria;
14:28-32   — Philistia;
15:1-16:14   — Moab;
17:1-14   — mostly about Damascus;
18:1-20:6   — Egypt;
21:1-10   — Babylon once more;
21:11-12   — Edom;
21:13-17   — Arabia;
(22:1-25   — domestic matters in Jerusalem;)
23:1-18   — Tyre.

But for chapters 1-12 we cannot make such a tidy outline. In fact, one of the first things that a careful reader notices about chapters 1-12 is that there seems to be a curious jump between chapter 5 and chapters 9-10. For example 5:25, 9:12, 9:17, 9:21, and 10:4 all end with an identical "refrain":

> *For all this his anger is not turned away*
> *and his hand is stretched out still.*

Since this refrain is found in chapter 5 and then in chapters 9 and 10, we wonder whether 5:25 and the material around it were not displaced somehow. Further, 5:26-30 has a vivid picture of the coming of a distant enemy at God's command, while 10:5-11 offers a similar picture of the coming of the Assyrians at God's command. But these similar passages in chapter 5 and chapters 9-10 are separated by the "call" of Isaiah (chapter 6) and much other material. It all looks so untidy. What has happened?

No single explanation is likely to be acceptable to every scholar, but it seems clear that much of what I have called the "helter-skelter" nature of chapters 1-12 is due to the habits of the Israelites when they first began to collect in written form the utterances of a given prophet. The early prophets themselves were evidently quite content with *word-of-mouth* proclamation, and with one proclamation at a time. The whole process of *collecting* and *writing down* all the various sayings of a prophet was done by other people later. But where you and I might be impelled to collect the material chronologically, or by subject matter, or in some way alphabetically, the early collectors of the Israelite prophetic sayings seem to have done it by various memory-devices like key words, or chains of key words, which lead from one utterance to the next. We can see traces of this technique even now in chapters 1-12.[7] Let us try some detective work.

In chapter 1, after an editorial note, we have an opening utterance (vss. 2-3). The collector of Isaiah's words evidently picked out the words "sons" (vs. 2) and "people" (vs. 3) as key words, because vs. 4 (at the beginning of the next utterance) opens with the same key words "people" and "sons." This unit evidently extends from vs. 4 to vs. 9; we notice toward the end of the passage the word "daughter" (vs. 8), which seems to balance "sons" at the beginning. Verse 9 ends with the words "Sodom" and "Gomorrah," and these are key words, too, as we can see—for the following unit begins with "Sodom" and "Gomorrah" (vs. 10). Verse 10 must begin a new utterance, because the words "Sodom" and "Gomorrah" are used quite differently in the two passages. In vs. 9 Isaiah says that God left Israel a few survivors, so that they *are not* quite *like* Sodom and Gomorrah, cities which had been altogether wiped out in the distant past (Gen. 19:24-25); but in vs. 10 Isaiah sarcastically *calls* his people "Sodom" and "Gomorrah," to show them how wicked he believes them to be. The two instances of "Sodom" and "Gomorrah" occur here side by side only because they are key words which link two utterances together in a chain. Then this new unit which began in vs. 10 continues through vs. 17 and ends with the words "fatherless" and "widow."

Now we find "fatherless" and "widow" again in vs. 23 (and indeed with the same accompanying Hebrew roots concerning "justice" as occurred in vs. 17), but there is a problem here. The utterance to which vs. 23 belongs evidently begins with vs. 21, not with vs. 18. Verses 18-20 seem to embody something else altogether, a unit which does not participate in the primary chain of key words. What seems to have happened is that the text of vs. 21 came *directly after* the text of vs. 17, so that vss. 18-20 were not originally there at all—they were inserted later by *another, later* collector who associated the ideas of "scarlet," "white," "snow," "red," "crimson," and "wool" in vs. 18 with the idea of "blood" and "wash" in vss. 15-16.

What we have established so far, then, we can set out in this way:

vss. 2-3   — sons, people

4-9   — people, sons (+ daughter); Sodom, Gomorrah

10-17 — Sodom, Gomorrah; fatherless, widow
[and blood, wash; + insertion,
vss. 18-20 — scarlet, white, etc.]

21-? — fatherless, widow.

We can trace this chain even further: vs. 21 begins an utterance about the "faithful city" (vs. 21) which evidently continues through vs. 26 (again "faithful city"), and the next key words that are included are evidently "judges" and "counselors" (vs. 26). We must take a great leap, however, to locate what must originally have come next, because these words turn up next only in 3:2, 3 ("judge," "counselor"). Evidently, then, the text of 3:1 originally came *directly after* 1:26. But how did these two utterances get separated so far?

Perhaps in this way. The unit in 1:21-26 is about the faithful city, that is, Jerusalem; so at a later stage there was added to it a short Zion-saying (vss. 27-28—Zion, by the way, is the name of the spot where the temple stood, in the center of Jerusalem). Then to vss. 27-28 was added still another saying about oaks and gardens (vss. 29-31), possibly because both vss. 27-28 and vss. 29-31 contain the Hebrew word for "together" (vs. 28 and vs. 31), a word which does not appear again in the book of Isaiah until 9:21. Then, to the Zion-poem in vss. 27-28 we have a longer Zion-poem added, in 2:2-4. *This* poem triggered the addition of quite a long poem to *it*, namely 2:5-22, because of words which the two shared: "mountains," vss. 2 and 14; and "raised," vs. 2, the same Hebrew word as "lifted up" and "lofty" in vss. 12, 13, and 14. All this seems complicated in the explanation but was a simple matter, at the time, of like being added to like, much as one layer of mother-of-pearl is added to another around a grain of sand.

(Incidentally, we may note in passing that the poem in 2:2-4 is found in an almost identical wording in Micah 4:1-4; the poem is probably a late one [see Chapter IX] and became so precious to the Jewish community that they preserved it in the prophetic collections of both Isaiah and Micah.)

Our chart then can continue in this way:

1:21-26 — fatherless, widow; judges, counselors, faith-
              ful city;

              [+ 27-28 — Zion, together;
               + 29-31 — together;
                           ——
               + 2:2-4 — Zion, mountains, raised
               + 2:5-22 — mountains, lofty, lifted up]
3:1-?   — judge, counselor.

Possibly our analysis can be continued in this way. The saying begun in 3:1 may continue through vs. 12, for vs. 12 is very similar to vs. 4 (vs. 4, "And I will make boys their princes, and babes shall rule over them"; vs. 12, "My people—children are their oppressors, and women rule over them"—though it is only fair to say that the verses in

Hebrew are not quite so similar to each other as they are in the English of the *Revised Standard Version*). In any event, this passage seems to be a long one in which the end imitates the beginning and so rounds it off. Then vss. 13-15 look as if they are a passage that picks up words from early in chapter 1 (with 3:14, "his people," and 3:15, "my people," compare 1:3, "my people"; and 3:14, "vineyard," compare 1:8, "vineyard").

Then 3:16 begins something quite new, an accusation against the "daughters of Zion" (placed here perhaps because of the "daughter of Zion" plus "vineyard" association back in 1:8). This accusation ends in vs. 24, having been interrupted by a curious long prose listing of women's finery, vss. 18-23, so that the original poem about the daughters of Zion would have been vss. 16-17 + 24. (Try reading the poem without the prose interruption.) Then 3:25-26 + 4:1 is a further passage describing a punishment meted out to women similar to that which has been meted out to the daughters of Zion. (Verses 2-6 of chapter 4 are evidently material that was added much later, here because of the phrase "daughters of Zion" in vs. 4.)

So far, our detective work has taken us only through the first four chapters. No wonder the casual reader of the book of Isaiah becomes bewildered. We shall continue our analysis of chapters 1-12 now without lingering over so much detail; but still, there are some matters to be dealt with.

Chapter 5 begins with a striking poem about a vineyard (vss. 1-7). It is possible that in an original collection of Isaiah's sayings this vineyard poem stood directly after 3:13-15, since the passages are united not only by "vineyard" but also by "house" (5:7; compare "houses," 3:14) and "justice" (5:7; the word "judgment" in 3:14 translates the same Hebrew word).

Then something new starts, a series of six "woes"; the same word "woe" is found at the beginning of 5:8, 11, 18, 20, 21, and 22. Two things we notice in passing. The first is that the opening "woe" passage contains the phrase "house to house" (vs. 8) and "houses" (vs. 9), and then "vineyard" (vs. 10), and even more curiously, the word *bath*. This word "bath" is a Hebrew word for an Israelite liquid measure, amounting to about six gallons or 23 liters; but since the Hebrew word for "daughter" coincidentally happens to be *bath* also, it may be that an earlier collector here perceived a pun on "daughter"—so that the first of these "woes" would then be tied in closely to earlier material. The other thing we notice is that the "woes" are unevenly spaced; it is possible that the passage beginning "therefore" in vss. 14-17 is an insertion made after the series of six "woes" was established (see the discussion on this passage in Chapter III).

Now we come to the puzzle we glimpsed earlier, as we noted the repeated "refrain" of 5:25, 9:12, 17, 21, and 10:4: why is material at the end of chapter 5 so far from similar material in chapters 9-10? Many commentators and translators try to solve the puzzle by main force, simply by shifting verses around. As we noted in the Foreword, the *New English Bible* inserts 5:24-25 after 10:4. The trouble is, other authorities have other solutions. For example, the translation of James Moffatt put 5:24-29 after 10:4, while two recent commentaries, those of Kaiser and Wildberger,[8] *exchange* 10:1-4 and 5:25-30. No one offers a good theory as to why verses of chapter 5 should find themselves so far from "home."

I think the best solution is the simplest after all: to leave the verses where they are, but to see 6:1-9:7 as a massive *insertion* between 5:30 and 9:8, similar to the large-scale insertion of 1:27-2:22 between 1:26 and 3:1 of which we have already taken note. I suggest that the reader read in sequence 5:8-30 and 9:8-10:4 to see what is going on. What do we have before us? One can sense the movement from one passage to the next, even though it is tedious to analyze what is going on; but let us try.

First we have the six "woe"-poems specifying the varieties of the people's wickedness—they stretch from 5:8 to 23. Let us arbitrarily call this type of accusation "Type A" material. Then we have the first "refrain"-poem, giving a message of destruction in general terms, making it clear that God is angry at his people (5:24-25). We can call this "Type B" material. This is followed by a little poem describing the distant enemy in quite specific terms; it is clearly Assyria that is being described, though the poem does not name her (5:26-30). We can call this "Type C" material. Then in 9:8 and thereafter we have three more "refrain"-poems, which seem to interlock with each other in words and phrases (for example, "open mouth," vs. 12, and "every mouth," vs. 17, are identical in Hebrew) and which speak both of God's anger (vs. 19—"Type B") and of the people's wickedness (vss. 20-21—"Type A"). These "refrain"-poems end at 9:21. Then finally there is a "woe"-poem which is also a "refrain"-poem (10:1-4) specifying the people's wickedness (vss. 1-2—"Type A") and hinting at the Assyrian threat (vss. 3-4a—"Type C"). In other words, the material in chapter 5 is of three different categories, and the material in chapters 9-10 combines the categories. This scheme offers a kind of symmetry and makes some overall sense.

Then we notice that what follows all this is a long sequence about Assyria (10:5-15) which begins by affirming that the Assyrians are a dreadful threat (10:5-11), something that was anticipated in 5:26-30, but which ends by proclaiming that God himself, after using Assyria, will *put down* the haughty boasting of Assyria (10:12-15). Indeed the opening word of vs. 5 in the *Revised Standard Version* ("Ah!") is actually the same Hebrew word as that "woe" of the "woe"-poems; thus there are really seven "woe"-poems, not six, the last "woe"-poem being against Assyria, however, not Israel. It is too bad, in a way, that the patterning of these passages has been so concealed from the reader by the insertion of the long sequence 6:1-9:7.

Let us go back now to that long insertion, 6:1-9:7, and see what *it* contains. This passage would appear to be an independent collection *about* Isaiah rather than words from him. The material here is both autobiographical (first-person narrative) and biographical (third-person narrative). Chapter 6 gives Isaiah's call, told autobiographically ("*I* saw the Lord," vs. 1). Chapter 7 gives two narratives of Isaiah's conversations with King Ahaz (vss. 1-9, 10-17) in third-person narrative (vs. 3, "and the Lord said to *Isaiah*"). The second of these narratives is the famous "Immanuel" passage (which we will discuss in detail in Chapter IV). The remainder of chapter 7 appears to be "commentary" material which attempts to give explanations for the conversations with King Ahaz. Then in chapter 8 we have an autobiographical item again (vs. 1, "Then the Lord said to *me*"). The material seems to be here because it offers the curious name of one of Isaiah's sons, Maher-shalal-hash-baz (vss. 1, 3), so the passage was attached to the two narratives in chapter 7, the first of which mentions another son of Isaiah's with a strange name, Shear-jashub (7:3), and the second of which speaks of the name of the wonderful child, Immanuel (7:14). We note that chapter 8 mentions the name "Immanuel" twice more (vss. 8 and 10— see the footnote in the *Revised Standard Version*). The remainder of chapter 8 (vss. 11-22) offers more autobiographical material, in which Isaiah speaks of the meaning of his teaching. And 9:1-7 is a familiar passage, also about *names*, for we have the names of the wonderful king (9:6). This little collection then turns out to be partly autobiographical, partly biographical, and to offer both the prophet's call and several items dealing with symbolic *names* which he bestows or announces. (We shall see more inner logic to the arrangement of this inserted "pamphlet" when we return to discuss it further in Chapter V.)

But why is this collection placed just *here*, interrupting the sequence of "woes" and "refrains"? Evidently because of several phrases and images in the collection which match phrases and images in chapter 5; for instance, "without inhabitant, and houses" in 6:11 matches "houses, without inhabitant" in 5:9. It is noteworthy that the phrase "without inhabitant" is found nowhere else in the whole book of Isaiah. There is also the contrast of "darkness" and "light," found in 8:22 and 9:1-2, which matches the same contrast in 5:20 (and in 5:30 as well, though that verse may be a later addition); and the Hebrew word *maher* ("hurry") in the first part of the name of Isaiah's son (8:1, 3) may reflect the occurrence of the same word in 5:26 (*Revised Standard Version*: "swiftly").

In the rest of chapters 10, 11, and 12 the same kind of ordering principles seem to apply. Thus 10:16-27a and 33-34 refer in various ways to "trees," "boughs," "forest," and so are appropriate after the passage about the axe and woodsman (10:15); 10:27b-32 looks like an intrusive passage which is there because the Hebrew words for "yoke" (10:27a) and "gone up" (10:27b) sound similar. Chapter 11 begins with another passage having to do with "trees" (vs. 1, "stump"), continues with "root of Jesse" (vs. 10) which mimics vs. 1, and goes on to use the words "ensign" and "nations" (vs. 10) which are then picked up in vs. 12. And chapter 12 serves as a general rounding off of the collection through chapter 11, as we have already noted.

We have already touched on the contents of chapters 13-23 in the list we made of the foreign nations referred to in them, so now we ask, what do we find in the book of Isaiah beyond chapter 23? Chapters 24-27 offer an alternation of passages of doom for the whole world (like 24:1-13) and passages of triumph (like 24:14-16a) that seems to make up a collection of material all its own. We shall deal with that collection in Chapter IX.

Then with chapter 28 we find ourselves back with "woes" again. Look at 28:1, 29:1 (the *Revised Standard Version* "ho" is the same "woe"-word in Hebrew), 30:1, and 31:1; these four chapters, it appears, form another collection all their own. Why this "woe"-collection should turn up *here*, so far from the earlier "woes" of chapters 5 and 10, we do not know; it might be that the collections of chapters 13-23 and of chapters 24-27 were inserted much later, in which case chapter 28 would of course originally have been much closer to chapter 10.

The ordering process of chapters 28-31 seems to be similar to what we found in chapters 1-12. Thus the reader can see the words "crown" and "glorious beauty" chasing each other through 28:1, 3, and 5, but what the reader of the English text cannot see is that the Hebrew word translated "they are confused" in 28:7 is a pun on the word "eats it up" in 28:4—for vs. 7 of course starts an entirely different passage.

Chapters 32-33 offer quite miscellaneous material; but still, we notice the patterns of "behold" (32:1), "woe" (33:1), "behold" (33:7). Chapter 34 is a wild poem of judgment on Edom (see 34:5) which curiously resembles some of the material in chapters 56-66 (compare 34:1-4 with 66:15-16). Chapter 35 is a lovely passage that sounds much like the material in chapters 40-55. We must admit, however, that how chapters 34 and 35 got into their present position is something of a mystery.

Chapters 36-39 are almost entirely in prose and duplicate the historical material in 2 Kings 18:13-20:19, except for the poem in chapter 38. Plainly, a scribe wanted to round off the Isaiah collection by a historical appendix which he had before him. (The last chapter of Jeremiah, Jer. 52, is the same kind of historical appendix; in that case it duplicates 2 Kings 24:18-25:30.)

Let us pause now and look over what we have learned. There seem to have been four small collections of material about Isaiah in the first instance:

(1) the opening collection—1:2-5:7;
(2) the first "woes"—5:8-30 + 9:8-10:4;
                              + 10:5-17 (+ other miscellaneous
                              material in chapters 10 and 11);
(3) the inserted biographical material—6:1-9:7;
(4) more "woes"—28:1-31:9.

To these collections there were added at a later period:

(5) the historical appendix—36:1-39:8;
(6) the collection on foreign nations—13:1-23:18;
(7) the collection on doom and triumph for the whole
                              world—24:1-27:13; and
(8) other miscellaneous material in chapters 32-35.

So much for a road-map through chapters 1-39. Even a quick road-map seems complicated to the non-specialist, and is no doubt over-simplified for the specialist, but at least it may serve as a kind of first-aid for the reader who wants to make sense out of what appears to be a crazy-quilt. We have found that these chapters give evidence from word-association and idea-association that they were built up over a long period of time indeed. It is clear, then, that these chapters were not written from scratch from beginning to end, but are the end result of a long process of collection.

But now, suddenly, in chapters 40 and beyond we are in a new world. Suddenly we find smooth sailing. We understand more of what is going on. We don't feel we need a commentary quite as much. In chapter after chapter we have an extended series of marvelous lyrical poems. God will save his people, we learn; he will bring them home, and all will be well. There was an elderly deaconess in a church I once served who used to say, "I just love the book of Isaiah," and I knew when she said this that she did not mean those hard, ugly passages like "And men shall enter the caves of the rocks and the holes of the ground, from before the terror of the Lord" (2:19) or whatever, but rather, "Comfort, comfort my people, says your God" (40:1).

But it is not only in readability and lyricism that we are in a new world in these chapters; we are also in a new world in vocabulary, geography, history, and theology. Thus if we ask who is Israel's enemy in war, then we recognize that in chapters 1-39 it is Assyria (there are 34 occurrences of the name "Assyria" in chapters 1-39, but none at all in chapters 40-66), while in chapters 40-66 it is Babylon (see 43:14, 47:1, 48:14, 20; the occurrences of "Babylon" in chapters 1-39 are only in the passages against foreign nations—13:1, 19, 14:4, 22, 21:9—and four times in chapter 39 in the narrative of an emissary from Babylon who has come to the king of Judah to try to hatch a plot against Assyria). Similarly we notice that in chapters 40-66 it is Babylonian gods which are referred to (46:1). In chapters 1-39 it is clear that the temple in Jerusalem is the very center of cultic life (6:1), referred to again and again by the phrase "the house of the Lord" (2:2, 6:4, 37:1, 14, 38:20, 22); but in chapters 40-55 (though not in 56-66) the temple must be rebuilt (44:28). All this evidence points to the fact that the material of chapters 40 and thereafter was produced in a very different historical circumstance than the material in chapters 1-39. Scholars have concluded that chapters 40 and beyond were composed not by the original Isaiah of Jerusalem

(1:1), but by an unnamed prophet who preached to the
Jews during the Babylonian exile two hundred years later,
about 540 B.C.

This conclusion is not a new one in biblical scholarship.
In the 12th century A.D. the Jewish commentator Ibn Ezra
hinted that the last half of the book, chapters 40-66, was
not written by Isaiah.[9] (For further discussion of Ibn
Ezra's work on Isaiah, see Chapter X.) The theory that the
material is from a later poet was first set forth clearly by
J.C. Döderlein in 1775 and popularized by J.G. Eichhorn in
1780-83.[10] Nevertheless many devout Bible readers have
rejected this view, convinced that the original prophet
Isaiah offered a whole series of predictions of Jesus Christ,
including 7:14, 9:1-7, and 52:13-53:12. For such readers
the unity of the book of Isaiah has been crucial, as I have
already noted in the Foreword.

In this regard it is significant that the question has been
approached in a new way in the last few years by Yehuda
T. Radday, a Jewish computer expert in Israel. Radday
evidently began his investigation by assuming the single
authorship of the whole book.[11] He certainly undertook his
computer work with a completely open mind on the
question,[12] simply submitting to the computer various
characteristics by which the sections of the book of Isaiah
might be compared with each other—any variations in style
of language *which are not open to the control of the author.*
One of his earliest tests, for example, and one of the most
striking in its results, was to compare the proportion of
"inflected nouns"[13] to all nouns in the sections of the book
of Isaiah. He found the percentage in chapters 1-35 is 17.1,
while the percentage in chapters 40-66 is 27.9.[14] These
percentages are in such contrast that there is no realistic
chance that the material is from the same author. As
Radday says, "In view of this test, one has to assume at least
one other author for the second half of the book."[15] This
test is only one of 41 linguistic tests on the book of Isaiah
which Radday carried out, most of which yielded similarly
significant results.[16]

Our perception, then, of being in a "different world" in

chapters 40 and beyond is substantiated by this kind of computer analysis. Scholars are accustomed to using the name "Second Isaiah" (or, using a Greek prefix, "Deutero-Isaiah") to refer to the anonymous author of chapters 40 and beyond.

Yet beyond all our awareness of the *contrasts* between what comes before chapter 40 and what comes in and after it, contrasts of authorship and of life situation, there is also a curious *unity* which we can perceive. For example, the term "Holy One of Israel" as a term for God is found 12 times in chapters 1-39, 14 times in chapters 40-66, but only five times in all the rest of the Old Testament—and only one of these occurrences is in a prophetic book.[17] Again, one of the constant affirmations of the original Isaiah was that God is to be described as "high," "exalted," "lifted up" (see 2:11, 12; 6:1; and other passages). "Second Isaiah," however, affirms the same theme (40:22) and then goes on to use the idea in a fresh way, when he describes the Servant of God as taking on the characteristics which up to then had been reserved for God himself: he shall be "exalted," "lifted up," "high" (52:13). (For a discussion of this theme see Chapter VII.) In short, it is no coincidence that the material of chapters 40 and beyond, though not written by the original Isaiah, is placed *with* material from the original Isaiah: the material does belong, in the sense that it is the expression of someone who stood *in a tradition*, an "Isaianic" tradition. One might almost say that the words of chapters 40 and beyond are the kind of thing Isaiah himself might have said if he had lived two hundred years later. There is a different style to the words, yes—we recall once more Radday and his computer—but there are similar themes set in new historical circumstances. We are in touch here with a quite specific prophetic heritage.

It is a little like a Lutheran hymnal: not all the hymns in a Lutheran hymnal are written by the man Martin Luther—in fact few of them are these days—but all of the hymns in the Lutheran hymnal are appropriate to the Lutheran tradition, and most of them have been written in the centuries after Luther by other Lutherans. Indeed there would have been no Lutheran hymnal at all if it had not been for Martin Luther and the theological perspective which he set forth.

That is why I have subtitled this study *Scroll of a Prophetic Heritage*, for what we have here is a fascinating phenomenon—a single prophetic viewpoint exercising itself over a long period of time in Israel. One has to assume some kind of community of prophets (this is evidently the meaning of 8:16) who not only remembered, preserved, compiled, and copied the words of an original prophet, but were alert enough to new needs in new times to produce further prophetic expressions which were authentic to that tradition.

But there is more, for chapters 40-66 do not seem to form a unity of their own. We sense a distinct letdown as we move from chapter 55, which ends in utter triumph (read 55:12-13), to chapter 56, with its concern for Sabbath-keeping (56:1-2) and the rights of the foreigner and the eunuch within the Jewish religious community (56:3-8). A good deal of the material in chapters 56-66, it is true, does give the same exalted impression as the material in chapters 40-55 (for example, 61:1-4, which, we recall, Jesus read at Nazareth), but not all of it does. In general the material in chapters 56-66 seems much more miscellaneous than does the material in chapters 40-55. Furthermore, if chapters 40-55 focus on Babylon and imply that the temple in Jerusalem has been destroyed, in chapters 56-66 the temple has been rebuilt (56:7), and in general our focus is on Jerusalem once more (60:8-14). It is true, there are a few scholars who insist on the single authorship of all of chapters 40-66,[18] but I feel most comfortable with the contrary assumption: that chapters 56-66 are not from "Second Isaiah," but from a person (or circle of persons) whom we shall call "Third Isaiah," who was then a follower (or, who were then followers) of "Second Isaiah" and who sought to apply the vision of "Second Isaiah" to the new situation faced by Jews who had come home to Jerusalem in 538 B.C. and thereafter.[19]

That we appear to have isolated three "Isaiahs" moves

us to raise the question whether all the material spoken by a prophet in chapters 1-39 can be attributed to the original Isaiah. I have already hinted that I assume not, though I have not explored the matter in detail. Thus I have suggested that 2:2-4, which appears in almost the same form in Micah 4:1-4, is later than Isaiah; here was an anonymous prophetic word which was too precious to lose, so that it was preserved in both the tradition of Isaiah and that of Micah.[20] There is other material in chapters 1-12 which gives every evidence of being added after Isaiah's time: the words on Jerusalem's restoration in 4:2-6 do not seem to be in the style of the original Isaiah; the four little paragraphs in 7:18-25 which amplify and frame explanations on the description of "the day" in vs. 17 seem secondary; and so do the amplifications and explanations of 10:16-27a, including what seem to be two contrary explanations of the meaning of the name of Isaiah's son Shear-jashub (10:20-23; compare 7:3 and the footnote in the *Revised Standard Version* to that verse). The material on the new age in 11:10-16 and the psalm-like material in chapter 12 likewise appear to be late.

At this point in the discussion the reader may react in two ways. First, he may feel that if what is said here is true, then there is not much left for the original Isaiah. This reaction is understandable; one can only reply that a great deal *is* left of one of the most remarkable figures in all of Israel's history, and we shall spend all of the next four chapters in exploring his words.

But the fact that some passages *seem* to fit a later period of time does not mean that they *have* to be dated late. Thus, the reader's second reaction may be to ask: Why could Isaiah not have said something very unusual to which people centuries later got accustomed and which they understood better? Or why could Isaiah not have predicted future events or circumstances if he spoke for God?

These questions go to the heart of Isaiah's own understanding of his work, of the understanding of his work *which his immediate hearers and later generations had,* and of the understanding of his work which we ourselves have.

Some of the answers to these questions must be saved for later chapters, especially Chapters II, V, VII, and X. But this much can be said now: scholars do not insist categorically that Isaiah *cannot* have been the author of this or that passage, but simply that he *is not likely* to have been the author. This, again, is a matter of raising the kind of questions which Radday raised by means of his computer— the whole way of speaking, the phrases, the style, do not appear to be Isaiah's. Scholars can develop an overall impression of an author's style, in much the same way that a wife, reading a note written by her husband who is being held hostage can tell the police, "That's not the way my husband writes; they must be twisting his arm." For some passages, scholars can say, That's not the way Isaiah speaks.

What we have said about chapters 1-12 also can be said for other collections in chapters 13-39. The "foreign nations" passages in chapters 13-23 seem mixed: some are from Isaiah, some from the century after his time. The collections of poems about the doom and triumph of the whole world seem to scholars *much* later than the time of the original Isaiah, perhaps from about 400 B.C., though I shall suggest in Chapter IX that the collection may have at its core a genuine word from Isaiah (24:1-3). But this collection in general, if it is to be dated as I have suggested, would have been compiled about three hundred years after the time of Isaiah and would be the last sizeable addition to the Isaianic collection.

With chapters 28-31 we are back with the original Isaiah, while with chapters 32-35 we have a mixture of later material from various sources. Indeed, chapter 35 may be from "Second Isaiah" himself.

Since we are surrounded by so great a cloud of Isaiahs, many questions occur to us. Who *are* all those other figures? What can we know about them? The answer, I am afraid, is, almost nothing. We know a few things about the original Isaiah (see Chapter II), and we can be almost positive that chapters 40-55 are the product of one person, whose circumstances we can guess (see Chapter VI). Beyond that, we hear only voices, various voices from various historical contexts, speaking out of centuries that happen to be badly documented (that is, the sixth and fifth centuries B.C.). So many unanswered questions leave us frustrated.

The ancient interest, however, was different from our own. They did not ask, Who spoke these words, and when? But rather, their question was, What words were to be spoken, and what is God doing, according to his spokesman? What is God like and what is he doing on a given occasion? This was the concern the Jews had, and this is what we have the resources to learn from the book of Isaiah. Many of the voices, under the circumstances, must remain anonymous, but what the voices have to say does come through loud and clear. Since these words were so carefully collected over so long a period of time, and since the collection was prized as scripture by the Jewish and then by the Christian communities, we are challenged to listen, to learn, and to heed their message.

We have come a long and rather tedious way in this chapter. We began with the discovery of a scroll in the Judean desert, a scroll which symbolizes the antiquity of the copying process which has brought the book of Isaiah to us. We have attempted to make a road-map of the long book. We have discovered various sub-collections in the book, and within these sub-collections have even found traces of the curious fashion by which the ancient collectors often built up these collections, using key words or association of ideas which reflect the memory devices of the earliest period of oral tradition. We have also glimpsed the number of prophets whose words have found their way into the collection, so much so that a modern hymnal was our ready comparison.

To discover this multiplicity, however, is only to rediscover what the author of the Epistle to the Hebrews sensed so long ago about Old Testament material in general: "In many and various ways God spoke of old to our fathers by the prophets" (Heb. 1:1). Multiplicity does not seem to have bothered the Old Testament community which brought these collections together, and multiplicity should not bother us.

Having made our initial survey, we turn to the first

order of business: making the acquaintance of the original prophet Isaiah, who started it all.

The First Isaiah

The First

CHAPTER II

God is High and Holy, and Isaiah is his Prophet

T HE BEST WAY to begin making our acquaintance with Isaiah is by looking carefully at the account which he has left us of his call to be a prophet, found in chapter 6. This passage focuses on one overwhelming incident in his life, the experience which launched him into his career of speaking out for God. As we read these verses we will find ourselves faced much more with Isaiah's view of *God* than with any description of the *prophet himself;* but indirectly, at least, our understanding of the prophet can begin to emerge as we face his view of God.

The first eight verses of chapter 6 are familiar ones to many people because they set forth a classic description of a person being addressed by God. Familiar though the verses are, a close look may reveal more than we have noticed before.

Verse 1 opens with the words, "In the year that King Uzziah died." Uzziah had ruled in Jerusalem over the southern kingdom of Judah for over 40 years (783-742 B.C.).[1] He had been an able and popular ruler, remaining at peace with King Jeroboam II in the north, whose capital was at Samaria. Over the years, the two kings had managed to push out the borders of their two kingdoms to nearly the same extent as King Solomon's realm of one hundred fifty years before. Trade routes had expanded, new buildings had gone up, population levels had increased, and there was prosperity past anyone's experience (compare 2 Kings 15:1-3, 2 Chron. 26:6-15). But during the last few years of his life King Uzziah was afflicted with leprosy and had to be isolated; his son Jotham evidently served as co-regent with him.

Then Uzziah died. One can surmise that the young Isaiah felt the same kind of shock and disorientation which older Americans will recall having felt when President Franklin Roosevelt died in 1945, or as many more felt when President John Kennedy was assassinated in 1963. What will we do without Uzziah? What will happen now? What will Jotham's policies be? It was with concerns like these that Isaiah had his vision of the *divine* king, the Lord, in the temple.

"I saw the Lord sitting upon a throne." Biblical Hebrew lacks any ability to specify a distinction between inner "seeing" and the seeing of outer, photographable objects: both are "seen," both are perceived. The Israelites hardly ever seem to have asked whether a given instance of seeing was "subjective" or "objective"; instead, they simply asked, Is God communicating through this perception? That was the important thing.

We must go on to affirm that many people, in many cultures and many circumstances, have reported and continue to report visionary experiences. Sometimes these experiences are purely personal and casual. Sometimes, however, they trigger a total reorientation of one's life; such was the case with Isaiah. The experience of seeing God in the temple was the beginning of his career as a prophet.

Nevertheless, Isaiah was extraordinarily bold in his description. Ezekiel, one hundred fifty years later, engrossed in a similar experience, was careful to indicate that his description of what he saw was a good four steps removed from reality: "*Such* was the *appearance* of the *likeness* of the *glory* of *the Lord*" (Ezek. 1:28). But such indirectness was not for Isaiah—"*I saw the Lord*"! Israelite tradition insisted this type of vision was impossible; for when Moses was dealing with God, we read, " 'But,' he [God] said, 'you cannot see my face; for man shall not see me and live' " (Exod. 33:20). Isaiah's words were bold enough to frighten off the ancient Aramaic translator and make him soften the phrase in his translation to "I saw the *glory* of the Lord."[2] But Isaiah did not avoid a straight-out statement; he says he saw the Lord himself, not his glory.

And he saw him "sitting upon a throne." This means, of course, that he saw God functioning as a king. For most people today the idea of a "king" is imprecise, and to use the image of "king" for God is just one more way to make God unreal and irrelevant. Kings are the stuff of fairy tales, of Shakespeare's plays, of faded photographs of royalty gathering for the funeral of Queen Victoria. It takes an effort of the imagination to remind ourselves that in Isaiah's day the king was the government—he was the ruler, usually the absolute ruler—and that authority and responsibility rested in him. His job was to command. One of the amazing things about the Servant of God whom Second Isaiah would later describe is that he shall so astonish kings that they will *shut their mouths* because of him (52:15). Who ever heard of kings shutting their mouths? Kings give orders, by definition. (For a discussion of this passage, see Chapter VII.)

Of course, Isaiah was not the first to glimpse God as king; long before Israelite times the high god was conceived of as a king—the god 'Ēl was called "eternal king," for example.[3] Evidently Moses' understanding of God's covenanting with his people at Sinai was an understanding based on the political model of an overlord in covenant with his vassals.[4] This was certainly Gideon's understanding when he rejected the offer of kingship for himself (Judg. 8:22-23), and the idea is assumed by many of the Psalms (see, for example, Ps. 24:8-10), notably in that oft-repeated phrase "The Lord reigns" (for example, Ps. 93:1).

Obviously the image of God as king was more straightforward in the days before Israel adopted human kingship than it was during the times of Saul, David, Solomon, and their successors. Human kingship, with all its outward pomp and circumstance, fed the images which the Israelites had of God; and the reverse was true, too—the human king, being "anointed of God" (compare 2 Sam. 19:21-22), gained ever greater stature in people's eyes from that very blessing of God. As a result, people were more and more tempted to assume that the human king represented ultimate authority (as the kings of other nations did), and that, as far as the

king's conduct was concerned, he was above the law—that
"anything goes." That is the meaning of the story of King
David's affair with Bathsheba (2 Sam. 11:1-12:23). It is
noteworthy, then, that in the year that Uzziah, the human
king of Judah, died, with all the attendant uncertainty of
the passing of power from one monarch to another, Isaiah
perceived, in a stunning vision, the authority and the power
of the divine king—of God himself.

But there is more to this than simply the reinforcement
of an old theological image. The fact is, if kingship in Judah
might take people's attention, the king of Assyria could
bring people to panic. There had been nothing in memory
to match the brutal bullying of nations by the kings of
Assyria (read 10:12-14). We shall have much more to say
about this matter in Chapters IV and V. The king of Assyria
could send people's morale down to zero with a threat, with
a mere glance. But if Isaiah's vision is convincing and
conclusive, then it follows that the king of Assyria is not
really the strongest figure in the universe; *God* is, sitting
upon *his* throne. God is stronger than Assyria. This simple
conviction would rule Isaiah's life for forty years and more.

"High and lifted up"—these words only reinforce the
point just made: God is high above everything else. One of
the psalmists uses similar language: "The Lord is high above
all nations, and his glory above the heavens!" (Ps. 113:4).

As we pointed out in Chapter I, the idea of the "height"
of God is one of the main emphases of Isaiah. In one
extended poem (2:5-22) he visualizes God as going on a
rampage, not only to bring mankind down to size (vss. 11,
17), but also to bring down everything else which is tall—
fortified walls (vs. 15), sea-going ships (vs. 16), and even the
stately trees and tall mountains (vss. 13-14). To ask, Does
Isaiah mean this literally? is to ask the wrong kind of
question. Isaiah is so caught up in the notion of the
awesome majesty of God, the notion of the immense
distance which separates him from all that is merely earthly
and human, that there is simply no comparison. The British
theologian J.B. Phillips wrote a book titled, *Your God is Too*

Small.[5] Isaiah would have understood the title. He would do anything to insist on the height of God.

"And his train filled the temple." Isaiah was worshiping in the temple. The temple in Jerusalem was not gigantic by present-day standards, but it surely must have given some scope to the sensibility of the worshiper. The historian has recorded for us the interior dimensions of the building (1 Kings 6:2): 60 cubits long, 20 cubits wide, 30 cubits high. Since a cubit is about a foot and one-half, or one-half meter, the temple would have been about 45 feet from floor to ceiling. And the skirts of God's robe filled this whole hall! Picturesque, but greatly impressive; as the skirts of his robe filled the temple, so the whole earth is filled with his glory (vs. 3).

Verse 2 reads, "Above him stood the seraphim; each had six wings: with two he covered his face, and with two he covered his feet, and with two he flew." The seraphim are winged beings, mentioned in the Old Testament only here. We are disappointed when we realize that we really have no idea of how Isaiah visualized them. On display in Baltimore there is a relief-carving of a six-winged figure[6] which was found in northeast Syria, at Tell-Halaf (ancient Gozan; compare 2 Kings 17:6), a carving which is evidently from the ninth century B.C., a century before Isaiah. Whether this figure is any clue to Isaiah's imagery we do not know. Others, again, have thought of winged serpents, but nobody really knows. What is clear is that "feet" here is a euphemism for the genitals (compare Deut. 28:57), so that with the six wings each seraph covers his nakedness, covers his face against the glow given forth by God, and then flies. As a king had his courtiers and bodyguards, so, we are given to understand, does the heavenly king; but we wish we could visualize in more detail Isaiah's conception.

Verse 3 continues:

> *And one called to another and said:*
>
> *"Holy, holy, holy is the Lord of hosts;*
> *the whole earth is full of his glory."*

These words have entered so deeply into our liturgies and our sense of what is fit to say of God that it is difficult to understand their meaning to Isaiah.

The term "holy," here repeated three times, did not center primarily in ethical purity, as it tends to do with us, but refers purely and simply to what is characteristic of God, what is special to him, what is separate from all common or ordinary use. Of course from a logical point of view God is "holy" by definition, and one does not feel much more informed than before. But we are not dealing here with the language of logic, but with the language of religious witness, and Isaiah perceives God's retainers to be affirming God's absolute distinctiveness, his distance from any share in the ordinariness of the world. In an old narrative, after the Philistines had superstitiously sent back the ark of God which they had captured, some Israelites said, "Who is able to stand before the Lord, this holy God?" (1 Sam. 6:20). No one can meddle with God.

"The Lord of hosts" is an old liturgical phrase in Israel. (We take note in passing that when the *Revised Standard Version* has "the LORD" in small capital letters, it is a code for the existence in the Hebrew text of the name of God, which is not "Jehovah," as people used to think, but is probably to be pronounced "Yahweh.") Now "Yahweh of hosts" is, I repeat, an old liturgical phrase (compare 2 Sam. 6:2), but so old that nobody knows what "hosts" are being referred to. A recent authority offers five suggestions of its meaning.[7] A reasonable assumption might be that the "hosts" are either other divine beings to whom Yahweh is superior, or are the armies of Israel which Yahweh commanded in early "holy wars," or perhaps (at a later stage of Israelite religion) angels of some sort. What might have happened is that a traditional designation of God received varying interpretations in the course of Israel's history. In any event, Isaiah perceived God's retainers to be referring to him in a traditional form of address.

"Glory" is the English translation of a Hebrew word (*kābôd*) with a remarkable range of meanings. In the first place, the word sometimes centers on the meaning of "weight" or "heaviness." For instance, in 22:24 we read, "And they will hang on him the whole weight (*kābôd*) of his father's house." Just as we speak of "weighty" people, people of influence and standing, who *make a great impression,* so our Hebrew word includes the idea of "respect, distinction." To "give glory" to someone is to show him respect (compare Prov. 26:8—the *Revised Standard Version* translates *kābôd* here as "honor"). Since those to whom respect is due are more often than not those with riches, splendid robes, magnificent appearance—such as the kings of the earth—the word also takes on the idea of "dazzling splendor." In Genesis 31:1 the word is rendered "wealth": Jacob has "gained all this *wealth.*" In Isaiah 35:2 we read of the glory (*kābôd*) of Lebanon which implies that for those who live near sea-level, the high mountains with their stately evergreens, cedars, and tall spruces make a deep impression.

So, if mountains or kings make a great impression, then Isaiah is convinced that God makes the greatest impression of all. The whole earth resonates with the impression he makes; the dazzling splendor of God is apparent to all those with eyes to see. Isaiah saw! The seraphim could see, but hid their eyes; Isaiah's ears rang with their shout.

The picturesque details of Isaiah's vision continue in verse 4: "And the foundations of the thresholds shook at the voice of him who called, and the house was filled with smoke." We are not sure of the translation "foundations of the thresholds"; the *New Jewish Version* suggests "doorposts," while other authorities suggest "door pivots."[8] *Everything* is filled with manifestations of God: the temple is filled with the skirts of his robe (vs. 1) and with smoke (vs. 4), the whole earth is filled with the bedazzling glory of him (vs. 3).

Here, plainly, is no cosmic buddy with whom Isaiah could easily identify; here is no deity of quiet beauty to whom Isaiah could offer calm devotion. Here, rather, is God the awesome king, from whom Isaiah shrinks in dismay, saying, "Woe is me, I am doomed!" (vs. 5, *New American Bible*). The Hebrew verb here does not really mean "I am lost" (as the *Revised Standard Version* and most other versions translate it) if by "lost" we think of "far from home" or "strayed." The verb has two ranges of meaning (unless, perhaps, Isaiah was deliberately punning with two quite different verbs that happen to be identical in sound):[9] one is "I am destroyed," as cities or countries are destroyed (so Moab in 15:1, where the same verb is used); the other is "I am struck dumb." This second meaning seems appropriate in view of the phrases that follow, which are concerned with Isaiah's *lips*. Isaiah feels crushed and silent in the face of what he has experienced.

Verse 5 continues: "I am a man of unclean lips, and I dwell in the midst of a people of unclean lips; for my eyes have seen the King, the Lord of hosts!" Why *lips*? What is so important about lips? Why not "heart," or "soul," or "ways"? The use of "lips" is plainly central for Isaiah, for vss. 6 and 7, concerned with the purification of his lips, move directly to his acceptance of the commission to speak for God.

The first and easiest answer is of course just that: if he is to *speak* for God, then his lips must be rendered fit for the task. But the matter runs much deeper and goes to the core of the Israelite view of how people function under God.

To the Israelite, what a person thinks up, and then says, and then does are all part of the same realm: plans, and words, and actions are all aspects of the same homogenized, personal expression. Plans begin in the "heart," which is the seat of the will (and not simply of the emotions, as it is for us). Then plans are put into words. "The heart of the wise teacheth his mouth, and addeth learning to his lips" (Prov. 16:23, *King James Version*). Words have power. For example, in Leviticus 19:14 we learn that cursing a deaf person is just as harmful as putting a stumbling-block out before a blind person. The Old Testament hardly knows what to do with our notion of "idle" words, for in the Old Testament, words are never idle but do good or ill to our minds and bodies. So people need to say what they mean. Isaiah denounces people who say "bitter" when they mean "sweet" (5:20), or perhaps even begin to believe that "bitter" *is* "sweet." Jesus made it clear that words are crucial when he diverted his hearers' attention from the problem of clean and unclean foods to the problem of the words which come out of people's mouths (Mark 7:14-23). The letter of James reminds us of the importance of our words, asserting that our "yes" must be "yes" and our "no" "no" (James 5:12).

Since the very word "word" in Hebrew also means "thing," words are central because they reflect what we really intend when we speak with each other. Here, then, is Isaiah, struck dumb by a sense of the presence of God in all his awesome height and holiness—and Isaiah knows that beside God all human beings shrink away—worse, they prove themselves unclean. The word "unclean" here is not what we mean by "dirty"; it means what is ritually unclean, what has no place in the presence of God. The poor leper must cry that he is "unclean" (Lev. 13:45) and cover his lips; does Isaiah here hint that before God the whole people is leprous? A corpse is "unclean" ritually, and defiles any who touch it (Lev. 22:4). All these ideas resemble our notion of taboo, but, for all that, they are powerful images of what is fit for the world of God and his people. "Polluted" is perhaps our best present-day equivalent.

Isaiah has the sense that he is wholly polluted, and his whole people is polluted, unfit to stand before God because of their unclean lips—that is, their polluted thoughts, words, and acts.

It is interesting that Isaiah sees himself as no different from anybody else. So far as this narrative goes, he has no sense of being special, of being "more religious," of being privileged to gain a glimpse of God. He is just Mr. Everybody, no different. Alongside of infinity, every finite number is the same, whether it be one or one million.

But Isaiah must be rendered fit for speaking on behalf of God, and so the stream of picturesque details of his vision continues. Verse 6 tells of his purification: one of the seraphim touches his mouth with a live coal and pronounces these words, "Behold, this has touched your lips; your guilt is taken away, and your sin forgiven" (vs. 7). Through this act that which has been implicit is made explicit: Isaiah's lips had been unclean because of "guilt" and "sin." The distance between God and his people, then, has not been a simple matter of taboos broken, but a profound disorientation resulting from rebellion, disobedience, and willful ignorance. One can describe the situation in many ways, as Isaiah himself would do (for example, in 1:2-4). We shall take up this matter in the next chapter. But now Isaiah himself is purged from any attachment to Israel's sin. Not, we note well, by anything he himself was able to do, but by the action of one of the seraphim, that is, by the initiative of one of God's retainers. It is by grace that he is purified, not by works, to use New Testament terms.

Finally, in verse 8, God speaks. He has been silent all this time: he has been king, but has not yet spoken or acted as king. His retainers have spoken and acted for him. But now he speaks, asking for a volunteer to be his messenger. "Whom shall I send, and who will go for us?" (vs. 8). Why does he say "I" in the first phrase, but then use the plural, "us," in the second? Who is this "us," if God alone is exalted in his glory? Evidently it is the same "us" as in Genesis 1:26, "Let *us* make man in our image." The word does not refer to the Trinity, in spite of what some traditional Christian commentators say, but simply to God speaking on climactic occasions with a royal "we," including his retainers and heavenly courtiers in his august moves.

"Whom shall I send, and who will go?" God asks. The answer is already apparent, if it is Isaiah whose lips have been rendered fit for the task. It would almost seem as if God's call for a volunteer here resembles those occasions in the army when the sergeant calls out, "I want four volunteers—you, you, you, and you." Yet Isaiah could have said, "No, thank you!" as Jeremiah did on a subsequent occasion (Jer. 1:6). Instead, Isaiah steps forward willingly to volunteer: "Here I am; send me!" He is free to accept, though God has taken the initiative and prepared the way.

Let us pause, now, to get our bearings, and to consider what it means for someone to undertake the task of being a messenger for God.

As far back as anyone could remember there had been prophets in Israel. We even have indications of men and women who spoke words from various gods and goddesses a thousand years earlier among the Amorites and Canaanites.[10] Some traditions remembered early figures like Abraham, Moses, and Aaron as prophets (Gen. 20:7, Deut. 18:18, Exod. 7:1). There were traditions regarding groups of prophets in the days of Saul, who were ecstatics (1 Sam. 10:5). But more relevant to Isaiah's situation was the precedent of men like Nathan, who spoke out God's word to King David (see especially 2 Sam. 12:1-23), and Elijah, who spoke out God's word to King Ahab of Israel (see 1 Kings 18, 21). In the view of these prophets, the king might be God's anointed, but the standards of behavior which God expects of his people apply to the king too.

If, as we have just seen, "word" and "action" are homogenized, then God's words, like God's actions, are supremely powerful. Read 9:8-10: "The Lord has sent a word against Jacob, and it will light [literally, "fall"] upon Israel; and all the people will know. . .who say. . .'The bricks have fallen. . . .' " In this poem, the "falling" of God's word on Israel is parallel to the "falling" of bricks. Or look at 31:2: "And yet he [the Lord] is wise and brings disaster, he does not call back his words." God's words bring disaster if he does not call them back. In Second Isaiah there is a classic passage about the power of God's word, 55:10-11, which states that God's word does not return empty (as an echo does) any more than rain falls up; God's word goes out and gets things done.

The enunciation of this word-with-power is the commission given to Isaiah. He is to be God's mouthpiece for his generation. And the content of his message is to be found in vss. 9-13 of the narrative in the chapter. It is ironical that when we deal with chapter 6 we usually avoid this part of it. I have heard many sermons and talks at summer camps on this chapter, but I have never heard a sermon on vss. 9-13. No wonder, for they are shocking! But we must persevere now, shocking though it is. What is Isaiah's commission to be?

> *Go, and say to this people:*
> *"Hear and hear, but do not understand;*

> *see and see, but do not perceive."*
>
> *Make the heart of this people fat,*
>   *and their ears heavy,*
>   *and shut their eyes;*
>   *lest they see with their eyes,*
>   *and hear with their ears,*
> *and understand with their hearts,*
>
> *and turn and be healed* (vss. 9-10).

This is an appalling task, and Isaiah is justifiably appalled. "Then I said, 'How long, O Lord?' And he said, 'Until cities lie waste, without inhabitant. . .' " (vs. 11).

No wonder we do not hear sermons on this part of the chapter! One cannot imagine any easy way to make this passage part of our proclamation to the present generation. (People in ancient times had trouble with the passage too; the rabbis softened it in various ways.)[11] What kind of prophetic ministry is this?

First, note that the Hebrew is quite faithfully translated into English, so far as I can see. Not only does it mean what it says, but the passage was even similarly used in Mark 4:12 to explain why Jesus spoke in parables. (It is noteworthy that both Matthew [13:13] and Luke [8:10] have eliminated Mark's final line which reads "lest they should turn again, and be forgiven." Also, though Luke does preserve the phrase "so that they may not" which Mark has and which reflects the meaning in Isaiah, Matthew has changed it to "because they do not," so that he has Jesus speaking in parables not "*so that* they *may not* see" but "*because* seeing they *do not* see"!) The adoption of the Isaiah passage in the Gospel of Mark shows that Isaiah and the New Testament community held a common perception of how God works. But let us return to Isaiah.

Yes, the Hebrew really means what it says. Isaiah was a man of unclean lips, and he dwelt in the midst of a people of unclean lips. God (through the seraph) had dealt with Isaiah. Now he must deal with the people. These words show how he will deal with them. Still, we ask, how can we see this monstrous assignment in the context of Isaiah's career?

The second thing to notice is that evidently this

prediction did *not* come true completely: a few people, at least, must have heard and heard, and then understood; a few people, at least, must have seen and seen, and then perceived; a few people, at least, must have understood and turned. Isaiah did gain some disciples, so far as we can tell from 8:16. Isaiah's words *were* remembered, collected, passed down from generation to generation, enlarged upon—we saw all that in Chapter I—and his words became a secure guide to Jews and Christians in their thinking about God.

Furthermore, Isaiah himself allowed for the possibility (at least theoretically he did—we shall pursue the matter in Chapter V) that people would change their ways (1:19-20). He named one of his sons Shear-jashub ("a remnant shall turn," or "return"—the Hebrew word is the same for both), and this son, so named, would be a permanent show-and-tell to remind people that at least a few will experience a change for the better. (We shall consider the problem of this name's specific meaning in Chapter V.) If a son is named "A remnant shall (re)turn," then the call to speak to people in such a way that they will *not* comprehend "lest they *turn* and be healed" cannot have been the full measure of Isaiah's understanding of God's will for him and his people.

Having said this much, we still have not grasped the enormity of the scandal of Isaiah's commission to go out and harden people's hearts. Needless to say, all kinds of suggestions have been made by commentators to explain the matter. Here are a few to think about.

(1) It is suggested that Isaiah understood this commission to be directed not to Judah, where he lived, but to *the northern kingdom of Israel*, centered in Samaria, which was to fall to the Assyrians in 721 B.C.[12] But this will not do, for the words "this people" (vs. 9) clearly refer to the people among whom Isaiah dwelt (vs. 5), and so far as the texts indicate, Isaiah lived in Jerusalem and dealt with the kings of Judah there.

(2) It is suggested that the call-narrative as we now have it is the meaning of the call-experience which took

shape in Isaiah's mind at the *end* of his career, as he looked back over 40 years of a disappointing ministry. In the light of what followed during his career, this is how he would have understood what the intention of God for him had been at the outset.[13] This is an attractive approach and not altogether implausible. If Isaiah recognized at the end of his career that the people had not responded to his speaking, then *either* he had misunderstood God's call to him (which would have been incredible!), *or* God had intended great things for his career but was too weak to follow through in Isaiah's ministry (which also would have been incredible!), *or* God must have intended it that way. But against this approach is the fact that Isaiah records that he was as appalled by the commission as we are ("Then I said, 'How long, O Lord?'" vs. 11); this reaction does not accord well with the kind of bitter hard-heartedness which we would have to assume for Isaiah if the suggestion were correct.

(3) It is suggested that Isaiah understands God to be speaking sarcastically here. Other prophets may have had positive assignments, but to Isaiah God gives a negative assignment, to give people ignorance. Isaiah would be commanded, as it were, to be an anti-prophet, to do the opposite of what a prophet ordinarily does, since an anti-people, a people who turned out to be all that God's people should not be, deserve an anti-prophet.[14] This is a suggestion that seems closer to the truth. Of course, to call any passage of scripture that seems implausible "ironic" or "sarcastic" is a dangerous device, for by this method one could explain away everything in scripture. But is certainly true that Isaiah could use the most biting sarcasm (read 29:9-10).

Finally, I suppose, we must come to terms with the words as they are. Elsewhere Isaiah affirmed that God's work is strange and alien (28:21); and certainly, according to a striking passage, Isaiah understood God to be about to trample down the vineyard which is Israel and Judah and make it a waste (5:1-7—see the discussion of this passage at the end of Chapter III). There is precedent for God's sending a confusing and misleading word, notably in 1 Kings 22:19-23. (All of vss. 1-28 in that chapter should be read to gain some sense of how people in those early days understood God to be working through the prophets.) According to tradition, God hardened Pharaoh's heart (Exod. 10:1); now he is about to fatten the heart of this people and harden their ears (the verb translated "make heavy" here in 6:10 is the same verb as "harden" in Exod. 10:1). Does Isaiah understand that as Pharaoh opposed God's intention at the beginning, so Israel and Judah oppose God's intention now? It would seem so.

Of course this grim program is in contrast to Isaiah's actual effectiveness. The sturdy memory of Isaiah's sayings which has come down to us proves his effectiveness. This grim program is also in contrast to the meaning of the name of Isaiah's son, Shear-jashub. But language in the Old Testament always tends to be of the all-or-nothing-at-all variety. Logical contradictions rarely bothered the Old Testament writers. The point is this: Isaiah really seems to have perceived, at the time of his call, that God's patience was at an end and that anything that could be done to hasten the day of judgment was to the good: that was to be the purpose of Isaiah's ministry.

But the idea of God's losing patience is just what we hate to face. God cannot really be like this; Isaiah must have misunderstood. This must surely be a curious relic of long-ago scare-tactics on the part of the religious leadership of Israel. In the light of Jesus' teaching of the fatherly love of God, we feel we must put all this aside.

I am not sure, however; perhaps we are too hasty. After all, Isaiah knew about the fatherhood of God, too. The opening saying in the collection which begins chapter 1 offers this:

> *Hear, O heavens,*
> *and give ear, O earth;*
> *for the Lord has spoken:*
> *Sons have I reared and brought up,*
> *but they have rebelled against me.*

Children of a father, yes; but what if the children are obdurate, what if they rebel? (There was a law about what,

ultimately, parents must do with a rebellious son—read
Deut. 21:18-21. Let us hope the law was not invoked too
often.) What can a father do? Jesus himself despaired of
Jerusalem. He wished to gather the people as a hen gathers
her brood, but his final climactic words were, "you would
not!" (Matt. 23:37). The whole of that narrative of Jesus
(vss. 29-39) should be read by those whose notion of Jesus is
one only of "happy" emotions. Jesus was scathing in his
denunciations too. We must understand that some people do
not respond to a vision of love and mutuality. Some people
did not respond to Jesus, and, according to Isaiah, God faced
people who had not responded to his own offer of love and
mutuality—and God wants to take steps with such people as
efficiently as possible. We don't like to face the problem of
human evil, but Isaiah's call forces us to.

> *Go, and say to his people:*
>
> *"Hear all you please, but do not understand;*
> *see all you please, but do not perceive."*

It is not a pretty picture, but we had best not try to tame
either God or Isaiah to our liking.[15]

The final verses of this chapter only reinforce the sad,
shocking finality of it all. "Then I said, 'How long, O Lord?'
And he said: 'Until cities lie waste without inhabitant. . . .' "

It is well to state here that the meaning of the last verse
in the chapter, vs. 13, is obscure in the Hebrew text. The
Hebrew literally says, "And still in it [that is, the land] (is?)
a tenth, and it [the land?] shall return and be for burning;
like a terebinth and like an oak, in which in felling (is?) a
stump; a holy seed (is) its stump." There is no way in
which these lines can be made to yield coherent poetry, or
coherent prose either, for that matter. The text has been
mangled and perhaps censored in some way. The last line
looks like a "gloss," that is, a marginal note which crept into
the text. With minimal change in the present text we could
read the words which begin "like a terebinth" in this way:
"like the terebinth [of the goddess?] and the oak of Asherah

[the name of the fertility goddess; see 2 Kings 23:4], cast out with the pillar of the high places."[16] In this understanding, the text would have referred to forbidden fertility cult practices (on this matter, see Chapter III). Although the verse is difficult, the thrust of the commission to Isaiah is clear enough if we remain with the material through vs. 12.

Though this study guide is not primarily concerned with New Testament problems, we do need to refer once more to the use made of vss. 9-10 in Mark 4:12 and parallels. This adaptation of the Isaiah passage in the gospels is striking and has understandably evoked much discussion. The consensus of judgment of scholars is that these words do not represent Jesus' own thinking about his parables but are a later reflection by Mark of the meaning of Jesus' mission as he saw it in the latter half of the first century A.D., when the lines between Christian and anti-Christian groups were hardening.[17]

We have spent most of this chapter exploring Isaiah's vision of God and what this meant to him and to his people. Inevitably, other kinds of questions arise. Is this vision *valid*? Does this material offer any secure clues as to what God is *really* like?

Of course many people will be content with the imagery as it is, for, they say, this is scriptural material, it has been channeled to us from a prophet who spoke for God, and that is the end of it. Of course it is valid!

But others will hesitate, and those who hesitate may have a great variety of reactions to such a vision. There are those who, while accepting a "high" view of God and understanding him as something quite different from human beings, are convinced that *love* is the key, and finding little here that they can call "love," they are repelled. They are repelled even more when they perceive someone embracing such a vision of God as Isaiah offers, but embracing it neurotically, craving the guilty status which such a vision warrants, eagerly seeking the punishment he or she feels is deserved but has been denied. There is no doubt that visions like Isaiah's can have such an effect, and there is little doubt that it is unhealthy.

Then there are others who are not sure what it means
to say that God is "high," preferring, let us say, to describe
God as Paul Tillich does, as "the Ground of all Being."[18]
These people may find some room in their own schemes for
the *judgment* implied by the holiness of God over against
the un-holiness of Isaiah and his people, but, after all, do
people's sensitized consciences not offer all the capacity for
self-judgment and the judgment of society which one needs?
So for these people, the awesome *otherness* of God implied
by Isaiah's vision seems unhelpful.

Still others think of "God" only as a kind of symbol for
one's highest principles and ideals, or the highest ideals of
society, or as an idea or concept, and to them the stark
personhood of Isaiah's vision is repellent, reflecting only
some outgrown primitivism.

And then there was the man who was asked his idea of
God, who paused for a moment and said, "Well, I guess my
idea of God is more of an oblong blur than anything else."
It is clear that Isaiah's sense of God is worlds apart from the
vagueness of an oblong blur.

Isaiah's God is specific, personal, involved with his
people and yet absolutely distinct from them; he is far, far
beyond any easy approachability. My family had a foolish
dog once who could sometimes be persuaded, when we
would yell "sick-'em" on moonlit nights, to chase the moon.
Needless to say he never caught up with it. One has the
feeling that Isaiah's God, to us, is something like the moon
to our dog. Thus, the ultimate question is, Does Isaiah's
vision have any claim on us and on our vision of God?

As we seek to answer this question, we must understand
that there were those in Israel who understood quite well
the *symbolic* nature of all God-talk. At the beginning of this
chapter we took note of Ezekiel's initial vision, which ends,
"Such was the appearance of the likeness and glory of the
Lord" (Ezek. 1:28). Israel knew that no words are adequate
for God. But perhaps Isaiah could agree to this: *any other
words* we could find to use to talk about God *would be
even less adequate* to say what needs to be said than the
words I use. When words fail, we do the best we can,

letting the words we do have do their work on our sensibilities.

So we are invited neither to swallow Isaiah's vision whole nor to reject it out of hand, but to take it seriously, to see where it leads, what its consequences are for our own understanding of God. Scripture constantly enlarges our perceptions. We sense this, or we should not be involved in a study like this one. The invitation is open to us, then, to discover how Isaiah's own sensitivity was shaped by his encounter with the high and holy God of his tradition.

We have become acquainted in this chapter with the man Isaiah—not biographically, as we might have wished, but instead in the only way we can, by reference to the call to prophesy which made him what he was. We would also like to know what he looked like, what kind of upbringing he had and where, how old he was when he felt the call of God, what his feelings were as he began preaching, how long a career he had, how people reacted to his words, and when and where he died. Unfortunately, we have few details of this kind, and we must be content with what memories did survive.

What few details we have from scattered notices here and there we may bring together now. We learn that his father's name was Amoz (1:1), but we are not told the place of his birth.

We have already mentioned that Isaiah accepted his vocation at the time of King Uzziah's death, 742 B.C. (6:1). Uzziah's son Jotham, who had evidently been co-regent with his father for a number of years after his father had become ill, became the next king. Jotham himself died after reigning in his own name for about seven years (around 735 B.C.). Though 1:1 states that Isaiah prophesied during Jotham's reign, nothing we have from Isaiah is specifically datable to the time of his reign. Jotham's son Ahaz took the throne next (735-715). Two incidents narrated in chapter 7 (vss. 1-9, vss. 10-17), and perhaps a third, narrated in chapter 8 (vss. 1-4a), involve Ahaz. During that period the northern kingdom of Israel fell (721). But it was during the reign of Ahaz's son Hezekiah (715-687) that the climactic crisis occurred in the history of Judah within the span of Isaiah's life: the invasion of Judah by the Assyrian king Sennacherib. We have an extended narrative of Isaiah's dealings with King Hezekiah during this emergency, reported both in 2 Kings 18-19 and in Isaiah 36-39, though we cannot be certain of the historical accuracy of every detail in these reports.[19] We shall give our attention to these incidents in the reigns of Ahaz and Hezekiah in Chapter IV.

Isaiah was married. We have the names of two sons, Shear-jashub (7:3) and Maher-shalal-hash-baz (8:3) (see Chapter V), but his wife is simply called "the prophetess" (8:3), leaving her anonymous. We do not even know whether her designation "prophetess" indicates that she, too, prophesied, or whether this is simply a way of referring to the wife of a prophet. We have a bare mention of "disciples" of Isaiah (8:16). Of Isaiah's death we know nothing, but the dates we have named for his ministry, 742-701, a 40-year span, match a normal adult career. When Jerusalem was saved from Sennacherib's battering-rams, when the crisis passed, Isaiah fades from our hearing. It may be reassuring to know that this dearth of knowledge about how Isaiah died bothered ancient people too: we have a legendary account, originating perhaps in the first century B.C., of how, in the days of King Manasseh (687-642 B.C.), Isaiah was sawn in two.[20] This legend is no doubt what is behind the curious statement in Hebrews 11:37. We would be wise, however, if we viewed this tradition as simply what imaginative people later on decided would be a fitting death for a remarkable life.

We are left, then, with what was central for both Isaiah and his hearers—his message. Next, we shall consider what manner of message this was, and whether, after all, it was delivered with an eye to the return of a remnant or with an eye to the utter deadening of the sensibilities of his hearers.

The opening oracle in the collection, to which we have already referred, sets the stage:

Hear, O heavens, and give ear, O earth;

> *for the Lord has spoken:*
> Sons have I reared and brought up,
>   but they have rebelled against me.
> The ox knows its owner,
>   and the ass its master's crib;
> but Israel does not know,
>   my people does not understand.

Since Israel had a tradition about God which went back at least to Moses, five hundred years before, why does Isaiah say that the people does not know? In what way has Israel rebelled? How is it that the dumb ox is smarter than Israel is? It is to these matters that we now turn.

CHAPTER III

The Breakdown of Community

A T THE END OF Chapter II we looked briefly at 1:2-3. This "oracle" (which is the term scholars use to refer to a single utterance of a prophet, one message delivered on a particular occasion), placed at the beginning of the Isaianic tradition, sets the theme for the message of the prophet. God has reared up sons, but they have rebelled against him; even the dumb ox is more responsive to its owner.

It may not be apparent to the present-day reader, but the background of this passage is the image of a cosmic *lawcourt*. Both Isaiah and his hearers assumed this. The "heavens" and the "earth" are addressed as witnesses or jurymen in a public disputation which is about to take place. One can find similar addresses to the "mountains," "hills," and the "foundation of the earth" in Micah 6:1-2, and in that passage the legal language is even more obvious. (There are other such passages too: Mic. 1:2—"peoples," "earth"; Jer. 2:12—"heavens"; Jer. 6:18-19—"nation," "earth.") In such a format God the king sits as judge *and* acts as plaintiff in a lawsuit against Israel.[1] In Chapter II, in our discussion of 1:2-3, we made reference to the law in Deuteronomy 21:18-21, how to treat a rebellious son. The law, we recall, prescribes that the parents are to bring such a son out to the elders of the city, sitting at the gate, and should make a public case of the matter. So here in 1:2-3 God is making a public case out of the dispute between himself and Israel.

But why should God's quarrel with Israel be assumed to involve a *lawsuit*, of all things? This imagery goes back to Israel's understanding of the *covenant* between God and

Israel, for a covenant, after all, is a contract, and Isaiah is proclaiming the fact that the contract has been broken by one of the signatories.

The covenant he has in mind, of course, was the covenant of Sinai. In Exodus 24:1-8 we can read a narrative of the ratification of this covenant, found after the presentation of the Ten Commandments and associated laws.

But what evidently seemed so natural to the Israelite, namely a description of the relationship between God and his people in legal terms, seems somehow offensive to us. Why should God's relation to his people be reduced, we wonder, to the level of a legal contract? Could they find no more appealing image for a relationship with God than something suggesting a lawyer's office?

The point is this: today, when *we* wish to clarify a relationship between two people, we often resort to psychological terms (we say, "She is ambivalent toward him," or whatever), while in *Israelite* times a relationship was clarified by a resort to legal language ("She is obligated toward him, and he toward her, in these ways. . ."). As we noticed in Chapter II, Moses' understanding of God's dealings with Israel was based on a political model, that of a treaty between a sovereign and his vassal prince. A sovereign in those days would make guarantees to a particular vassal—for example, military support against common enemies, and assurance of the economic well-being of the vassal's realm. At the same time the vassal made guarantees to the sovereign: to provide a certain amount of military and economic support to the sovereign (so many troops, so much tribute), to agree to submit all disputes between himself and another vassal to the sovereign for settlement, and so on. The various obligations of the vassal were his responsibility in the treaty; if he broke them, then the sovereign could punish him in a variety of ways, and the gods would, too, as we see by the various curses spelled out that would be invoked if the treaty were broken.

Since early Israel understood its status under God in the same way, we can see how such a "contract"-form would be suitable to a view of God who is characterized as a king, as

personal, and as quite other than the sum-total of Israel's own
goals or ideals. Isaiah shared this vision of God with his
people.

The obligations of Israel in her contract with God are
exemplified (though not exhausted) by the Ten Commandments. The Ten Commandments do have a kind of legal
"air" about them, it is true, but it is noteworthy that they
specify no punishments for those people who break them.
We are not told what was to be done to someone when he
bore false witness against his neighbor; we are only told,
"Don't do it!" The Ten Commandments do not offer a list of
crimes to which penalties are attached, but rather an outline
of the behavior appropriate to a new community characterized by trust and mutuality among its members and by
loyalty to God who is their king (the only king they had,
until the rise of the monarchy, as we saw in Chapter II).
Later collections of laws were gathered around the Ten
Commandments, some of them with penalties attached,
some without. All these laws helped characterize this new
community.

Read through Exodus 21-23. Here are all kinds of laws
which a rural community needs to be able to live together.
Try to catch the spirit of them. If there is sometimes inten-
tional murder, then sometimes there is involuntary man-
slaughter too (Exod. 21:12-14). There are oxen who might
gore someone unexpectedly, but then there are also oxen
whose owners have been repeatedly warned (Exod.
21:28-29). Don't be a party to malicious gossip (Exod.
23:1); don't pervert justice in the courts (Exod. 23:2). Bring
back your neighbor's straying ass even if this particular
neighbor happens to be someone you hate (Exod. 23:4).
Don't take economic advantage of non-citizens; remember,
you were once non-citizens yourselves (Exod. 23:9). Of
course there are also many laws which seem irrelevant
today—laws involved with taboos, with curious cultic details
(Exod. 23:14); laws regarding slaves, who were not treated
the way freemen were (Exod. 21:20-21); laws regarding
women, who were not treated the way men were (Exod.
22:16-17). Of course, we are dealing with a community

whose ethical standard leaves much to be desired; but these laws, and many like them, indicate the shape of a community which sensed from the beginning that to be in covenant with God meant to be responsible to him and to be sensitive to the obligations of justice within the whole community.

It is precisely this sense of justice within the whole community which Isaiah saw lacking in the people of his generation. In passage after scathing passage he speaks words of judgment in the name of God to those who have perverted the justice which God expects.

These oracles of judgment are found in chapters 1, 3, 5, 10, 28, and 30, and it is these which we shall be examining in this chapter. Let us begin with 1:10-17. In vs. 10, as we already noted in Chapter I, Isaiah addresses his people as "Sodom" and "Gomorrah"—cities blasted by God in the distant past for their wickedness. What name today could match it for contempt and horror? "Huns," perhaps?

Then Isaiah moves in to criticize the people for their religious rituals—their sacrifices (vs. 11); their festivals (vss. 13-14); even their prayers (vs. 15), for in those days the "spreading forth of hands" was the attitude of prayer. The problem with those hands spread forth in prayer is that they are bloody with social injustice (vs. 16). In short, Isaiah is rebuking the people in the name of God for being "religious," as that trait is ordinarily understood. In a stunning series of short lines of only two Hebrew words each, a simplified check-list for the dull of mind, he ticks off God's rules:

> *Cease to do evil.*
> *Learn to do good,*
> *search for justice,*
> *help the oppressed,*
> *be just to the orphan,*
> *plead for the widow* (vss. 16-17, *Jerusalem Bible*).

Now you and I take it for granted that somebody ought to be looking after the widows and orphans, whether it be their families, the church, the county, or the state. But the reason we take it for granted is at least partly because people like Isaiah have reminded us of our obligations. Of course, looking after the widow and the orphan had been a part of the mandate of the total Israelite community at the beginning, but by Isaiah's day the basic economic and social unit had become the large extended family group. In such a society a widow or orphan (who could not claim such an extended family, and therefore had no man for economic support or for a spokesman in court) could lose out. Read the story that Jesus told about the widow who kept bothering the judge (Luke 18:1-6) and get some sense of the widow's desperation.

Social justice, then, was a prime concern of Isaiah's, a concern we understand ourselves (though we are not always much better than Isaiah's contemporaries were in responding to it). But why is Isaiah against religious ritual? Does he want to do away with sacrifice and religious observance altogether? If so, he would immediately be a hero to many people today who look back upon animal sacrifice in Israel as a barbarous, bloody waste. We would not "delight in the blood of bulls" (vs. 11) either.

Something quite different is at stake here, however. There are few scholars today who would maintain that Isaiah really wanted to do away with all public religious observance completely and permanently, as we might too easily assume. Religious communities in ancient (and modern) times always need some kind of religious observance. A curiosity of Hebrew grammar may give us some perspective in the matter, for the Hebrew language lacked any easy way to express a preference, any easy way to rank items in order of *priority*, to say "rather this than that." In Genesis 29:31 we are told that Jacob "hated" Leah, but the context makes it clear that the Hebrew word "hate" here really means "loved less." Jacob did not want to get rid of Leah—he simply *loved* Leah *less* than he did Rachel. (Compare Deut. 21:15, where the English word "disliked" in the *Revised Standard Version* is the same Hebrew verb "hated." Here, too, it clearly means "loved less.") Isaiah's message in 1:10-17 seems to be that God does love sacrifices, but he loves them *less* than justice. He wants *justice first.* Sacrifices may be good and necessary, but they are never sufficient. Justice is distinctive to the covenant community, and justice is what God is yearning for. (The same assessment should be made of other anti-sacrifice sentiments in the Old Testament, such as Amos 5:21-24.)[2] This view of sacrifice would bring Isaiah close to Jesus' teaching (see Matt. 23:23, especially vs. 23b).

Since justice is missing, God accuses Israel of rebelling (vs. 2), forsaking God, despising him (vs. 3). Israel seems unable to take the hint when God punishes her (vss. 5-6), even when the country appears ravaged and left desolate by foreign armies (vss. 7-8); lucky that a few have survived! (vs. 9). This oracle, following the opening one, sets forth many of the key themes of the prophet Isaiah: the refusal of the people to be the community God wants them to be (vs. 4), the theme which we are exploring in the present chapter of this study; the ravaging of the countryside by foreign armies (vss. 7-8), which we shall discuss in Chapter IV; and the bridge to a better future which the surviving remnant offers (vs. 9), which we shall discuss in Chapter V.

What has made the community forget its vocation for justice and righteousness? It is the *leaders*, it seems, who are to blame, according to vss. 21-23. It is the princes who are rebels; it is they who do not defend the orphans or widows. The men who should be offering leadership, who should be setting the pace, are not doing so. They are a part of the problem, not a part of the answer.

The theme of leadership is expanded in the long oracle (or collection of oracles) in 3:1-15, and this passage will repay our close attention. Verses 1-8 say, in effect, that since the leaders of Judah have failed, God is going to take them away altogether and replace them. They are the "stay and staff" (vs. 1), and out they must go. (We must note in passing that the words "the whole stay of bread and the whole staff of water" do not belong; they appear to be a "gloss" [see Chapter II], an insertion by a later copyist who did not understand Isaiah's use of "stay and staff" to refer to the leaders listed in the lines of vss. 2-3.) Isaiah is convinced that God will "make the punishment fit the crime." If the leaders of Jerusalem and Judah—the military man, the judge, the prophet—have been unfit, then God will replace them with youngsters, so that there will be utter anarchy (vss. 4-5). (Incidentally, a recent study indicates that the Hebrew word for "boys" [vs. 4] and "youth" [vs. 5] means a servant of high rank, like the medieval *squire*;[3] but Isaiah's point here is still that society will be turned upside down.)

Today, this might not be seen as a punishment at all. In Western culture in the last couple of decades there has been an upsurge of "youth culture," so that in our context Isaiah's concern for *order* in society, his view that to make boys their princes (vs. 4) is a punishment rather than a liberation, will strike some as reactionary. Why *not* make boys their princes? They might do better than the old guard!

The Old Testament in general is *not* automatically pro-the-older-generation and anti-the-younger-generation—this must be emphasized. Abraham was told to *leave* his father's house (Gen. 12:1); God had better things in store for him. Joel preached that old men shall dream dreams *and* young men shall see visions (Joel 3:28). Jeremiah tried to excuse himself by saying he was too young to prophesy, but God overruled him (Jer. 1:6-7). Isaiah himself looked to a child for a sign of new hope (7:14-16).

But the fact remains that Isaiah had a keen sense of the need for *stability* in social structures, and the society of his day was held together by a thin veneer of leading families whose skills in leadership were based upon the traditional lore and wisdom which one absorbed with experience and years (see Job 12:12). Strip that veneer away, Isaiah feels, and all is chaos. That social structure[4] was a different matter from the social structure of present-day Western culture with its mobility, its communications network, its literacy. Few of us have had any first-hand experience with real social chaos—the kind that overcame mainland China in the months before the Maoists took power in 1949, or overcame Lebanon during the civil war of 1975-1976—when there is no agreed-upon authority, and power is in the hands of local chiefs of one sort or another. It is nightmarish. It is this experience which Isaiah means to depict as he foresees the present corrupt leaders being stripped away by God. And the nightmare gets worse (vs. 6), for one says to another, You have an overcoat, so be our leader! What a reason for leadership, when one's realm is nothing but a smoking ruin anyway! And worse, Mr. Overcoat says no (vs. 7), leaving people with no leader at all. The passage winds back on itself in vs. 12 with a reinforcement in which the leaders are not only children but women as well. The remarks I have already made about Isaiah's view of a stable society obviously imply that he could not conceive of the leadership of women any more than he could of leadership by the young. The passage ends by summarizing the themes upon which we have already touched: God will judge his people (vss. 13-14) because they have ground down the face of the poor (vss. 14-15).

The next passage deals with women, but deals with them centrally, not glancingly as vs. 12 did. The passage includes vss. 16-17 + 24 (for the sequence, see the remarks on this passage in Chapter I). Isaiah offers here what amounts to a parody of the glitter and the clatter of women parading up and down the street. Again, says the prophet, the punishment will fit the crime, for God will substitute the badges of humiliation for the emblems of beauty. In passing, let me remark on two matters of text. First, in vs. 17 the word translated "secret parts" in the *Revised Standard Version* is a rare word in Hebrew, and may mean "foreheads" (*New English Bible*) or "pates" (*New Jewish Version*) instead. And second, the last word in vs. 24, "shame" in the *Revised Standard Version*, is almost certainly "branding" (*Jerusalem Bible* and *New English Bible*) or "a burn" (*New Jewish Version*). Present-day women who are concerned for parity in sex roles will not like the emphasis on finery and decoration here, but we must remind ourselves that Isaiah spoke out of a society where sex roles were clearly defined and traditional. The point is that he was convinced that neither the male leadership (vss. 1-8) nor the women (vss. 16-17 + 24) were behaving responsibly, and that for both sets of people God had prepared an appropriate punishment.

In chapter 5 we find a whole series of "woes" pronounced against various groups in the population who exhibit behavior that works against community. One by one he ticks them off. There are first of all the covetous (vss. 8-10), who buy up the real estate of poor people until they are left to their lonesome selves in the middle of their huge holdings (vs. 8). We react differently to aloneness: for us, solitude is something to which we look forward from time to time—some time in the woods to get away from the press of people in our cities. But for the Israelites of that time, who lived with a far lower population density than most of us experience, the good life consists of clustering together for security and community; for them, living alone is a terrible fate. (Compare the image of loneliness in 1:8.) As for all their houses, they will be empty (vs. 9), and as for their fields, they will yield hardly anything (vs. 10)—the Hebrew measures indicate this. We saw in Chapter I that a "bath" is about six gallons or 23 liters—not much wine from ten acres; and since there are ten ephahs to a homer (compare Ezek. 45:11), one certainly cannot get ahead by *sowing* ten times as much seed as one *harvests*. The punishment, again, will fit the crime: greed brings its own reward.

Then there are the carousers (vss. 11-13). We should understand that the word translated "strong drink" in vs. 11 does not mean distilled liquor, for the process of distillation was not developed until the European Middle Ages. This Hebrew word originally meant a kind of barley beer, but later was extended to refer to any alcoholic drink brewed from grain or fruit. If we are looking for a single word, "beer" would be best. The Israelites did not disapprove of wine as such—it gladdens the heart of man (Ps. 104:15). But, plainly, people who seek wine and beer from early morning till late at night and do nothing but carouse (vs. 12) are not taking Yahweh's will seriously. The *Revised Standard Version* has a white space separating vss. 12 and 13, but I think this is in error, since vs. 13 states the punishment for the carousers, and again the punishment fits the crime—they will go into exile, fainting from hunger and thirst.

Verses 14-17 appear to be either an insertion here, or else a parallel picture of doom which uses another "hunger" image: Sheol (the world of the grave, the abode of the dead) "gapes with straining throat" (in the vivid phrasing of the *New English Bible*). People are gobbled up by the grave. In this way God is exalted while people are humbled (vss. 15-16), and here we have that same note of contrast between the exalted God and humble humanity which we explored in Chapter II. And in the day of punishment who besides Sheol will have enough to eat? Animals will, who feed among the ruins (vs. 17). The ancient Orient knew what ruined cities are, and the Orient is dotted with them still. As one drives along a highway in Syria today one may come upon ruins; and if he stops the car and strolls off to explore them, he may unexpectedly come upon a shepherd pasturing his flock. It is hard to imagine a more vivid reminder of the impermanence of human societies than to see fatlings and kids feeding among the ruins.

More "woes" follow: first a "woe" on the people who doubt that God really is at work—who say, "Come on, show us what the purposes of God really are, so we can see for ourselves!" (vss. 18-19). The meaning of vs. 18 is not as certain as we could wish; several commentators favor an understanding of the text as follows:

> Woe to those who draw guilt with sheep cords
> and sin with calf ropes.[5]

If this is a correct understanding, then the passage would link up with the "lambs, fatlings and kids" in vs. 17 and suggest people who drag sin along with about as much speed as they can drag a heifer along, but who at the same time want Yahweh's work to hurry along at double time. One has the feeling that Isaiah is here burlesquing conventional phrases in people's minds, but it is no longer possible to be sure of the joke.

Then come three more "woes," quickly sketched (vss.

20-23). First, those who call things by their opposites, and who do the opposite of what they imply they are doing (vs. 20). We can understand what Isaiah means since there has been a similar devaluation of the currency of language in our own day. For example, the American government has spoken of "preventive reaction strikes" when they mean "bombing raids"; there are "preservatives" in foods that turn out to cause cancer. Of course usage in a language does change in the course of time, but one cannot help feeling that there is sometimes a deliberate avoidance of reality in the expressions we favor. In Chapter II we referred to Isaiah's concern that people say what they mean. There are also people whose every action makes one wonder what they are *really* up to. This is what Isaiah is talking about here. And then quickly, in vss. 21-23, the conceited (vs. 21), and, once more, the drunken (vs. 22), who corrupt the legal process for a bribe (vs. 23).

It is common to say that the Old Testament was concerned with people's actions, while Jesus was concerned with people's attitudes as well. But Isaiah, too, was concerned not only with the unjust things people *do*, but also about the wrong use of words, about wrong attitudes. This string of vignettes presents people who are thoughtless, devious, unscrupulous, who run after beer and doubt the justice of God, who enjoy foreclosing mortgages and think nothing of depriving the poor of their rights. It is not a pretty picture Isaiah paints of his community. But it all sounds quite familiar; these are people we know, too.

There is one more "woe" in the series, as we saw in Chapter I; it is found in 10:1-4. No explanation of the passage is so good as the passage itself, particularly as the *Jerusalem Bible* has it:

> Woe to the legislators of infamous laws,
> to those who issue tyrannical decrees,
> who refuse justice to the unfortunate
> and cheat the poor among my people of their rights,
> who make widows their prey
> and rob the orphan.
> What will you do on the day of punishment,

when, from far off, destruction comes?
To whom will you run for help?
Where will you leave your riches?
Nothing for it but to crouch with the captives
And to fall with the slain.
Yet his anger is not spent,
Still his hand is raised to strike.

Here, then, is Isaiah's description of a society whose genuine community had broken down altogether. The description is so scathing that we are impelled to ask, Is Isaiah's description fair? Was it really like this? Was he justified in such an overwhelming judgment?

Of course a moment's thought will make it clear that there is no way we can possibly get a "reading" on the moral tone of Isaiah's generation or any other in ancient times. It is hard enough to get a reading on our own. In *every* generation there are people who are better than our expectations and people who are worse. One's comparison of his own generation with earlier ones is always skewed by sentimentality and faulty memory; the "good old days" always seem a little better, maybe, than they really were. But we must understand that the people of Israel had become involved, by the time Isaiah was preaching, in practices of agriculture and of the marketplace which put new stresses and strains on their society. When the Israelites had lived as nomads in the desert and when they had first settled down in Palestine, they *had* to look after the widow and the orphan; it was only common sense to be one for all and all for one. But new agricultural and mercantile ways brought on new temptations to take economic advantage of one's neighbor, so that Isaiah's dismal description had a basis in fact. It really does seem to have been harder to be good than it had been in earlier, poorer times. On the other hand, it is quite possible that Isaiah and the other prophets of his time may have been more sensitive to subtle sorts of wickedness than religious spokesmen had been in earlier times. But whatever the basis in fact for Isaiah's denunciations, they struck Israel like a thunderclap. If the people were truly as insensitive as Isaiah said they were, then it is no wonder he was convinced that the more he preached, the less they would understand (6:9-10).

There is a related question which we must consider: to whom was Isaiah speaking, anyway? We recall from Chapter II that some commentators have thought Isaiah's mandate to increase people's insensitivity was a mandate directed to the *northern* kingdom (Israel) rather than to the southern one (Judah). There is no doubt that *some* of the material in Isaiah was directed to the north (for example, 28:1-4, to which we shall turn in a moment, since this passage mentions "Ephraim," and Ephraim was a northern tribe). But the place names in the passages which we have so far examined are all southern: "daughter of Zion" (1:8), "Jerusalem" and "Judah" (3:8), "daughters of Zion" (3:16). Isaiah lived in Jerusalem, so far as we know, and though he had a concern for the north until that kingdom fell in 721 B.C., his focus was plainly on the south.

Let us turn now to chapter 28, which begins with that passage about Ephraim (vss. 1-4) of which we just took note. Verses 1-4 + 7-13 make up a passage with several remarkable features. The drunkards of Ephraim are complacent because they feel safe. The word "crown" (vss. 1, 3) is evidently an image for the circle of the defense-wall on the round hill of Samaria, which will be cast down (vs. 2) and trodden under foot (vs. 3) by a military force which will come on like a hailstorm or flood of waters (vs. 2). ("Overflowing waters" is an image for the enemy force in another of Isaiah's oracles [8:7] which we shall study in detail in Chapter IV.) So this "crown," the defense-wall, will fall into the hand of the enemy as easily as a sweet, fat fig falls into somebody's hand on a hot day of early summer and is swallowed whole (vs. 4). And, of course, it did happen; the northern capital of Samaria was besieged by Shalmaneser of Assyria (2 Kings 17:3-5) and then fell to his successor Sargon in 721 B.C. (compare 2 Kings 17:6). Complacency and drunkenness, it seems, were characteristics not only of the south; the north had manifested them too and had become ripe for the plucking.

Verses 5-6 are, so far as we can tell, a later insertion

that reinterprets the "crown," "glory," and "beauty" of vs. 1 to refer not to Ephraim's pride but instead to God, who will restore justice to his people.

So it is in vss. 7-13 that we find the completion of vss. 1-4. Verse 7 begins, oddly, with "these." Who are "these"? Does Isaiah accompany the word with a gesture? We must assume, I suppose, he means those in the south. And how do the southerners behave? Verses 7-8 offer a remarkable set of lines in which the interwoven words, by their very organization, suggest the weaving gait of the drunkards. Word by word the passage reads:

> And also these with the wine reel
>   and with the beer stagger,
> priest and prophet reel with the beer,
>   are confused from the wine,
>   stagger from the beer,
> reel in vision,
>   totter in decision;
> for all the tables are full of vomit,
>   filth without any space.

What's more, there is a nice pun here: in the fourth line the verb "are confused" is a homonym with another verb which means "are swallowed"—the same verb which appears in vs. 4, where the ripe fig "is swallowed." Thus, the fourth line here could be translated not only "are confused from the wine," but also "are swallowed by the wine." The drunkards thought they were doing the swallowing, and all the while the wine was swallowing *them*. Who is boss, they or their wine?

I would suggest that what we have here is Isaiah's own later extension to the south, his later reapplication, of an earlier oracle he had directed against the northerners. Some years before, evidently, Isaiah had expressed his contempt for the drunken complacency of the people in Samaria; but now, he sees, the southerners are in even worse shape, and so he took the old words against the north and used them as a backdrop for a longer oracle against the south. The two parts (vss. 1-4 and vss. 7-13) are linked not only by the obvious descriptions of drunkenness, but also by the pun on "swallowed" in vss. 4 and 7 and by the word "sees" (vs. 4) and "vision" (vs. 7), which are the same in Hebrew. This phenomenon of what I shall call the "self-extended" oracle occurs again in Isaiah: two examples from chapters 29 and 31 will be discussed in Chapter IV. (The book of Jeremiah evidently offers two more of these as well.)[6]

The scene of the drunken brawl prompts a mocking follow-up (vss. 9-13) which is evidently quite vivid but at the same time is not easy for us to reconstruct. We start with vss. 9-10: What do they mean? Who is speaking? The "he" of vs. 9 could well be God (compare "the Lord will speak" in vs. 11; admittedly the Hebrew text in vs. 11 does not say "the Lord," simply "he," but "the Lord" is certainly implied). Isaiah may be asking, If the leaders of the people are drunk, then to whom can God communicate his message? To babies, maybe (vs. 9). Part of the shock of the contrast between the drunken leaders and the babies is the contrast between the wine and beer which the leaders continue to imbibe, and the milk which the babies have quit imbibing.

In vs. 10 it is doubtful if the Hebrew words in the first two lines really have a meaning: to translate them "precept upon precept. . . , line upon line. . ." is to force these syllables to have a meaning which they probably do not have. The Hebrew words are *ṣaw lāṣāw ṣaw lāṣāw qaw lāqāw qaw lāqāw*, and were obviously chosen more for their sound than for any sense; so the *Jerusalem Bible* is probably right simply to write the Hebrew syllables here. The suggestion has recently been made[7] and accepted by many scholars that these are the original names of the letters *ṣ* and *q* in the Hebrew alphabet (*q* comes right after *ṣ* in the Hebrew order of letters ("*ṣ* for your *ṣ*, *ṣ* for your *ṣ*, *q* for your *q*, *q* for your *q*"). In this case the word "little" in the last line may be the schoolmaster's address to one "youngster" or another: "Here, youngster; there, youngster." If, then, in vs. 9, Isaiah says God is going to have to start giving his message to babies, then in vs. 10 we would have his depiction of God the schoolmaster at work, starting from scratch with his people, letter by letter.

Or, alternatively, "he" in vs. 9 may not be God at

all, but Isaiah, and Isaiah may be quoting the sarcastic reaction of the drunkards to himself: "Who does he [that is, Isaiah] think he's teaching anyway? Why does he treat us like babies?" In this case, the syllables in vs. 10 would be the drunkards' imitation of Isaiah's prophetic discourse, making hash of it.

In any event, whether God through Isaiah must turn to babies or whether the drunkards accuse Isaiah of treating *them* like babies, God himself will do some speaking through people whose language Israel really *will* not be able to understand (vs. 11). The people who had ignored the true "rest" (vs. 12) which is an aspect of confidence in God (compare 30:15, and the discussion in Chapter IV) will soon be forced to cope with a *real* babble—the syllables of foreigners this time, *ṣaw lāṣāw* and all the rest (vs. 13)—and will be utterly defeated in war.

There is one more theme which emerges from our study of 28:7-13, namely the contempt with which the Israelite leaders treated Isaiah's message. We have another angle of vision on this matter, evidently, in 28:23-29. Isaiah sounds here like a teaching assistant in the School of Agriculture, offering a lecture in Ag. 1-A, saying the obvious to the farmers. Isaiah is saying that although one can grasp God's message to farmers on how to plant dill and barley, nobody, he implies, seems able to understand God's message to the people about justice. Jesus would say the same thing about people who know the signs of the weather but not the signs of the times (Matt. 16:1-3).

The contempt of Isaiah's hearers for his message is made crystal clear in 30:8-14; they are a rebellious people, lying sons (vs. 9—reminiscent of 1:2, 4, where we started), who say, "Prophesy not to us what is right; speak to us smooth things, prophesy illusions" (vs. 10). What an indictment of congregations who wish only good news, only comfortable words, from their religious leaders! This is really the equivalent of saying, "Let us hear no more of the Holy One of Israel" (vs. 11). The terrible words of the call of Isaiah have turned out to be true in this case: the people really are opaque to God's word. Therefore, God's action on these people will be like a wall about to buckle, which comes down with a crash; nothing will be left (vss. 13-14).

Perhaps the best succinct presentation of the breakdown of community in Israel and Judah is to be found in the remarkable song back in 5:1-7, a passage with which we have not yet dealt. This passage is a fitting one to round off this topic.

Isaiah takes the part of someone singing to the "beloved" (the Hebrew word is masculine) a love-song concerning his vineyard (vs. 1). Who is the beloved, and what is this all about? On the face of it, Isaiah could be singing a song to a friend in the context of the harvest festival, the feast of ingathering (Exod. 23:16b). Alternatively, it might be a wedding-song addressed to the bridegroom: evidently the image of "vineyard" often referred to the bride (compare Song of Songs 2:15, 8:11-12).[8] Or again, Isaiah may be embarked upon a parody of a fertility-cult hymn, in which case the "beloved" would be taken as the fertility deity. But this is a song which turns out to have a stinger in it (vs. 7), as we shall see. So if Isaiah seems to be talking about a friend at harvest time, then the friend turns out to be God; if Isaiah seems to be talking about a bridegroom, then the bridegroom turns out to be God; and if Isaiah seems to be talking in pagan terms about a fertility deity, then the real deity who gives fertility will be the true God. We wish we had a better grip on the ancient context of this song. Perhaps a modern equivalent would be trying to sing "Holy, Holy, Holy" to the tune of "Let Me Call You Sweetheart"? In any event, the first verse does not offer lush vocabulary which reminds one of the Song of Songs, or of the early Canaanite fertility-cult texts, for that matter.[9]

Verse 2 is, on the surface of it, a description of the patient work of a farmer digging, terracing, planting, building a tower to guard against thieves and birds. He planted vines which were to yield lush, red grapes. This is the meaning of the Hebrew phrase translated "choice vines." Since by looking ahead we know that the farmer will turn out to be God, we can sense here that Isaiah really has in mind the patient work of God in settling the people in the land of Palestine and working with them in a steady, patient fashion through the years. In the phrase "he looked for it to yield grapes," "looked for" is not strong enough; the Hebrew verb (*qiwwā*) means "hope earnestly," "strain with expectation."[10] God *longs* for the vine to turn out right. But it doesn't.

Verses 3-4 involve the hearers in the problem: what should I do, you farmers, that I have neglected to do? Now comes the first hint that there is more here than just agricultural advice asked for; the hearers are asked to "judge" between the farmer and his vineyard, as if there is a *dispute* between them. Compare the same phrase in Genesis 16:5 in the context of a squabble between Abraham and Sarah. Why did the grapes want to go and turn bad (as if it was deliberate on their part!)? Again we have the phrases of vs. 2, of God's *longing* for the vine to turn out right, when it doesn't.

Verses 5-6 go back to the agricultural activity of vs. 2, but now it is destructive activity. The farmer will remove the hedge, break down the wall, stop the pruning and hoeing so that it becomes a waste; and, in a second, much more awful hint that there is more here than agriculture, the "farmer" will command the rain to stop. But farmers hope for rain, wait for rain, pray for rain—so what kind of farmer is it who will turn off the rain, who *can* turn off the rain, even? The fertility deity was supposed to turn *on* the rain, but since God is the real God, it is he who can and will turn off the rain.

This is not a human farmer at all, of course (vs. 7), and the secret now tumbles out in a single line: "The vineyard of the Lord of hosts is the house of Israel," and, given the key, we can deal with all the earlier details of the song in the way we are intended to. In seven Hebrew words we have the climax at the end of vs. 7: God had *longed* for good grapes (vss. 2, 4), but his intention in doing so was to *long* for justice and righteousness; but all he got in the bad grapes was the opposite of justice and righteousness—bloodshed and the cry of the oppressed. What we cannot see in the English translation is the Hebrew pun here: he looked for *mishpāṭ*, but instead got *mispāḥ*; he looked for *ṣedāqā*, but instead got *ṣeʿāqā*. Years ago, the commentator G. H. Box tried his hand at a pair of puns in English to match the Hebrew:

> *For measures He looked—but lo massacres!*
> *For right—but lo riot.*[11]

One may add that the Zurich Bible in German tries a similar venture:

> *Er hoffte auf Guttat, und siehe da Bluttat,*
> *auf Rechtsspruch, und siehe da Rechtsbruch!*[12]

One more point should be made about this passage. We have taken note of the occurrences of the Hebrew verb "long for" in vss. 2, 4, and 7. What we have not yet said is that these three occurrences are the only occasions in the whole Old Testament where this verb has *God* for its subject—all the other occurrences use it for the longing of human beings. Most people today have trouble imagining how God's loving care for his people can be squared with his wrathful anger at his people. But Isaiah had no problem: the God of grace, who expends all the labor in clearing the hillside of stones for terraces and in planting and tending the vineyard, is at the same time the God of judgment who pulls down the stone walls and allows the briers and thorns to choke the vineyard if the grapes he longs for never come into existence, and all he has is poor, sour grapes. God cares, he longs, he waits: his people disappoint him. What else can he do?

In this chapter we have surveyed the evidences Isaiah saw for the breakdown of God's community: God's people are more interested in the details of sacrifice than in taking care of widows and orphans; the civil and religious leaders are particularly guilty; women pay attention to their bracelets, men to their beer and wine; people twist words, they bribe judges, nobody cares. As we said, it is not a pretty picture. It is a long way from the behavior outlined in those laws in Exodus 21-23. Furthermore, God cannot stay idle while his people flout his will. God will take steps, and the steps he will take are actions of which we have had hints, as we heard talk of sheep feeding among the ruins of the land (5:17). Hovering at the edge of our attention has been that threat of military defeat implied in 1:7, in 3:6, in 10:3-4, in 28:11-13, as well as in 5:17. Clearly Isaiah has in mind the march of foreign armies. But what armies, when, and how? It is the stuff of the headlines, and we must next turn to see what the headlines were all about in Isaiah's day, so that we can make sense out of his message of what God is about to do to his community.

CHAPTER IV

Nations on the March

THERE ARE SEVERAL hurdles we face as we try to understand Isaiah's message to his people regarding the international events of his time. For one thing, we have to become somewhat familiar with the affairs of those days—what nation was threatening what other nation about what; and we have a hard enough time, it seems, keeping track of the events of our own times. For another thing, Isaiah seems to have had a taste for *ambiguity* in referring to some of these events: as if he left people saying, "Now what did he mean by that?" Again, Isaiah had a conviction that God in these international affairs was "free-lance," leaning sometimes to one side, sometimes to another. This free view of God tends to bewilder us, who feel more comfortable if we think we know which side God is on (American dollar bills say "In God We Trust," and many people assume this implies God stays on our side). Finally, as events of world history continued to shift through the decades after Isaiah's time, the collectors of Isaiah's words often added material, shifted material, reshaped material to keep it abreast of the times, so that we often have difficulty discerning Isaiah's own perceptions. But still, it is important to try, because he had some remarkable lessons to teach.

The main thing to remember is that there were two military crises during Isaiah's career: the first in 734-733 B.C. (the "Syro-Ephraimite" crisis), and the second, the great Assyrian crisis, which began brewing up around the year 714 B.C. and came to a climax in 701 B.C. Both were three-sided conflicts. In the first, Jerusalem was threatened by a combination of Samaria and Damascus, while Assyria stayed alert in the background. In the second, Jerusalem was besieged by Assyria, while Egypt was in the background. Both these crises then involved Assyria, the first indirectly, and the second directly. In both of them, as I have indicated, Isaiah sees God at work, not permanently on any particular side, but doing his own will quite independently. How this works out we shall now see.

The first crisis, in 734-733 B.C., is normally called the "Syro-Ephraimite" war. Ephraim, we saw in the previous chapter, was one of the principal northern tribes of Israel, and Israel had its capital at Samaria. Syria, of course, had its capital at Damascus, as it does today. The narrative that deals with the affair is found in 7:1-8:4—a passage that contains a verse which has been a great focus of interest for Christians (7:14). Directly following the call narrative of chapter 6, then, we find this account of the crisis which occurred early in Isaiah's career.

The first verse of this passage is one of those heavy biblical sequences that tend to put us off. "In the days of Ahaz the son of Jotham, the son of Uzziah, king of Judah, Rezin the king of Syria and Pekah the son of Remaliah the king of Israel came up to Jerusalem to wage war against it, but they could not conquer it." What is this all about?

Uzziah, who had died the year of Isaiah's call (6:1), was succeeded by Jotham, who ruled over Judah until the year 735. Toward the end of Jotham's reign an effort was made among several of the smaller powers to the north to form a military coalition against the growing pressure of the great Assyrian empire to the east. The two chief nations in this plan were Israel ("Ephraim") and Syria. The kings of these two states began pressing Judah to join their coalition, the idea being that hanging together is better than hanging separately. This is the meaning of 2 Kings 15:37, which describes the situation.

When Jotham died in 735 his son Ahaz took the throne. Ahaz was at that time only 20 years old (2 Kings 16:2), young and inexperienced. The military pressure upon Judah the following year (734/33) took the form of an invasion by both Israel and Syria (2 Kings 16:5, and compare now Isa.

7:1); their purpose was to force Ahaz off his throne and replace him with a man named Tabeel (7:6), a person who presumably would be more pliable to their wishes. In this way Israel and Syria could be sure to secure their southern flank against any stab in the back and could stand unitedly against Assyria.

The words of Isaiah 7:2 are contemptuous: when "the house of David" heard of the military coalition marching against him, his legs shook in his boots. There is certainly a contrast between the military ability which David himself had had and the nervousness of this 21-year-old descendant of his, 250 years later!

So Isaiah gets a commission from God to go out with his son and meet Ahaz. Quite specific directions for the meeting-place are given. Isaiah's son plays no direct part in the proceedings, but the son had such a curious name—"A remnant shall return"—that it was remembered and much brooded over by both contemporaries and later generations. (We shall have to postpone until Chapter V our consideration of what the son's name meant to Isaiah and his contemporaries.)

Now if vs. 2 speaks of Ahaz with contempt, it is with similar contempt that Isaiah, in his word to Ahaz in vs. 4, refers to the two threatening kings: they are "these two smoldering stumps of firebrands." The erstwhile firebrands have gone out and now simply smolder, smoke—and anyway, the firebrands are nothing but "stumps." The Hebrew word for "stumps" is literally "tails," and since the combination "head and tail" is on Isaiah's lips elsewhere (9:14), one suspects that what Isaiah is saying here is that the "heads" of their respective peoples (vss. 8 and 9) are really nothing but "tails." Not an elegant description, certainly; but the point is, they are nothing for Ahaz to lose sleep over: don't go to pieces, Ahaz (vs. 4).

Why does Isaiah not call Pekah, the king of Israel, by name—why does he call him "the son of Remaliah" (vss. 5, 9)? It may be because his name is so much like that of his predecessor Pekahiah (2 Kings 15:25);[1] but it may again be out of contempt. There is also the suspicion that "Rezin" was not the correct form of the name of the Syrian king, but that again Isaiah was twisting the name out of contempt,[2] but we are not sure. One has the impression, in any event, that Isaiah was indicating to Ahaz not only by his words "do not fear" but also by the very way he refers to these kings that they do not really amount to much. The invasion will not succeed: what is Syria anyway but Damascus, and what is Damascus but Rezin? He implies that Rezin is not nine feet tall, nor is the king of Samaria (vss. 8a, 9a). Then Isaiah ends (vs. 9b) with a sentence offering a nice play on words: *'im lō' ta' amīnū kī lō tē'- āmēnū*, which reads, as Moffatt translated, "If your faith does not hold, you will never hold out."

(By the way, we have a short judgment-word against these two invaders which Isaiah evidently spoke against them at this time, 17:1-6. In vs. 4 of that passage "Jacob" refers to Israel [that is, the northern kingdom]. Four or five olives at the top of a tree [vs. 6] are not much of a remainder of the harvest of olives, and not much will be left of Israel or Syria either.)

But Ahaz, in the narrative of chapter 7, cannot take his mind off that invading army, so Isaiah tries another tack. (The words "the Lord" in vs. 10, by the way, are evidently a copyist's mistake for "Isaiah," as was already recognized in ancient times, for the Aramaic translation reads "the prophet of the Lord.") He says, Ask a sign from God to reassure yourself: make it anything, high or low (vs. 11). But Ahaz refuses to dare. He takes refuge in a pious excuse (vs. 12); it is for God to test *us*, he claims (thinking of traditions like Gen. 22:1), not for us to test God. Here he is hypocritically "playing to the galleries," all the while avoiding the issue.[3] This reaction angers Isaiah, who now calls him "house of David" to his face (compare the comment above on vs. 2); and notice how Isaiah refers to "my God" rather than to "your God," or "our God," or simply "God," as if Ahaz has taken himself beyond any sound relation with God at all. Then Isaiah offers Ahaz the sign for which he did not dare to ask.

The narrative of this sign is given in vss. 14-17. Given the importance of vs. 14 to Christians, and given the fact that the interpretation of these four verses has always been

among the most disputed in scripture, we would do well to
pick our way carefully. In particular, we must first read the
Old Testament text as it stands and postpone for a moment
the use which Matthew made of vs. 14 (see Matt. 1:23).

Isaiah says, literally, "Look, the young woman is pregnant and bearing a son, and shall call his name 'Immanuel'." (For those who are curious about the grammatical
details, it may be stated that the Hebrew for "young
woman" has the definite article; the Hebrew for "is
pregnant" is a participle, not a past verb, and the Hebrew
for "bearing" is likewise a participle.)

Two things need to be said here. First, the Hebrew
noun at the beginning of the verse, *'almā*, really does mean
"young woman" and not "virgin." It is used elsewhere in the
Old Testament in contexts that do not imply virginity at all
(compare its occurrence in the Song of Songs 6:8, where the
"young women" are part of a *harem*—though the *Revised
Standard Version* there translates "maidens"!). It was the
later Greek translation of the Old Testament, which
Matthew then subsequently used, which employed a Greek
word for "virgin" in 7:14.

Second, the name "Immanuel" seems deliberately to be
ambiguous in meaning. It is true that it means "God is with
us," as we all know, but it may also be translated "God is
against us." That is, the preposition in Hebrew is ambiguous
in the same way the English preposition "with" is
ambiguous: the English "with" can mean "alongside of,"
but we also speak of "fighting *with*" or "contending *with*,"
where "with" means "against." The same is true in Hebrew.
One can check Hosea 4:1, 12:2, and Micah 6:2, all prophetic passages from the same century as Isaiah, where God
has a "controversy" or a "lawsuit" *with* (the same preposition), that is, *against* Israel or Judah.[4] Indeed the use of
"Immanuel" in 8:8 looks like a threat rather than a promise
(see the discussion of 8:5-8 below). The later Greek translation removed any possibility of ambiguity, choosing the
meaning "God is with us," and Matthew followed this.

Let us summarize the situation. Isaiah speaks of the
"young woman"—perhaps he gestures toward her—and of

her future son whose name suggests that God is to take action with his people, but whether for or against his people is
a bit uncertain. Isaiah wants to insist that God is active in
the situation, something which Ahaz had not borne in mind
(compare vs. 12). But who is the young woman? Many
suggestions have been made. A persistent suggestion is that it
was the wife of Ahaz—a son who would be born to her
would be a son whom the king would constantly have in
sight. (Thus many scholars have held that "Immanuel" is
Hezekiah, who succeeded Ahaz on the throne; on this, see
the discussion of 8:8 below.)[5] In recent years, however,
the opinion has grown stronger that the young woman is
Isaiah's wife, so that the son would be a third one alongside
Shear-jashub (7:3) and Maher-shalal-hash-baz (8:2, 3).[6] No
firm solution is possible with present evidence.

The sign continues: the future son will eat curds and
honey, evidently baby foods after weaning,[7] before he knows
right from wrong; and before he knows right from wrong, the
threat of these two kings will vanish—that is, in a couple of
years or so. The emphasis of the sign, then, is not on a marvelous *birth*, but on the time-lapse at the end of which God
will see to it that the threat is gone.

Isaiah adds these words in vs. 17:[8] God will bring
upon Ahaz and his people "such days" as have not come
since the north split from the south 200 years before. Isaiah
evidently intends *this* verse to be ambiguous too. (The final
words, "the king of Assyria," are evidently a marginal note
added by a later editor who insisted on clarifying the ambiguity.) Is this good news or bad news? Isaiah does not make
it plain, any more than he made plain what "Immanuel"
means; he intends to leave the judgment in the mind of his
hearers. It could be *better* days than you've seen since the
day of David and Solomon, but then again it might well be
worse days than you've ever seen. Who knows?

The rest of the chapter consists of a variety of material,
some evidently from Isaiah, picturing in vivid detail the
devastation which Assyria will work (like vss. 19, 20), some
evidently from later prophets of hope, picturing a restored
land (like vss. 22a and 25). It is no longer possible to dis-

entangle all this with much confidence, or to tell whether the words about the devastation to be wrought by Assyria were intended by Isaiah to round off vss. 10-17 or whether they were added later. But it is clear that Isaiah's message was: do not worry about these two bumptious kings of the north; the real threat, which you can hardly bring yourself to notice, is Assyria.

Isaiah evidently offered Ahaz still a third reassurance (8:1-4), this time with the name of another of Isaiah's sons, Maher-shalal-hash-baz (vs. 3), whose name means "the spoil speeds, the prey hastes," and is to be inscribed on a tablet for all to see (vs. 1). But whose spoil, whose prey is referred to? Isaiah explains that it is that of Damascus and Samaria, shipped off to Assyria before his son can say "Daddy" or "Mommy" (vs. 4)—again, an assurance parallel to 7:10-17.

It was not a two-sided conflict, then, but a three-sided one; Isaiah was insisting that it was Assyria that was the real threat. So in an ironic kind of way Isaiah was agreeing with Damascus and Samaria, which also saw Assyria as the real threat. That was why they were trying to force Jerusalem into their coalition.

This is evidently what Isaiah means by 8:5-8. The people of Judah have refused the quiet waters of the Jerusalem water-supply (vs. 5)—an image for the resources of God; and as a result the River (that is, the Euphrates) will flood its banks all the way to Judah and inundate it (vss. 6-8). In other words, Assyria will invade your land. The word "wings" in vs. 8 may refer to the *branches* of the flood waters. It is noteworthy that when he says "your land" in vs. 8, the "you" in Hebrew is singular; he is talking to Immanuel alone. Does this suggest, again, that Immanuel is one of Ahaz's sons, expected to rule over Judah? At any rate, the use of the name "God is involved with us" here suggests once more the ambiguity of the name; for the flood of the Assyrian army over Judah is bad news indeed.

But Ahaz could not see it that way. To him Damascus and Samaria were the actual threat, while Assyria was only a theoretical one. So instead of following Isaiah's advice and counting on God to defend him against the two kings of the north, he begged help from Assyria herself against the two kings—just what Damascus and Samaria were afraid he would do. He sent an enormous gift to Tiglath-pileser, the king of Assyria, and became his vassal:

> So Ahaz sent messengers to Tiglath-pileser king of Assyria, saying, "I am your servant and your son. Come up, and rescue me from the hand of the king of Syria and from the hand of the king of Israel, who are attacking me." Ahaz also took the silver and the gold that was found in the house of the Lord and in the treasures of the king's house, and sent a present to the king of Assyria. (2 Kings 16:7-8)

And it worked: Assyria did march against Damascus and conquer it, and she would also march in the next few years against Samaria, the northern kingdom of Israel, and conquer it. But then again, in a few more years still she would march against the southern kingdom of Judah and threaten *it*. Assyria's embrace was not benevolent.

Now we must touch on the use Matthew later made of 7:14. It has upset many people that the *Revised Standard Version* uses "young woman" in 7:14, in view of "virgin" in the *King James Version*, and in view of "virgin" in Matthew 1:23. Indeed the *New International Version*, which has a more conservative and evangelical sponsorship, has recently used "virgin" in 7:14. When the *Revised Standard Version* was first published, Professor Luther A. Weigle, for many years chairman of the Revised Standard Version Bible Committee, received in the mail the ashes of a *Revised Standard Version* Bible burned by some earnest Christians because of this translation of Isaiah 7:14.[9] (But we forget how much opposition the *King James Version* evoked in 1611 when *it* was first published: the translators were accused of "blasphemy," "most damnable corruptions," "intolerable deceit," and "vile imposture"!)[10]

However, it has become clear by this point in our discussion that the whole narrative of 7:1-17 is not that of the birth of a Messiah but the reassurance of a weak young king in the eighth century B.C. who was threatened by an invasion led by two kings from the north. In a couple of years, said Isaiah, the threat will have vanished. Clearly, then, we shall have to accept the fact that Matthew was using 7:14 in a context other than the one in which it first figured.

But we want to be fair to Matthew and to respect his integrity too. Matthew knew his Old Testament scriptures in Greek, and, as we have seen, the Greek version of 7:14 did use "virgin." Matthew, then, wishing to set forth his conviction of the virgin birth of Jesus, found in this passage not only what he was convinced was an anticipation of that birth of Jesus, but also a perfect symbolic name for Jesus—"God is with us." What better summation of God's incarnation in human form could one wish for? Matthew was utterly convinced of the exciting news which he wanted to share, the news that the God who had worked in times past was still working, and indeed had worked his climax before their very eyes. To share that news, Matthew combed the scriptures to find passages to reinforce his witness. Some passages fitted well, some not so well. But the collection of passages he found represented a shorthand way of his conveying the massive unity of God's purpose. So if Isaiah had rather ambiguously insisted that God was involved with his people (for good or for ill), Matthew affirmed the positive: God has visited his people with a permanent parable of his gracious ways with them, the permanent parable of Jesus Christ. Matthew's use of 7:14 has entered deeply into the liturgical language of the Christian church, and into hymns like "O Come, O Come, Immanuel." This intentionality of Matthew we can honor without in the least losing our grip on the initial context of these words of Isaiah's, even if this means maintaining a tension between the mind of Isaiah in the eighth century B.C. and the mind of Matthew in the first century A.D.

Now we must return to the matter of Assyria. It was Isaiah's lot to live at a time when Assyrian power was expanding to its utmost. From her center at various capital cities near the present-day Mosul on the Tigris River in northern Iraq, her realm had spread south to the Persian Gulf, northeast to touch Lake Urmia in present-day Iran, north to Lake Van in what is now eastern Turkey, and west toward the Mediterranean. Even beyond these frontiers she exacted tribute from vassals and client tribes and nations, such as the Medes in central Iran.

If we wished to follow a detailed history of Assyria,[11] we would chart her expeditions in various directions from her center; but we are concerned in this study simply with her westward expansion toward Judah. One reason for her expansion westward, of course, was sheer expansionism. A dynamic empire constantly wants more, as Hitler's realm did in the years before and during the Second World War. But there were specific reasons for Assyria's wishing to gain a foothold on the Mediterranean: there was timber there, especially in the mountains of Lebanon; there was access to sea trade on the Mediterranean; and there was the chance to plant troops against any possible expansion of Egypt northward, since Palestine was always no-man's land between Egypt and the powers in the east, just as Poland has always been security for Germany against Russia, or for Russia against Germany.

Assyria's westward expansion began intermittently. In the century before Isaiah, she had marched on looting and punitive expeditions, but in Isaiah's own century her marches were for permanent conquest. She captured Damascus, as we have noted (in 732 B.C.), she captured Samaria (721 B.C.), and she exerted her control over Philistine territory (what we call today the "Gaza Strip") in the following year. Then in 701 she was besieging Jerusalem. (By 663 B.C., we may add, she would go on to invade Egypt and march all the way up the Nile to Thebes and sack it.)

Assyria maintained a high culture, an elaborate religion, a busy bureaucracy; but she ruled by deportation and terror, as we have already mentioned in Chapter II. Sargon II was the Assyrian king who finished the capture of Samaria in 721 B.C. Here is his description of how, in 717 B.C., he handled the incipient rebellion of the king of Carchemish (a city which stands on the present-day border of Turkey and north Syria):[12]

> In the fifth year of my rule, Pisiri of Carchemish broke the
> oath sworn by the great gods and wrote messages to Midah,
> king of Mushki [a people in central Turkey, perhaps the
> Phrygians], full of hostile plans against Assyria. I lifted my
> hands in prayer to my lord [god] Ashur with the result that
> I quickly made him, and also his family, surrender from
> Carchemish, all in fetters and with the gold, silver and his
> personal possessions. And the rebellious inhabitants of
> Carchemish who had sided with him, I led away as
> prisoners and brought them to Assyria. I formed from
> among them a contingent of 50 chariots, 200 men on horse-
> back and 3000 foot soldiers and added it to my royal corps.
> In the city of Carchemish I then settled inhabitants of
> Assyria and imposed upon their neck the yoke of Ashur, my
> lord.

Stalin managed in our own terrible century to use similar
transplantations of whole populations as a technique of
statecraft.

If Assyria aroused such terror in her subject peoples as
this inscription implies, then we can understand why Ahaz
moved to become subject to her king, why he sent treasure
from temple and palace, why he imitated an Assyrian altar
for the temple area in Jerusalem (read 2 Kings 16:10-18)—
anything to insure peace, even the peace of subjection. But
it must have been a lonely reign for Ahaz: Assyria came and
captured the northern kingdom and deported many of its
leading citizens (2 Kings 17:1-6),[13] leaving Judah to stand
alone, her territory only a little larger than that of our state
of Rhode Island.

King Ahaz died when he was 40 years old, in 715 B.C.
He was succeeded by his son Hezekiah, who was 25 years
old when he became king (2 Kings 18:2). It was during
Hezekiah's reign that the second military crisis of Isaiah's
career occurred, that crisis climaxed by the siege of Jerusalem of which we have spoken, by the Assyrians in 701
B.C. But that crisis had a long build-up, having been anticipated by events in the previous decade. At about the time
Hezekiah became king, Assyria was weakened temporarily
by a whole series of rebellions: by the Babylonians to her
south, by other peoples to her north and northeast. What

interests us is the attempt by various peoples in the Palestinian area to rebel. We saw a moment ago that Assyria had
taken over the Philistine territory (the Gaza Strip) by 720
B.C.; but by about 714 B.C. the Philistines were revolting
against Assyria, beginning with their city of Ashdod and
then drawing in other cities. They expected Egyptian aid in
this revolt—though Egypt by this time had been so
weakened that it was being ruled by a foreign dynasty, an
Ethiopian one (the 25th dynasty). This situation seems to be
the background of chapters 18-20 in Isaiah. Evidently, am-
bassadors (18:2) have been sent to Jerusalem to discuss
common action against Assyria, the same notion that
Damascus and Samaria had had 20 years previously!
Though the poem of chapter 18 is difficult to interpret
clearly, there is obviously a great contrast between all the
military agitation (vs. 3) and God's quiet work (vs. 4).
Isaiah clearly counsels Judah not to enter the scheme. Now
whether chapter 19 fits into this period or not, it is clear
that the prophet sees no stability in Egypt, only internal
fighting (19:2) and poor leadership (19:11-15).

Chapter 20 offers a narrative specifically dated to this
revolt of the Philistine city of Ashdod. According to this
narrative, Isaiah went around naked for three years to symbolize the long, sad lines of Egyptian prisoners of war being
led away when the Assyrians would crush the revolt.

But, we ask, did Isaiah really go around naked for
three years? To our way of thinking, it would seem shocking, given Israel's feelings of modesty about the human
body. But then again, prophets did often undertake symbolic actions, not only in sometimes giving their children
symbolic names (compare 7:3, 8:1-3) but in even stranger
actions. Thus Hosea married a prostitute (Hosea 1) as a sign,
and Jeremiah carried a yoke on his shoulders (Jer. 27:2,
28:10) as a sign. We have Assyrian depictions of prisoners of
war being led away naked, and there are bronze bands now in
the British Museum that show prisoners from the town of
Hazazu (in north Syria) being led away naked, some with
hands tied behind their backs.[14] On the other hand, Isaiah
might have worn a loincloth. But the point is that he

demonstrated what he intended to communicate, the situation of a prisoner of war.

We suspect Hezekiah trusted Isaiah and did not join the revolt. We know that when Assyria came into Ashdod in 712 she put down the revolt ruthlessly and reorganized the city as an Assyrian province, but that she did not go on to attack Judah. We also know that the leader of the Ashdod revolt fled to Egypt for sanctuary when the revolt failed, but Egypt turned around and gave him over to the Assyrians—so much for the trustworthiness of Egyptian help against Assyria!

Yet the reprieve for Judah was only temporary. As soon as Assyria could put her full attention to the west, she pressed the attack. Of course Assyria's goal was not to conquer Judah alone; she simply wished to secure her western front against a threat from Egypt or any other quarter. It was in 701 B.C. that she invaded Judah and besieged Jerusalem. We shall postpone the details for a moment and simply think about the crisis which Judah had to face.

Isaiah had been warning of Assyria's coming for years, and we have a whole array of pronouncements of his which deal with the threat of Assyria and the hopelessness of depending on military aid from Egypt. There is no way to date these words; they may have been delivered at the time of the Assyrian attack on Ashdod in 712, or at the time of her attack on Jerusalem in 701, or at any time in between. We listen to them now to gain an understanding of Isaiah's view on the *theological* meaning of the Assyrian threat.

Let us look first at a quite general oracle, 5:26-29. Assyria seems still to be a mere shadow on the horizon, and the threat of her invasion is part of the general array of punishments which God can inflict. Read the passage aloud. (Verse 30 does not belong with what precedes; it seems to be a stray verse included here because of the duplication of the word "growl.") Like present-day soldiers who, when put on alert, keep their uniforms on even when they sleep, ready to tumble into trucks on a half-hour's notice, so were the Assyrians: hardly sleeping, underwear tied, sandals laced, ready for action (vs. 27). Look at their weapons and chariots—arrows sharp, bows bent, horses' hoofs like flint, wheels like the whirlwind (vs. 28). Who could rescue their victims? (vs. 29).

Now let us turn to 10:5-15, perhaps the most important passage of all in setting forth Isaiah's view of the place of Assyria in God's scheme of things. The first verse of this passage has a grammatical difficulty which the translations have not caught. The Hebrew should be read:

> *Woe to Assyria, the rod of my anger*
> *and a staff is he in the hand*[15] *of my fury.*

The first word in the verse is the word "woe to," just like the opening word of 10:1 and the woes in chapter 5.[16] (For the splitting of similar material between chapter 5 and chapters 9-10, see the discussion in Chapter I.) This verse then concentrates on the affirmation that Assyria is both the instrument of God's will and the object of God's antipathy. How does this work? We shall see.

Verse 6 affirms that God is sending Assyria against a "godless" nation—the godless nation of course being Judah. It may be remarked in passing that a verse like this is a standing rebuke to anyone who casually assumes that the Old Testament is simply tribal lore about a tribal God for the Jews, for God is here bringing the most hated and feared nation the Orient had ever seen against his own beloved people, whom he calls "godless." And what will Assyria do? What she always does—loot, plunder, and stamp the nation down like mud in the streets.

Is it Assyria's intention to do God's will? By no means: *he* (Assyria) does not so think (vs. 7—the pronoun in Hebrew is emphatic). Assyria is just "doing its thing," and its thing is destruction and annihilation of "nations not a few"—what an understatement! Listen to her boasting as she ticks off one conquered city after another, one nation after another (vs. 9).

I take vs. 10 as an addition by a later editor,[17] so in our reading we shall jump from vs. 9 to vs. 11. The As-

syrians have boasted of all their cities conquered, ending
with Damascus and Samaria, the two capitals which figured
in the Syro-Ephraimite crisis back in the time of Ahaz.
Verse 11, as translated in the *Jerusalem Bible*, which follows
the Hebrew word order, reads: "As I have dealt with Samaria and her idols, shall I not treat Jerusalem and her
images the same?" It is a nice irony on Isaiah's part: there
must have been many in Judah who were convinced that
Samaria was half-pagan and deserved to fall, but to equate
Jerusalem and *her* images with Samaria and her idols was a
low blow. As we shall see, this was actually the point of
view of Assyria, at least as the Judean historian recalls it (see
the discussion below on 2 Kings 18:34-35); but can this
really be the sentiment of God as well, who is sending
punishment on Judah?

By now the naive hearer could easily come to the conclusion that Isaiah is proclaiming a God who has simply
changed sides: having once been pro-Judah, he is now pro-
Assyria and anti-Judah. But no, Isaiah's viewpoint is more
subtle than that. God is not *pro*-Assyria, he is simply *using*
Assyria to punish his covenant people, and after he is done
with this task, he is going to punish Assyria for being too
haughty. This is the meaning of vs. 12, which, though it is
not part of the original poetic sequence of Isaiah (the verse
is in prose), does explain the course of the argument. The
poetic sequence begins again in vs. 13. "I have done it"
picks up "shall I not do" and "I have done" in vs. 11, and
"my hand" ironically picks up the "hand of my fury" in vs.
5. Assyria thinks she is supreme and altogether in control,
she thinks all she is doing is of her own power; but really
she is nothing but a tool in God's own hand. Listen again to
her boast of kings dethroned, of treasures plundered (vs.
14). And who would dare to let out a peep?

And now the pay-off (vs. 15)! Is a tool more important
than the worker, or does the saw lord it over the carpenter?
Assyria is really nothing but a *rod* or *staff* in God's hand (vs.
5), so how can the rod or staff take over the universe?

Verse 15 nicely refers back to vs. 5 in the imagery of
"rod" and "staff," suggesting that we are at the end of this

unit of prophecy. Of course people wanted to know specifically what God was going to do with Assyria; vss. 16-19 are evidently attempts by later hands to fill that need, so we would do well to stop at this point.[18] What is abundantly clear from vs. 15 is that God is sovereign even over Assyria, and that is the main thing. Now we see why vs. 5 began with "woe." The whole passage, which at first hearing seems to be about the brutality of Assyria, is really about God's retribution on Assyria.

As I say, it is a subtle point of view. Judah has been free to be godly or godless. Assyria is free to pursue her hobby, which is destruction and death. But God in his sovereignty works his own pattern in and through and even against these human freedoms: Assyria feels free, *is* free, but at the same time is a tool in God's hands, nothing more. God is not permanently pro-Judah or anti-Judah, anti-Assyria or pro-Assyria. People today often wonder how the Bible sorts out the problem of human freedom and God's sovereignty. The Bible never sorts out the problem on a theoretical basis, but it affirms both human freedom and God's sovereignty in the specifics of the headlines. For the Bible, the territories of human freedom and of God's sovereignty are not separated by some Berlin Wall—they interpenetrate, however hard it is for our logic to grasp.

Now we turn to a series of passages found in chapters 28-31, considering first 28:14-22. As with the passage in chapter 10, this one is complicated and needs careful analysis. Verse 14 offers a remarkable double play on words. The leadership of the nation are addressed as "scoffers" (in Hebrew, more literally, "men of scoffing"). Actually, since we have "those who rule. . .in Jerusalem" in the second line, one might have expected "men of Zion" in the first line, since "Zion" is often a parallel to "Jerusalem" in the prophets (for example, Micah 3:10, 12). But instead of "Zion" (Hebrew *ṣiyyōn*) we have another word that sounds similar, "scoffing" (Hebrew *lāṣōn*). But there is another twist to this line, since Proverbs 29:8 states that "scoffers [the Hebrew again is 'men of scoffing'] set a city aflame." The clear implication of Isaiah's words is that the leadership is not really leading at all but is rather destroying the city. The second line carries a double meaning, since the word "who rule" can also be translated "who make clever sayings" or "who make proverbs" (the same verb occurs in Ezek. 16:44). This alternative meaning for the word is appropriate here: if those who rule are *scoffers*, then they no doubt pride themselves on their *clever words* as well. An English translation can hardly do justice to the richness of texture of these lines.

Now Isaiah mocks the pretensions of the leaders; for what are they saying? Listen to the news announcement (vs. 15): "We have just concluded a mutual aid pact with—" with whom? With *miṣrayim* (Egypt)? With *'asshūr* (Assyria)? No! says Isaiah; rather, with *māwet* (Death) and with *she'ōl* (the Grave)—that's all your diplomatic negotiations will come to.[19] "So we will be safe when the flood [so the *New English Bible* and the *New Jewish Version*, rather than 'scourge'] comes over us," continue the leaders; because—where have we found our refuge? In God, who is our refuge and strength (Ps. 46:1)? No, says Isaiah; "we have made lies and falsehood our shelter." And what will God do to this jerry-built structure the leaders have produced? Hail and waters will overwhelm the refuge of lies (vs. 17b); the treaty with death and Sheol will not stand, when the flood [again, rather than "scourge"] comes by (vs. 18). The "flood," of course, is the Assyrian invasion (compare 8:6-8, already examined).

Then overlying this ironic taunting by Isaiah is a fresh set of affirmations (vss. 16-17a, 19-22).[20] God is going to erect on Zion a better shelter than the shelter of lies which the leaders have erected; God's shelter will have a firm foundation-stone. Isaiah seems to suggest a firmness to Zion, but we must save until Chapter V a full exploration of this conviction.

Verses 19-22 continue the contrast between the terrible flood represented by Assyria and God's relation to it. The flood will sweep you away (vs. 19)—that is clear, and understanding this news will be nothing but terror. But what is the meaning of the proverbial expression in vs. 20— the bed too short, the blanket too small? Is it the message of

J.B. Phillips' book *Your God is Too Small*, a work referred to in Chapter II? Did Judah have a conceptual world too small for God's work? It would seem so, for his deeds really are strange and alien (vs. 21), not at all what we would expect. God will act, no question about it, as he acted at Perazim (2 Sam. 5:20) or at Gibeon (Josh. 10:9-14). But in the old days God had acted *for* Israel, while now he will act against her; it *is* strange. So, don't scoff (vs. 22), you scoffers; and we pick up that word from vs. 14, to round off the message.

To summarize this passage, we see that Isaiah mocks Judah's hopes for a military solution as faith in a paper tiger. The flood will sweep you away, he tells them, because God is a God of action. Security in God is real (vs. 16) but of a very different sort than you had thought.

Three passages deal with the foolishness of expecting help from Egypt—30:1-7, 30:15-17, and 31:1-3. In 30:1-7 we can be grateful for a passage that is easy to read and understand. The first three verses of this passage are quite clear. Verse 4 can be understood against the situation which prevailed in Egypt at the time. We have already mentioned the chaos in Egypt in the years 730-715 B.C. and the resultant Ethiopian dynasty (the 25th). This dynasty established control, first in the south of Egypt, then in the north, where the two cities were located which are cited here. The verse means, "Though Pharaoh's representatives have established a coherent government as far north as Zoan and Hanes. . . ." Verse 5 of course simply reinforces vs. 3: the Egyptians are a no-account people.

Unfortunately we lose our grip on the meaning of the first line of vs. 6 and the last line of vs. 7. "An oracle on the beasts of the Negeb" cannot be right; the present Hebrew words do mean this, but they make no sense in the context. The word "oracle" is literally a "burden," so the old Aramaic translation may be right in reading "they carry on beasts in the Negeb"—this would at least make sense in the context.[21] Who is carrying all these riches by ass and camel through a desert ridden with lions and snakes? The verse does not say, but the context suggests the Judeans (compare 31:1).[32] Egypt, according to vs. 7, will turn out to be "hot air" (the basic meaning of the Hebrew word translated "worthless" here). But what is the joke in the last line of vs. 7? What is the meaning of the new name Isaiah gives Egypt? "Rahab" we can understand; it is an old term for the sea-dragon whom God had crushed (Ps. 89:9-10); and evidently because the dragon was understood to live in the Nile (Ezek. 29:3), the name Rahab became attached to Egypt (Ps. 87:4). It is this designation which Isaiah is mocking: this Rahab is a do-nothing. (The Hebrew may be slightly askew in the text; it may mean "Rahab the silenced" or the like.)[23]

A similar passage is 30:15-17: God expects you to be saved by returning to him, in quiet confidence and trust (compare 8:6-8, which we have already examined), but instead you insist on depending, of all things, on horses (no doubt part of the expected military aid from Egypt). The result is that a thousand of you will flee at the threat of one of the enemy, till you are left all by your lonesome self (an echo, again, of 1:8—and perhaps an ironic reversal of Ps. 91:7).

The message of 31:1-3 is again one of the hopelessness of relying on Egypt. "Woe to those who go down to Egypt for help and rely on horses." The whole passage is a scathing denunciation of all those who depend on military hardware. "When the Lord stretches out his hand, the helper will stumble. . . ."

But the material of vss. 1-3 seems to have been extended later by Isaiah himself. This is another specimen of the category of "self-extended oracle" which we met in Chapter III. The extension is contained in vss. 4-5 + 8-9 (vss. 6-7 are in prose and interrupt the continuity of the poetry). Verse 4 is teasingly ambiguous; suddenly we no longer know where we are. Who is the lion? Who are the shepherds? What is God doing, since the word "upon" is a preposition as ambiguous as the one we have dealt with already in the name "Immanuel"? Is God fighting "upon" Zion, or "with" Zion, or "against" Zion? Once Isaiah used "lion" to mean Assyria (5:29), but then once Amos used "lion" as a simile for God (Amos 3:12; and the simile is also

implied in Amos 1:2, where the verb "roar" is used specifically of a lion). Is Assyria growling over Judah, not
frightened away by Egypt? Or is God growling over Judah,
not frightened away by Assyria? Verses 1-3 are definitely a
threat; but in vs. 5 it is clear that God is delivering Jerusalem. So vs. 4, which is ambiguous in itself, is clarified by vs.
5—and it is good news; so God is the lion, whom Assyria
cannot scare away. And Assyria will fall some day too (vss.
8-9). It looks, then, as if Isaiah has himself extended a
threat oracle (vss. 1-3) by later good news (vss. 4-5 + 8-9).
Notice how vs. 8 mimics vs. 3—just as the Egyptians are "not
God," so the Assyrians shall fall by a sword "not of man."

The last oracle to be discussed here is also a self-extended oracle: 29:1-8.[24] A question arises at the very beginning: what does "Ariel" mean (vss. 1, 2, 7)? The answer
is that nobody knows. The best guess is that it was a name
given to the altar-hearth used for burnt offerings in Jerusalem. But since Isaiah seems to have been prone to use names
or expressions which were ambiguous or far from obvious,
we suspect that the name here involved a word-play, or a
nickname, or some other mode of expression whose key we
have lost.[25]

The first word of vs. 1 is the same old word "woe"
which we have already met so often. "Ariel" in vs. 1 is used
for the whole city, the city where David encamped; and
Isaiah is pronouncing a woe on it. The end of vs. 1 is clearly
sarcastic: "Oh, yes! Just keep up your observance of the
New Year's festival, business as usual at the altar-hearth"—
like fiddling while Rome burns.

There is no warrant for the "yet" at the beginning of
vs. 2 in the *Revised Standard Version*; the *New English
Bible* and the *New Jewish Version* are correct simply to use
"and." Verse 1b was sarcastic, so the consequence is that
God will distress Ariel. The last line of vs. 2 evidently contains whatever word-play "Ariel" offers, perhaps meaning
something like "I shall make of her a *real* sacrificial fire!" As
David once encamped around Jerusalem to take it (vs. 1), so
now God will encamp against her (vs. 3), so that people will
gibber and whimper like ghosts in the grave (vs. 4).

The Hebrew of vs. 5 does not imply a contrast; the "but" of the *Revised Standard Version* (and the "yet" of the *New English Bible*) should be "and" (as the *New Jewish Version* has it) so that the complete thought is: you will whisper from the dust (vs. 4), and your enemy will be as numerous as grains of dust (vs. 5). The word for "multitude" here and in vss. 7 and 8 is the Hebrew *hamōn*, a curious word which refers to the "turmoil" or "uproar" of a loud noise or a large crowd, so that it indicates either loud confusion or numerousness or both.

The verb "be visited" in vs. 6 is ambiguous in Hebrew; it means "be attended to"—either for reward or punishment, whichever is appropriate. So the question arises: is the turmoil which God creates (vs. 6) the same turmoil as that of the enemy (vs. 5), or is it a counter-turmoil? Is God rewarding us or punishing us by his visitation? My own answer is this: the acoustic effect of the Hebrew lines of vss. 7-8 is quite different from that of vss. 1-6, so that I suspect vs. 6 ended the original oracle of Isaiah.[26] If that is the case, then God's turmoil expressed in vs. 6 was intended as a threat, but later the extension took the matter in a quite different direction; Isaiah, exploiting the possible ambiguity of "be visited" in vs. 6, now states that the *hamōn*, the "multitude" (vss. 7, 8), is nothing but a *halōm*, a "dream." In other words, the nations that fight against Zion will turn out in the end to be nothing more than a passing nightmare.

The reader who has managed to follow the argument through this chapter has come a long way and deserves congratulations. Let us try to summarize now. We have looked at a large array of passages on the Assyrian crisis: first at a passage in which Isaiah speaks of the terrors of Assyria (5:25-29); then at a passage in which he affirms the horrid plans of Assyria as God's own plans, but states that God will punish Assyria for her assumption that she is number one (10:5-15); then at a passage in which the leaders are addressed as "scoffers" and their proud efforts to gain military help against the enemy are mocked, since God himself is the only source of security and is himself working against his own people (28:14-22); then at some passages in which

Isaiah specifically deals with the hopelessness of expecting military aid from a nation like Egypt (30:1-7, 30:15-17, 31:1-3). The last of these passages was extended by later material from Isaiah which insists that though Assyria threatens Zion, God is not scared away but will protect Jerusalem, and that eventually the Assyrians will fall (31:4-5, 8-9). Finally, we looked at another oracle which begins with God's distressing Jerusalem, no doubt through an enemy here unnamed, but which was later extended by Isaiah to indicate that this threatening multitude is nothing but a dream in the night (29:1-6 + 7-8). So there are three protagonists in the Assyrian crisis—Assyria itself, Judah, and Egypt. Judah oscillates between Assyria and Egypt, and God is independent of any of them. It is a subtle and liberating viewpoint. The self-extended oracles which we have just examined indicate that though God is punishing Judah, he is also protecting Judah. We must save until Chapter V a detailed discussion of Isaiah's view of Jerusalem and Zion; for now, we shall round off our study of the international events of Isaiah's day by reading the account of the siege of Jerusalem which the historian of the seventh century B.C. has left us.

The record is found in both Isaiah 36:1-37:7 and 2 Kings 18:13-19:7. These are largely duplicate accounts, but the fuller and more original account is in 2 Kings, to which we now turn. (Scripture references for the rest of the present chapter, then, will not be to Isaiah but to 2 Kings.)

The year, we know, is 701 B.C. Let us begin with 18:13; but let us not read this verse too hastily. Imagine Sennacherib, king of Assyria, marching into Judah and taking its fortified cities. In a famous inscription text from Sennacherib himself, he boasts of the number of these cities: he states that he took 46 of them and deported their population, while shutting King Hezekiah and the remnant of his troops in Jerusalem "like a bird in a cage."[27] This simile is uncomfortably close to Isaiah's phrasing of the boasting of Assyria in Isaiah 10:14 (see our study of the passage above). Isaiah was not far wrong!

Sennacherib set up his headquarters at Lachish (2 Kings

18:14), a city 25 miles (40 kilometers) *southwest* of Jerusalem. The Assyrian power is now locked firmly around Jerusalem. There are stone bas-reliefs in the British Museum vividly depicting Sennacherib's siege of Lachish before its surrender.[28] Hezekiah sued for peace (vs. 14), and the Assyrian king set a price of 22,500 pounds (over 10,000 kilograms) of silver and 2,250 pounds (over 1000 kilograms) of gold (again, vs. 14), an enormous sum which set King Hezekiah to emptying the treasures of temple and palace and to stripping the gold facings of the temple doors (vss. 15-16).

Then the king of Assyria sends his lieutenants to parley with the Judean authorities across the defense-wall of Jerusalem. What a scene! They ask for the king himself to come out, but the king sends three of his officials instead (vs. 18). Through these officials the Assyrian lieutenants relay the terrifying message: "What are you trusting in anyway? Do you think mere words are a substitute for military power? Do you think to depend on Egyptian military aid? But Egypt is not a walking-stick; it is a splintered piece of cane that will run through the hand of anyone leaning on it! Do you think to depend on Yahweh? But Yahweh has been victimized by your king's religious reforms! Look—we will make you a bargain: we will give you 2000 horses on the spot if you can find anyone in Judah who knows anything about cavalry technique. How can you repel any of my military horsemen if you have to depend on Egypt for such know-how? And, by the way—according to your theology, is it against Yahweh's will that I am coming to destroy your land?" (vss. 19-25). That last thrust fits hand-in-glove into Isaiah's own message. It is diabolical; it would be hard to imagine a speech more inclined to lower the morale of the inhabitants of the city.

The first response of Hezekiah's officials is, "Shhh: not so loud! Please don't talk Hebrew—you're lowering the morale of the townspeople. Talk Aramaic. We speak it." To which the Assyrians replied: "Don't you think your townspeople ought to be told what's going on? After all, it is they who are doomed, in the siege we are laying, to eat their own dung and to drink their own urine" (vss. 26-27).

Then the Assyrian spokesmen went on: "Don't trust your king, particularly when he says that Yahweh will preserve your city. Surrender to me: I'll grant you better food and drink at home—your own grapes and figs and water from your own cistern. Until (yes, there is a catch in it) I deport you to another land, just as lovely, off to the east somewhere. After all, one land is pretty much like another. Besides, where are the gods of all the cities I have already captured? What evidence do you have that Yahweh will fare any better in *this* siege?" (vss. 28-35).

No one had any answer to this horrid taunt. What answer could there have been? The Judean officials came back to the king with their clothes torn in humiliation. The king in turn, when he heard the news, tore his clothes and put on sackcloth and went to the temple to pray, and then sent a delegation to Isaiah.

This delegation came to Isaiah with a word from the king which begins with a remarkable expression of frustration—perhaps it was proverbial: "This day is a day of distress, of rebuke, and disgrace; children have come to the birth, and there is no strength to bring them forth" (19:3). And the king asked Isaiah's prayers for those left in the city.

Isaiah's answer to Hezekiah (19:6) is his answer to Ahaz a third of a century before (Isaiah 7:4): do not fear. And he goes on to say that the king of Assyria will be unsuccessful against Jerusalem and will return home.

And he did; Jerusalem did not fall. Sennacherib did pull his troops out. We are not certain whether a plague afflicted them (so 2 Kings 19:35, with details that are somewhat legendary),[29] or whether news reached Sennacherib of trouble at home that needed his presence (so, by implication, 19:7). Indeed, the sequence of events in chapter 19 seems garbled enough that some scholars have argued for *two* campaigns by Sennacherib in Palestine.[30] But a detailed reconstruction of these events need not concern us, since the attitude of Isaiah seems clear enough: Assyria is not number one—God is, and God moves back and forth among the combatants accomplishing his will. (Compare the remarks on this matter at the end of Chapter II.)

We have not yet discussed in detail one item which has kept cropping up in this chapter, and that is that Isaiah seems to have become convinced by the time of the siege of Jerusalem that God would keep his foothold in Jerusalem and that Jerusalem would be the basis for the future renewal of Israel. So we must ask, What was to be the shape of Isaiah's idea of renewal for Israel? What did he anticipate for the future after the crisis of Assyria had subsided? We shall find that this is as complex a question to answer as the question of Isaiah's understanding of the meaning of the political events of his time, but it must next engage our attention.

CHAPTER V

Renewal After Disaster?

*T*HE TITLE OF THIS chapter ends with a question mark
because we cannot necessarily take it for granted that
Isaiah preached a happy future. Of course we do find many
expressions of hope within chapters 1-39, but we have seen
enough of the additions of later copyists and editors to acknowledge that the question must be dealt with systematically.

There is much evidence that speaks *against* the existence
of authentic hope within the message of Isaiah. There is the
word of Jeremiah, a century later, spoke to the prophet
Hananiah:

> The prophets who preceded you and me from ancient times
> prophesied war, famine, and pestilence against many
> countries and great kingdoms. As for the prophet who proph-
> esies peace, when the word of that prophet comes to pass, then
> it will be known that the Lord has truly sent the prophet (Jer.
> 28:8-9).

That is, Jeremiah seems to be saying that traditionally
prophets speak bad news; so prophets who speak good news
are not in the tradition, and their words cannot be accepted
without firm evidence that their good news is coming true
after all.

Then there is the terrible desolation of Isaiah's own call,
which we examined in detail in Chapter II. Bad news is
everywhere in the call, and the deformed text of 6:13 is hardly
good news; vs. 13 looks more as if someone later tried to
squeeze a bit of good news out of the bad news of the original
form of text.

Many people have found good news in 1:18-20, which is surely a word authentic to Isaiah. It certainly is good news, if the Hebrew text means what the English versions render it to mean: "though your sins are like scarlet, they shall be white as snow. . . ." Many evangelistic sermons have been preached from this text. The problem is that Hebrew verbs cannot be as specific as English verbs are in expressing the shades of meaning which our modal auxiliaries do ("could," "might," and all the rest); we are sometimes unsure whether we have statements or questions in a Hebrew line. Such is the case in 1:18. The verb "let us reason together" has implications of "let us argue out a legal case," and since God acts as judge, we have here the kind of covenant lawsuit which we explored in Chapter III. The word "though," which occurs twice in vs. 18, translates the normal Hebrew word for "if," and the Hebrew passage leaves us with the impression that the judge is scornfully quoting the argumentation of the defendant (Israel): "Come now, let us work through your argument: 'if your sins are like scarlet, then they are to be white as snow'? 'If they are red like crimson, then they are to become like wool'? Is that it?" Then the judge counterposes his own argumentation: "*If* you are willing and obedient, then you shall prosper; but if you refuse and rebel, then you shall die. . . ." *These* are the *big* "ifs"; these "ifs" overwhelm your own "ifs."[1] The placement of this verse in the context of other passages early in the book of Isaiah does not encourage an optimistic view of Israel; Israel continues to rebel (1:5).

But the reader will be impatient if we simply take one hopeful passage after another from chapters 1-39 and analyze them without any attempt to see an overall pattern. The reader knows there are many great and moving passages of hope within chapters 1-39. True, the passage about "swords into plowshares" in 2:2-4 may be shared with Micah and be unoriginal to either (see Chapter I), and the "Immanuel" passage in 7:14 may need to be seen in the light of the Syro-Ephraimite crisis (see Chapter IV), but there is "The people who walked in darkness have seen a great light" in 9:2, "There shall come forth a shoot from the stump of Jesse" in 11:1, and much else. The Christian in particular has steadily gone to Isaiah to find words about the Messiah; "Isaiah 'twas foretold it," says a line of a well-known Christian hymn. We have reached the last of the chapters in this study guide to be devoted to the original Isaiah. So what shall we say about this vast problem?

The first thing to say is that the picture of Isaiah which has emerged so far in our study is not the picture of a crystal-ball gazer. We have seen Isaiah hearing the call to preach, and to preach judgment upon the people (Chapter II), since they have broken community with each other and broken covenant with God (Chapter III); as a consequence, says Isaiah, God is sending Assyria upon the people as a rod to beat them with (Chapter IV). All of our investigation so far suggests a person deeply engaged in his own time, both diagnosing the sicknesses of its people and suggesting prognoses for his people in their near-future as the logic of their choices in their time works out under God's sovereignty. We have found no room yet in our picture of Isaiah for a figure who projects events 700 years into the future.

Part of our difficulty may be that we have a rather different view of past, present, and future than the Israelites did. Our own understanding of the reality of past, present, and future may be based much more than we realize on the simple fact that there are three such tenses of Latin verbs (*amo, amabam, amabo*), and philosophers were accustomed for hundreds of years to thinking of this as normal. But I myself have never been sure how long the present lasts: five seconds, five minutes, five weeks? When does the present get to be the future? The fact that there are only *two* forms of the finite verb in Hebrew, one roughly corresponding to *past* time (or at least to action understood as *completed*) and one roughly corresponding to *future* time (or at least to action *anticipated, under way, habitual,* or the like), suggests to me that for the Israelites the categories are only two, after all, and the present is simply the knife-edge boundary between past and future.

Further, we vaguely assume that we are striding forward into the future but that the landscape is foggy and we can't see ahead very well. The Israelite image, on the other hand, was that what is "ahead" of us in space is what has happened *formerly*, in the past; while what is "behind" us in space is what will happen *hereafter*, in the future. Thus in 1 Samuel 9:9 the word "formerly" is *lepānīm*, literally "to the front"; but the opposite word, *'aḥar*, must be translated "after that" in one passage of Genesis (Gen. 18:5) and "behind him" in another passage four chapters later (Gen. 22:13). (Incidentally, this perspective was the ancient Greek one too.)[2] The mental picture, then, is that we are móving *backwards* into the future, as when we row a boat on a lake—we row backwards and thus see where we have been but see new trees and inlets only as we come abreast of them. This view of past and future seems thoroughly realistic, and it also emphasizes the twofold division of time about which we have been speaking: the past (what can be seen) and the future (what cannot yet be seen.)[3]

Now for most Israelites most of the time, the world would go along in a given year as it had the previous year; the patterns of life were established, and the instruction of priests and the counsels of wise men were enough. Like the rower on a placid lake, one pull on the oars produces an effect not different from the previous pull on the oars.

But from time to time there are kinks in history, crises, the tumble of events, when all is suddenly confusion; and then, the Israelites assumed, God sends a spokesman to warn what is about to happen. In the same way, if the lake suddenly issues into a tumbling stream with rapids, then it is handy for the rower to be alert to the fact beforehand. In early days the prophet was called a "seer"—he can see what the rest of the community is unable to see (compare again the same verse, 1 Sam. 9:9, cited a moment ago with regard to the word "formerly"). The prophet not only occasionally "saw" God (Isa. 6:1), but he "saw" events as well (compare Amos 3:7). It is handy to have someone around who sees not only "ahead" (to what is past), but also sees "behind" (to what is to come). But the prophet's task to see through the kinks of history is not a task to see 700 years ahead; his task is to see the immediate future which is the unexpected outgrowth of the actions and the decisions and the relationships of the people. This seems to have been the conviction of Israel. The prophets predicted—yes; but they predicted the near-future, not the far-future. (This perspective began to change when prophecy developed into apocalyptic; we shall discuss the process in Chapter IX.)

The situation becomes far more complicated, of course, when words of a prophet like Isaiah become not simply words of *immediate* application to the events of his time but become something else—when they become words *for every age*, for *general* application. Then succeeding generations find their own sets of meanings in the old words and see them as relevant to their own fresh specificities; so we ourselves find difficulty separating later perceptions of meaning from earlier ones. We saw a striking example of this difficulty in the use Matthew made of 7:14 (see Chapter IV).

With these general observations, let us see what can be made of these words to Judah of hope and renewal which can be defended as authentic to Isaiah. We begin with the curious names which Isaiah gave his two sons: Shear-jashub, "A remnant shall return" (7:3) and Maher-shalal-hash-baz, "The spoil speeds, the prey hastes" (8:1, 3).

In the literary contexts in which these names appear, they seem to function as reassurance. This is fairly clear for Maher-shalal-hash-baz; as we saw in Chapter IV, 8:4 indicates that by the time this son is old enough to say "Daddy" or "Mommy," the loot from Damascus and Samaria will be on its way to Assyria. Though it is by no means so clear for the meaning of Shear-jashub, the general mission of Isaiah to Ahaz (in chapter 7) is to bring reassurance, and the presence of this son would presumably reinforce the purpose of his mission.

But the immediate application of the names to the Syro-Ephraimite crisis hardly exhausts the meaning of these names to Isaiah when he gave them to his sons.

Both names are odd. It is not just that to us they are odd; they were undoubtedly odd to Isaiah's contemporaries too. The only other prophet who gave symbolic names to his children (of whom we have record) was Hosea (Hos. 1:4, 6, 9), and these names were straightforward in meaning: "Jezreel" (the site of a terrible atrocity a century before [2 Kings 10:7]), "Not pitied," and "Not my people." All were terrible judgments leveled against an erring people; the meaning of these names was crystal clear.

But Isaiah's names were odd because, I strongly suspect, they made people wonder, "Now what does he mean by that?" We saw in Chapter IV that the name of the boy "Immanuel" was ambiguous—is God for us or against us?

Let us begin with the second name, Maher-shalal-hash-baz. This is really a double line of poetry, with full parallelism:

> *The spoil speeds,*
> *the prey hastes.*

One wonders, why a double line of poetry, when just *Maher-shalal* would have gotten the point across? For awesomeness? For fuller impact of the message? The predicates are odd, not at all what one would expect with their subjects. The subjects are words referring to plunder or loot in battle: garments, gold and silver, jewels, flocks and herds, women and children, slaves—Judges 5:30 gives a typical picture of such plunder. "The plunder is hurrying." How could that be? One could imagine slaves, women and children, even flocks and herds "hurrying" under the whiplash; but how could clothes, gold, silver, and jewels be said to "hurry"? God hurries, people hurry, but *plunder*? What makes the plunder hurry? Whose plunder is hurrying, and to where? Who has captured the plunder? Isaiah does not answer any such questions. How much better, we might think, if Isaiah had just been more specific, had named his son, say, "Maher-kedmah-shelal-zaphon"—which would mean "spoil of the north speeds to the east." That would make it all clear, and no more of a mouthful than the name Isaiah did use! But he didn't. He gave us a mouthful which gives us no clues, and forces us therefore to ask the questions we do ask.

The only answer I can think of is that the name is both

good news and bad news. It is good news in that Damascus and Samaria, the potential despoilers, will themselves be despoiled; the pressure will soon be off Judah. But it is bad news in that there is a power, Assyria, which is powerful enough to despoil Damascus and Samaria, and therefore powerful enough to despoil Judah as well. Some day we ourselves might be the plunder! The boy's name serves, therefore, as a steady reminder that good news and bad news are intertwined.

So with the older son's name, Shear-jashub. Here there is no double line of poetry, only the single statement. But in a way this name is just as odd, because the subject ("a remnant") comes in this Hebrew name before the predicate ("shall return"), whereas the normal Hebrew sentence (and the normal Hebrew name when it is made up of a sentence) has the predicate before the subject (the sequence Maher-shalal-hash-baz is normal in this respect). If the subject comes first here, then the subject is underlined; the name then means something like "It is a remnant which shall return."

Now if "remnant" is underlined, the word "remnant" would also hit a raw nerve for people in Isaiah's day. It was, alas, a common experience to see whole populations decimated by war and pestilence. A quarter-century before Isaiah's time, the prophet Amos had spoken quite mathematically of the experience:

> *The city that went forth a thousand*
> * shall have a hundred left,*
> *and that which sent forth a hundred*
> * shall have ten left*
> * to the house of Israel* (Amos 5:3).

In a passage resembling Isaiah 1:18-20, which we examined earlier in the chapter, Amos states the bare possibility of God's grace. To whom? to Israel? No, to the *remnant* of Joseph (one of Israel's sons):

> *Hate evil, and love good,*
> * and establish justice in the gate;*

> *it may be that the Lord, the God of hosts,*
> *will be gracious to the remnant of Joseph* (Amos
> 5:15).

People were not only decimated or altogether wiped out by war and pestilence, they were also subject to deportation. Isaiah knew this well, and all his people knew it; this fact was built into his very call (6:12): "[Until]. . . the Lord *removes men* far away, and the *forsaken places are many* in the midst of the land."

It was Assyria, of course, that ruled by deportations. When Assyria captured Samaria in 721 B.C., they deported its leadership off to the east (2 Kings 17:6). King Sargon boasts that he deported 27,290 of its inhabitants,[4] though this figure may be inflated. Archeologists recently dug up a pathetic echo of the existence of Israelite deportees from Samaria who had been settled at Nimrud (the biblical Calah, Gen. 10:11-12), the capital of Assyria at that time: a single potsherd on which were scratched the names of 11 Israelite deportees[5]—11 out of the thousands—a remnant whose word to the world, "Here we are!" had to wait to be heard by archeologists 2700 years later. To those who first heard the name of Isaiah's son, then, the name had potential for bad news, sending a shudder through the soul. "It is (only) a remnant which shall return."

But still, for Isaiah, the name comes as a mitigation of the terrible words of his call. The Lord may remove men far away, but a remnant *will* return; so that, though the name of Isaiah's son might at first strike a chill into people's hearts, on second thought it is modestly reassuring. If only 10 percent survive, even so, we tend to assume (it is only human nature) that we will be among that 10 percent. Isaiah said a remnant will return, so it is good news, too, in a way. Some *will* return, and there will be some continuity between past and future.

There is another way by which Isaiah and his contemporaries might have perceived the name "A remnant shall return," other than returning *from deportation*, and that is returning *to God* in repentance; and the clue again is found in a line of Isaiah's call, this time in 6:10. We have already touched on the matter when we were dealing with the difficult question of the meaning of Isaiah's terrible call to drive people away from comprehension (see Chapter II). The line in the call is: "lest they see with their eyes . . . and *turn* and be healed." The verb translated "turn" here is the same verb as "return" in the name of Isaiah's son. Here again we have a mitigation of the terrible message of the call. The call had indicated that people in general would be pushed further from understanding. But now comes the mitigation: not that *nobody* will turn and be healed, but that a *remnant will* turn. Here, then, Isaiah discovers that he can count on a few, a faithful remnant; and his naming of his son may suggest the point at which he felt released from the awful totality of universal condemnation which his call bespoke. This faithful remnant will be able to grasp the message of being willing and obedient to God. (1:19); and *they* will be the basis for a better future.

But everybody hates ambiguity; people want to know what an expression *really* means. Thus we have the interesting spectacle of a passage within the book of Isaiah in which two followers tried to pin down what Shear-jashub *really* meant. The passage, 10:20-23, offers commentary on the word "remnant" which is dependent on the word "remnant" in vs. 19. Follower #1 composed vss. 20-21, declaring that some day the survivors will no longer be dependent on their enemy (who, it is implied, is Assyria), but will *return to God*. So this is good news, news of ultimate repentance. Follower #2 (who was not necessarily later than #1) composed vss. 22-23, declaring that in contrast to the enormous number of Israelites which had been promised to Abraham (Gen. 22:17), only a remnant will return from destruction. This is basically the bad news of the destruction of a population.

If we may summarize, then: we see Isaiah doing a balancing act during his entire life, offering judgment when people are confident, offering hope when people are in panic. Isaiah's call comes on heavy with doom: his mission is to speak so that no one will understand, no one will turn,

and this incomprehension will continue until God removes
men far away. But then a message of mitigation comes:
Isaiah is moved to name a son "A remnant shall return,"
and this ambiguous name reminds people that though God's
judgment will fall heavy upon the people, a few *will* turn
back to God, and a few *will* return from deportation. This
ambiguity was presented to Ahaz along with the ambiguity
of the name of the new child, "Immanuel," and the
ambiguity of Isaiah's new son, Maher-shalal-hash-baz. There
is new hope for the immediate future, in that the threat to
Judah presented by Damascus and Samaria will evaporate
(by God's grace), but ultimately there is a worse threat to
Judah from Assyria (by God's judgment). Now we can
understand better the inner logic of the arrangement of the
intrusive pamphlet, 6:1-9:7, which we examined in
Chapter I, a pamphlet that begins with the desolate call and
is mitigated by the three names; this pamphlet ends, of
course, with the names of the marvelous king (9:6), as we shall
shortly see.

Then, two or three decades later, as the Assyrian threat
became real and terrifying, Isaiah's perceptions of that
judgment, his pronouncements of doom on Jerusalem (like
29:1-6) were extended by fresh material that suggested hope
for Jerusalem (29:7-8; compare 31:1-3, supplemented later
by vss. 4-5 + 8-9). These self-extended oracles we discussed
in Chapter IV.

Isaiah does seem, then, to have become convinced of the
inviolability of Jerusalem. One senses this in many passages
whose genuineness to Isaiah would seem to be un-
challengeable, for example, 31:5—"Like birds hovering, so the
Lord of hosts will protect Jerusalem; he will protect and
deliver it, he will spare and rescue it"; 31:9—"The Lord,
whose fire is in Zion, and whose furnace is in Jerusalem"; and
28:18—"Behold, I am laying in Zion for a foundation a stone,
a tested stone, a precious cornerstone, of a sure foundation:
'He who believes will not be in haste.'" The plunder may
hurry to Assyria or wherever, but he who has faith will not
hurry. The word of Isaiah to King Hezekiah, which the later
historian quotes, may be the piety of the following century

looking back on the deliverance of Jerusalem, but it does seem
to reflect the convictions of Isaiah:

> And the surviving remnant of the house of Judah shall
> again take root downward, and bear fruit upward; for out
> of Jerusalem shall go forth a remnant, and out of Mount
> Zion a band of survivors. The zeal of the Lord will do this.
> Therefore thus says the Lord concerning the king of Assyria,
> He shall not come into this city or shoot an arrow there, or
> come before it with a shield or cast up a siege mound
> against it. By the way that he came, by the same he shall
> return, and he shall not come into this city, says the Lord.
> For I will defend this city to save it, for my own sake and
> for the sake of my servant David (2 Kings 19:30-34).[7]

The last sentence of this quotation offers two emphases
to Isaiah's message of hope which we must now examine:
the first, as I say, is the matter of the inviolability of
Jerusalem, and the second is his concern for the dynasty
inaugurated by King David. We shall take up the matter of
Jerusalem first.

Jerusalem was plainly much on Isaiah's mind. We have
seen this even in chapter 1 of his oracles where the daughter
of *Zion* (an expression which means something like "poor
Zion"—the *New Jewish Version* translates it "Fair Zion") is
left alone when the assault comes (vs. 8); the faithful *city*
has become a harlot (vs. 21). But after God punishes her, he
will restore her leaders, and she shall be called the city of
righteousness (vss. 24, 26). No other prophet from Isaiah's
century whose word survives offers this conviction that God
had so much invested of himself in Jerusalem. For Amos,
Jerusalem is simply a place from which God utters his voice
of judgment (Amos 1:2); Hosea does not mention Jerusalem
at all; and Micah, who was close to Isaiah in time and
message, sees Jerusalem simply as the target of God's destruction—"Jerusalem shall become a heap of ruins, and the
mountain of the house [i.e. of the temple] a wooded height"
(Mic. 3:12; compare Mic. 1:5-9). Isaiah is then quite distinctive in his conviction of God's protection of Jerusalem. What
lay behind such a belief?

A long tradition supported it, of course. Every ancient

people looked to a spot, their own focus of worship, which they considered to be the very center of the universe: here the gods gathered, or at least here was the earthly symbol of the heavenly meeting place of the gods.[8] In particular, the Canaanites who lived in Syria and Palestine before the coming of the Israelites had a "mountain of the gods," a mountain where they believed the gods held council, under the leadership of 'Ēl, the high creator god. It was located in the far *north*, and is to be identified either with Mount Cassius, along the Mediterranean coast at the point of the present-day frontier between Turkey and Syria, south of the Orontes river,[9] or the Amanus mountain range, north of the Orontes river,[10] or both.[11] Other Canaanites looked to other lofty mountains as their local perception of where the gods gathered: mountains in Lebanon, or Mount Carmel in Palestine (where Elijah had a contest with the prophets of Baal, 1 Kings 18:17-46).

When King David captured Jerusalem and made it his own royal city (2 Sam. 5:9), he evidently took over many of the pre-Israelite traditions of its "Jebusite" population (which is what the previous inhabitants were called), whose beliefs had much in common with those of the Canaanites. Among these traditions was that of the centrality of Zion, the holy center of the city. This tradition was then joined to the Israelite tradition regarding God's presence with the ark of the covenant at the time when David brought the ark into Jerusalem (2 Sam. 6).[12] The Psalms are full of images of Zion as the "city of God" or as the "mountain of God" (Ps. 2:6, 46:4, 5, and others). This is not surprising, but what is surprising is that Mount Zion is spoken of as being in the "far north" (Ps. 48:2)—that is, that the images of the old Canaanite mountain of the far north have now been transferred to Zion in Jerusalem.

(The notion of Jerusalem as the very center of the universe continued in later generations: there is Ezekiel's phrase "the center [literally, 'navel'] of the earth" (Ezek. 38:12), thought to apply to Jerusalem;[13] there are medieval maps which show Jerusalem in the center of the world; and there is a grotesque carved navel today for all to see, on the floor of the Chapel of the Greeks in the Church of the Holy Sepulchre in Jerusalem.)

But if Canaanite imagery was used to talk about Jerusalem, the great danger was the development of a complacent, pagan attitude: that God would protect Jerusalem no matter what.

The prophet Micah would evidently have viewed these pretensions of Jerusalem as purely pagan (compare the remarks on Micah above); but Isaiah was convinced that this notion of the centrality of Jerusalem could be tamed to the Israelite faith. God would protect Jerusalem (31:5), yes. But Jerusalem had become a harlot (1:21) and needed to be purified by God (1:25); indeed God himself must lay the cornerstone for the true security of Jerusalem (28:16). God will protect Jerusalem, yes. But the basic necessity of her citizens was trust and faith in God (compare 30:15). Trust in God's protection of Jerusalem is good, but it must be a trust in God, not a trust in Jerusalem; and this trust in God must be in partnership with a sense of *justice* in the community (again, 1:21).

Isaiah's conviction that God would protect Jerusalem was mightily reinforced when she *was* protected, when the Assyrian army did not capture her after all. Forever afterward the Isaianic tradition continued to amass passages dealing with the centrality and coming purity of Jerusalem; for a fine example, see 4:2-6, which can hardly be from Isaiah himself (see Chapter I) but shows what later generations did with that tradition. (We shall discuss that passage in detail in Chapter IX.)

The other motif in Isaiah's theology which speaks of hope is the twin of the motifs of the inviolability of Jerusalem: God's concern for the dynasty of David. This motif is not found simply in that last phrase of 2 Kings 19:34; it is found supremely in two passages which have become central to Christians, namely, 9:2-7 ("The people who walked in darkness have seen a great light") and 11:1-9 ("There shall come forth a shoot from the stump of Jesse"). To many people these two passages of hope for the future, hope embodied in a righteous king, are the high points of Isaiah 1-39.

We recall what was said at the beginning of Chapter II about the monarchy in Israel: that in the days after David and Solomon people were more and more tempted to assume that the king who happened to be ruling at a particular time represented ultimate authority (as the kings of other nations did); and that, as far as the king's conduct was concerned, he was above the law—"anything goes." This view of kingship in Jerusalem would have been reinforced by pagan ideas coming in with the Jebusite tradition, just as was the case with the people's view of Jerusalem.

This view of kingship was reinforced by another factor also, namely the prophet Nathan's oracle to King David (2 Sam. 7:8-16) that God would covenant specifically with David to keep him and his descendants on the throne forever. We are so accustomed to this idea that we must remind ourselves that at the time the oracle was spoken it represented a real innovation for Israel. In the beginning, of course, kingship was out of the question. Before the time of Saul and David, Gideon had said, "I will not rule over you, and my son will not rule over you; the Lord will rule over you" (Judg. 8:23). Even when the monarchy was inaugurated with Saul, there is evidence of great uneasiness in Israel over the innovation.[14] The prophet Hosea, preaching in the same century as Isaiah, was convinced that embarking upon kingship had been a mistake and had gone against the will of God (Hos. 8:4 and 13:10-11 are the clearest formulations of this conviction; compare also Hos. 3:4).

But the Israelites did adopt the institution of monarchy, and the Davidic dynasty did persist. By the time Hezekiah was crowned, the dynasty of David was only 15 years shy of being three hundred years old, and it would persist for a total of 414 years—a remarkably long span of time for one family of kings. People's sense of security in the Davidic monarchy, like their sense of security in the temple in Jerusalem, was reinforced by various psalms (compare Ps. 20, a psalm of prayer for the king's victory in battle, which speaks also of the "sanctuary" and "Zion" in vs. 2).

As with Jerusalem, so with the monarchy; Isaiah (in contrast to Hosea) believed that such a view of monarchy could be tamed to the Israelite faith, and that conviction evidently forms the basis of 9:2-7 and 11:1-9; monarchy in the line of David, yes (9:7, 11:1), but a Davidic monarchy which is a source of justice and righteousness for the community (9:7, 11:4).

It is virtually impossible for a Christian to read these passages without Christian associations (the lines of Handel's *Messiah* ringing in one's ears). But, as with 7:14, before we turn to the use Christians have made of the passages, let us try to see them in Isaiah's world, see how he intended the words and how his own hearers heard them.

We begin with 9:2-7. We may note in passing that the genuineness of this passage has been widely questioned, but that most scholars today accept its authenticity to Isaiah.[15] The vocabulary of vss. 2-5, at least, is quite militaristic: there will be a great change of morale from gloom to joy as the people throw off the burden of their oppressor by the help of God's direct intervention. Indeed, it will be as overwhelming a victory as was Gideon's over the Midianites (Judg. 6:1-8:17)—that is the meaning of the reference to "Midian" in vs. 4. And all the muddy boots and bloody clothes of the enemy will be burned (vs. 5).

Is the oppressor the Assyrian? It would seem logical. It is likely that this passage is connected with vs. 1, because vs. 1 seems to reflect the Assyrian invasion of the territory of Zebulun and Naphtali in 733/2 B.C. (2 Kings 15:29). In this case the great reversal described in vss. 2-7 will be the reversal of this particular invasion of northern territory by Assyria.[16]

God will intervene and this great reversal will be a holy war, like the old holy wars in the time of the judges. The intervention will be accomplished by the gift of a king. It is striking, however, that the word "king" itself is never used; he will have a throne (vs. 7), he will have a kingdom (vs. 7), but he is not called "king"—"prince," yes (vs. 6), but not "king." There were princes in the days of the judges (see Judg. 5:15), but not kings. So here Isaiah is evidently trying to reshape the Davidic monarchy after the old pattern of the time before the first king, King Saul.

Now curiously enough the words "child" and "son" in vs. 6 do not necessarily imply an infant or a youngster, as we might assume. This is the language of Oriental monarchy, by which the king, specifically on the day of his coronation, is called a "son" of the deity.[17] One finds traces of such wording elsewhere in the Old Testament: thus in the oracle of the prophet Nathan to King David, already referred to, in 2 Samuel 7:14, the statement is made that God will be a father to the descendant of David who rules after him, and he will be a son to God. Again, in Psalm 2:7, part of what is evidently a coronation psalm for kings in Israel,[18] we find the wording, "I will tell of the decree of the Lord: He said to me, 'You are my son, today I have begotten you.' " (Psalm 72:1 has similar wording. This psalm evidently had a purpose similar to that of Psalm 2.) One has the impression, then, that Isaiah 9:6 begins with royal language appropriate to the coronation of a king (or to the anniversary of a coronation).[19] The verse continues by stating that the "government"—the meaning of the word is uncertain; it may be some symbol of office (the *New English Bible* reads "symbol of his dominion")—shall be upon his shoulder.

At the end of vs. 6 we have a list of throne-names for the new king. Throne-names were well known in the ancient world; an Egyptian pharaoh would adopt them when he began his reign. So the pharaoh Haremhab (1333-1306 B.C.) adopted these names: "Strong bull, able in counsels, great in wonders at Karnak, filled with the truth, creator of the two lands, splendid is the character of Re, elect of Re, beloved of Amon, Horus at the festival, on whom life is conferred."[20]

The throne-names in the Isaiah passage form the climax of the passage. The first word of the first name in Hebrew is a well-known governmental title, "counselor" (see, for example, 1:26 and 3:3). The whole phrase here could mean "a marvel of a planner" (so the *Revised Standard Version*: "wonderful counselor"), but is more likely to mean "a planner of marvels."[21] These "marvels" are evidently prodigious acts (such as in battle) effected with God's help; the same word appears in the "Song of Moses" in Exodus 15:11 (God is "doing *wonders*").

The second name can be nothing other than a title for God: the first word (*'Ēl*) is the old word for the creator-god in Canaanite belief, now accommodated to the Israelite God. It is the same word for God found in the name "Immanuel." The second word (*gibbōr*) means "champion, war-hero." This combination appears as a divine title in 10:21, a verse we studied earlier in this chapter: the remnant of Jacob will return "to *the mighty God*"; and it appears, again as a divine title, in Jeremiah 32:18 (again translated "mighty God"). Isaiah is referring to *God* here in 9:6 by this title, and any attempt to water down the meaning of the phrase to apply it to a human king (such as the translation in the *New English Bible*, "in battle God-like") is simply inadmissible. We have just heard (in vs. 4) of God's prowess in battle; so this name means "God the war-hero." We referred a moment ago to the Song of Moses in Exodus 15; vs. 3 of that chapter offers a similar affirmation: "The Lord is a man of war" (though the Hebrew phrase there is a different one).

The third article is again a divine title: "Father forever" or "Father of everlastingness." "Father" is a term applied to God in the Old Testament, but never unequivocally to the king. Specifically, as we saw in the oracle of the prophet Nathan to King David in 2 Samuel 7:14, God is father *to the king*. At the beginning of Isaiah 9:6 a "son" is born; that is, the king has become a "son" to God. Now God is affirmed as everlasting Father to the king.

The fourth title again offers in its first Hebrew word a governmental title, "prince"; this term is found in 3:3 (although the *Revised Standard Version* there translates it "captain") and in other places. This prince will be a prince of *shālōm*. This well-known Hebrew term covers much more than the absence of war: it refers to community well-being, safety, health, prosperity. It can even mean military success. When Gideon the judge was pursuing the Midianite kings, he said to the men of Penuel who were impeding him, "When I come again *in peace*, I will break down this tower" (Judg. 8:9). Here *shālōm* clearly means "military success" rather than "peace" in our sense. The *Jerusalem Bible* translates this passage as "when I return *victorious*. . . ." So a "captain of *shālōm*" in Isaiah refers to the king as successful against foreign threats as well as a sponsor of prosperity at home.

So here are the throne-names: a governmental title, two divine titles, and a governmental title once more. Is the marvelous king *receiving* divine titles here? I submit that he is not, in spite of all the commentators.[22] We saw in Chapter II that for Isaiah only God is supreme; it is inconceivable then that Isaiah would call the king "God."

The solution, I suggest, is that the two middle titles are *theophoric* names (and I must now explain the meaning of the term "theophoric"). Israelite personal names were in general of two sorts. Some of them were *descriptive* names; for example, "Zeruah," the name of the mother of Jeroboam I (1 Kings 11:26), is evidently a descriptive name meaning "leper." But most Israelite personal names were *theophoric*: that is, they involve a name or title or designation of God, with a verb or adjective or noun which expresses a theological affirmation. Thus "Hezekiah" is a name which means "Yah (=Yahweh) is my strength," and "Isaiah" is a name which means "Yah (=Yahweh) has brought salvation." It is obvious that Isaiah is not called "Yahweh"; he bears a name which says something *about* Yahweh. So I suggest that the marvelous king is not *called* "mighty God" or "Father forever," but that the middle titles of his throne-names are theophoric. (It may even be that the Hebrew phrases imply an "is": "God the war-hero is Father forever.") If we think back, we will see that "Immanuel" is likewise a theophoric name: the new child is not *called* "God"; he bears a name which makes an affirmation about God.

Let me point out one more aspect of this matter. The name of Isaiah's son Maher-shalal-hash-baz made up a symmetrical pair of poetic lines. The throne-names of the marvelous king here make up another kind of symmetry—an A-B-B-A form: the governmental title, the middle divine titles, and a governmental title again. Isaiah uses this A-B-B-A form frequently, as do other poets in the Old Testament. A simple example will do; in 11:6a the Hebrew reads, word by word, "And shall dwell the wolf with the lamb, and the leopard with the kid shall lie down." Here the line begins and ends with the two verbs, and between them are the subjects and prepositional phrases. The A-B-B-A form of the throne-names helps to keep the categories clear, and the two categories—the governmental titles that are descriptive, and the divine titles that are theophoric—are quite distinct in Isaiah's mind. Thus the king bears these names: "Planner of wonders; God the war hero (is) Father forever; prince of well-being."[23]

It is curious that the throne-names continue the rather militaristic tone of the poem; we had not quite expected this. Just as *shālōm* speaks both of success against foreign threats and well-being on the home front, and as vss. 2-5 speak of success against foreign threats, so vs. 7 speaks of well-being on the home front: the king's reign will be confirmed by God's grace and the characteristics of his ruling will be justice and righteousness.

Now what would have been the circumstance that would give rise to such an oracle? I have already suggested that it served as a coronation ode for a king, or an ode for the anniversary of his coronation. (For a description of the coronation of a king over Israel, see 2 Kings 11:12.) There is no way to prove the suggestion, of course. But we do have psalms which were evidently composed for great occasions in the life of a king. Psalm 45 was composed for a royal wedding, and we have already looked at two psalms (Pss. 2, 72) which offer phraseology similar to that of the Isaiah passage. These examples suggest that we are dealing with a common literary type, evidently songs for a coronation. A coronation is a joyous occasion, an occasion when one hopes a corner has been turned, when one hopes that the government will become responsive to human need, when one hopes that things will go well for the realm. This explains the mood of these psalms, and the mood of the Isaiah passage. One can imagine that Isaiah, a confidant of kings (7:3-4, 2 Kings 19:2-7), might have been approached with a request to speak a word from God on the day of the crowning of Hezekiah, perhaps, when the people hoped for a reversal of the terrible military situation of the kingship of Ahaz. At least this is the persistent Jewish tradition, and it may well be correct.[24]

Such a glad ode, by its very idealism, would lend itself admirably to *re-use* for any later king of Judah. Americans do the same thing. They sing the "Star Spangled Banner" on every patriotic occasion even though the "rockets' red glare" of the British attack on Fort McHenry near Baltimore on the night of September 13-14, 1814, is no longer of great excitement to them. It would always be possible for those in Judah to take heart from the affirmation that "the people who walked in darkness have seen a great light."

Then, when Jerusalem fell to the Babylonians in 587 B.C. and kingship was at an end, the promise of ideal kingship became one of the top items on the agenda for the future: when kingship is restored, this is what it will be like! The old song of Isaiah's became a nucleus for Jewish dreams of restoration.

Of course this passage has entered deeply into Christian sensibilities. It helped shape the language which records the angel Gabriel speaking to Mary (Luke 1:32-33), it was used by the church fathers in referring to Jesus,[25] and it is embodied in many lectionaries as one of the readings for the liturgy on Christmas Day. Christians are quite justified in doing this. The passage is about kingship, and Jesus saw himself as a king—a humble king, it is true, but a king nonetheless (Matt. 21:3-5). He who taught that the peacemakers are blessed (Matt. 5:9) is appropriately called "Prince of Peace" (with a shift of meaning for *shālōm*). If one follows the perspective of the early Christian affirmation which Paul sets forth in Philippians 2, "Therefore God has highly exalted him and bestowed on him the name which is above every name, that at the name of Jesus every knee should bow" (Phil. 2:9-10), then even the old title of the warrior-God, "God the war-hero," is appropriate now (not

as a theophoric title, but as a descriptive one) for Jesus—
transposed by the power of the way of the cross to the
simple title, "mighty God." Renewal after disaster? Isaiah's
words have given both the Jewish and the Christian communities hope for greater renewal than he imagined, after
disaster deeper than he imagined.

The companion piece to 9:2-7 is 11:1-9, to which we
now turn. Verses 1-5 enlarge upon the theme of 9:7, the
theme of a Davidic king who will rule with justice and
righteousness and be concerned for the poor and the meek
of the earth.

Many people have assumed that this passage refers to a
restored Davidic kingship after it had ceased to be, a
dynasty renewed after the exile. They have assumed this
simply because of the occurrence of the word "stump" in vs.
1, for a stump is, after all, what is left after the tree is cut
down.[26] But the Hebrew word in question does not necessarily mean "stump." It appears only twice elsewhere in the
Old Testament: it does mean "stump" in Job 14:8, but in
Isaiah 40:24 it clearly means "stem" (so rightly in the
Revised Standard Version). So with one vote either way we
can take the usage in 11:1 on either side. If it means "stem"
(and I myself think it does here), then we could be dealing
with intact kingship in Isaiah's own day.

What about the authenticity of the passage? That has
been widely questioned, and some who affirm the authenticity of vss. 1-5 believe vss. 6-8 or 6-9 are a late addition.[27] But it is clear that the vocabulary in vss. 1-5 is
Isaiah's. We have seen how similar it is in motifs to the vocabulary in 9:7, and the concern for justice for the poor is
plainly one which Isaiah preached (see Chapter III). It is
also clear that the vocabulary of vss. 6-8 is found in genuine
passages of Isaiah—for example, "lamb" in 5:17, "lion" in
5:29 and 31:4. I am convinced that the passage must be
taken as a whole and that it is all genuine to Isaiah.

The problem is that vss. 6-8 appear to speak of a re-
creation of nature so that wild animals are no longer destructive, and that such a view, which became a convention

of the apocalyptic world-view in the centuries *after* Isaiah, hardly seems appropriate to Isaiah himself. (Thus 65:25 is part of a passage uttered two hundred years later than Isaiah. We shall study this passage in Chapter VIII. This verse summarizes 11:6-9 in the context of a re-created nature when there will be no more infant mortality; see 65:20.) (But we may note in passing that the idea of the permanent taming of wild beasts is very old indeed. We find the following lines in the Sumerian paradise myth of Enki and Ninhursag, to be dated before 2000 B.C.: "The lion kills not, the wolf snatches not the lamb.")[28]

The passage in 11:6-8 appears to suggest that when the new king comes, things will be as they were in a golden age of primeval paradise. It is a beautiful idea, but the question is, does it fit *Isaiah's* mental furniture? I believe the passage is authentic to Isaiah but that we have misunderstood his message. I should like to propose that vss. 6-8 are a description not of a re-created nature but of international peace, and that the wild animals are symbols of predatory nations.[29] One notes that in one of the early passages on Assyria Isaiah likens the enemy to lions (5:29). Jeremiah, in a noteworthy passage shaped in the following century, cites the first three wild beasts of Isaiah 11:6 as a figure for the Babylonians (Jer. 5:6)—the lion,[30] the wolf, and the leopard. (Here may be an indirect bit of evidence in favor of the suggestion that this passage was *Jeremiah's* understanding, a century later, of Isaiah's oracle.) We also have Amos's sarcastic comment about "rescuing" from the mouth of the lion two legs, or a piece of an ear, suggesting that this is the way the inhabitants of Samaria will be "rescued" (Amos 3:12). All these examples suggest that in Isaiah's time predatory animals were mentioned to symbolize predatory nations.

In this view, then, the new king will rule his realm with justice (vss. 3-5) and there will be international security without the threat of oppressive military power. Such a poem might serve as a coronation ode in the same kind of way as we assumed for 9:2-7.[31]

But such grand language, like the grand language of

9:2-7, outlived its context, and in the terrible days of the Babylonian exile and beyond, the Jewish people used these words to feed their hopes for the future. When they craved relief from both injustice and hostile nature, the words became a program for an apocalyptic re-creation of the world, and the imagery has continued to move us: witness the 19th century painting of the American Quaker artist and preacher Edward Hicks, called "The Peaceable Kingdom," a bucolic scene of animals wild and tame, resting side by side with children.

Hope for renewal is in Isaiah's words, but a hope tempered by a realistic appraisal of the situation of his day. It is a measure of the power of his images that they continue to feed the imaginations of those communities who share the biblical heritage down to the present day.

Perhaps we should underline the word "communities" here. Isaiah's hope for renewal was never to individuals one by one; his "prince of peace," upon whom the "Spirit of the Lord" rested, was no Savior to individuals one by one. His hope for renewal was to his community, a community knit together by ties of covenant and clan relationship far closer than most communities today. The earliest church was another such close-knit community (Acts 2:44-47), and one can hope that Isaiah's images of renewal can aid in knitting together communities of God's covenant in our own day.

We have completed our study of the first Isaiah, and we turn now to the words of his greatest successor, who shaped the words of chapters 40-55.

"Second Isaiah"

CHAPTER VI

A Return For Exiles

*I*F OUR EXPLORATION of hope and renewal within the message of the original Isaiah was decorated with a question mark, there is no question now: chapter 40 opens a sequence of 16 chapters of the most sustained, lyrical expression of hope and renewal to be found within the Old Testament. Not until the pages of the New Testament do readers of the Bible find the same reassurance which they find in chapters 40-55. In Chapter I of this study I quoted an elderly deaconess in a church I had served who used to say, "I just love the book of Isaiah," and I pointed out that it was such chapters as these that she had in mind.

What are our own first impressions of this material? They are of spaciousness and a lack of interruptions, of lyricism and soaring images, and of a kind of self-explanatory quality to the lines. Let me spell out these impressions a bit. First, we sense spaciousness and a lack of interruptions. When we studied material in chapters 1-39 we were always dealing with short passages, bits and pieces that stand cheek-by-jowl with other bits and pieces, additions, insertions, and the like. But in chapter 40 and beyond we feel able to read and read and read without stopping. Next, we find lyricism and soaring images. The images we met in chapters 1-39 were exciting, stimulating, sometimes shocking, but rarely did they soar as these do in chapter 40 and beyond. One has the sense here of being on a long downhill ski-run, or in a glider a mile above the earth; one could go on forever.

Above all, we find a self-explanatory quality to the lines. Suddenly we do not need the lines explained or the Hebrew words defined; we believe we understand without help. (This impression is not altogether accurate, as we shall see, but it *is* a first impression.) No wonder the responsive readings and unison readings in our orders of service are often drawn from Isaiah 40-55.

These first impressions are striking enough that we should trust them awhile. It is good to begin by reading chapter 40 aloud, and to do so in a recent translation other than the *Revised Standard Version*. It is not a bad translation, but it reflects so much of the familiar phrasing of the *King James Version* that we must find a way to hear the words as freshly as did the first hearers. So just because it is a fresh translation with a high style, I like to use the 1950 version prepared by Ronald Knox, a British Roman Catholic. Here are vss. 27-31 of chapter 40:

> What, then, is this thought of thine, Jacob, what is this complaint of thine, Israel, that the Lord does not see how it fares with thee, that thy God passes over thy wrongs? What ignorance is this? Has not the rumour of it reached thee? This Lord of ours, who fashioned the remotest bounds of earth, is God eternally; he does not weaken or grow weary; he is wise beyond all our thinking. Rather it is he who gives the weary fresh spirit, who fosters strength and vigour where strength and vigour is none. Youth itself may weaken, the warrior faint and flag, but those who trust in the Lord will renew their strength, like eagles new-fledged; hasten, and never grow weary of hastening, march on, and never weaken on the march.[1]

There is an almost Shakespearean grandeur to the scope of this English which nicely matches the grandeur of the Hebrew lines.

What is the good news that we hear? That there is comfort for the people (vss. 1-2), that a straight road will be made through the desert for God (vss. 3-5), and that though people are as transitory as grass, God's word stands forever (vss. 6-8). We hear that God comes with might but will feed his flock like a shepherd (vss. 9-11), that this God had no one to coach him in his creative work and alongside him the nations of the world shrink to nothing (vss. 12-17), that the idols of the nations are nothing alongside God (vss. 18-20). We hear that this God has numbered all the stars of the heavens and brings princes to nought (vss. 21-26), and that therefore Israel has no reason to feel sorry for herself, for God gives power to the faint so that they shall walk and run once more (vss. 27-31).

As we move into chapter 41 we find many of these themes once more: the reassurance to Israel (vss. 8-10), the foolishness of idols (vss. 7, 29), and refreshment even in the desert (vss. 17-20). But there are other themes that strike us as less comprehensible: God is stirring up someone from the east (vs. 2) or the north (vs. 25) who will trample on rulers. What is that all about? We also hear echoes of legal language: the coastlands are to listen while we (who are "we"?) draw near for judgment (vs. 1); someone is addressed by God and told to set forth his case and bring his proofs (vs. 21). We begin to wonder whether we have understood quite so well as we had thought.

As we have done earlier in our study, we shall try to turn aside from the familiar strains of Handel's *Messiah* ("And the glory, the glory of the Lord shall be revealed," 40:5) to see this material in the context of a particular time and place for the Old Testament people.

We have already found some provisional answers in our survey of the book of Isaiah in Chapter I. Chapters 40-55 are the work of a prophet who stood in the tradition of Isaiah but who spoke to his people in exile in Babylon, two hundred years later than the time of the first Isaiah, about 540 B.C. He is an anonymous prophet whom we call (for lack of any more specific knowledge) "Second Isaiah." The situation of these people in exile was so different from the situation of the hearers of the first Isaiah that we need at least a thumbnail sketch of what had happened in the meantime.

Assyria, as we know, was not able to capture Jerusalem in Isaiah's time, but she did extend her control deep into Egypt during the next century (see Chapters IV and V). King Hezekiah's successor, his son Manasseh, had a long reign of 45 years,[2] and, according to the records of the Assyrian king of the time and the hints in 2 Kings 21:2-9, he paid heavy tribute to Assyria and conformed public worship to the paganism of Assyria.

By the time Manasseh died, Assyria was growing weaker under pressure from her many subject peoples, led by the Babylonians (a people related to the Assyrians) to the south. During the reign of Manasseh's grandson Josiah, Assyria fell (612 B.C.), defeated by Babylon. There was a brief time, then, when neither Assyria nor Babylon was strong enough to bother Judah, and during that time, in the kingship of Josiah, Judah enjoyed her last reassuring days.

After Josiah was suddenly killed in battle (609 B.C.), however, Judah quickly fell to pieces. Josiah's son Jehoahaz ruled for only three months, only to be deposed by the pharaoh of Egypt and deported there, never to be heard from again. His brother Jehoiakim was put on the throne and paid tribute first to Egypt, but then, suddenly, when Babylon threatened, to Babylon. When he thought he could, Jehoiakim rebelled *against* Babylon. While the Babylonian king Nebuchadnezzar besieged Jerusalem, King Jehoiakim died, and his 18-year-old son Jehoiachin was put on the throne. But this boy-king lasted only three months before Jerusalem fell to the Babylonians (598 B.C.), and the king, the queen mother, and many of the nobility were deported to Babylon. The Babylonians picked another member of the Judean royal family, the brother of Jehoiakim, named Zedekiah, and placed him on the throne of Judah—but under Babylonian control, where he lasted 11 years. He, too, got notions of independence, and King Nebuchadnezzar came in to besiege Jerusalem once more. When the city fell in 587 B.C. the Davidic monarchy was at an end. The temple was also destroyed, several hundred leaders were deported, and Jerusalem became virtually uninhabitable. This is the period, by the way, through which the prophet Jeremiah lived and preached.

The Judeans who were deported to Babylon were evidently not put into internment camps, as we might imagine, but were settled in various colonies; their labor was doubtless useful in constructing some of the new building projects in which Nebuchadnezzar was engaged. Over a period of time many of the deportees managed to settle down. They were allowed to build houses, to farm, and no doubt to set up small trading enterprises.[4] Nevertheless, no one likes to be held against his will, and the tradition of Israel's tie with the land of Palestine was so strong that there must have been constant yearning to return home.

But it was not only a simple homesickness; there were deeper questions that appear to have shaken people's spirits in those long years of exile.

The first Isaiah, we recall, had encouraged people to trust that Jerusalem would be inviolable and that the Davidic line of kings would be unbroken. This trust was challenged, in the decades before the exile, by the prophet Jeremiah, who said that, to the contrary, Jerusalem and Judah would be destroyed, and that God was doing it deliberately to punish his people. The central question, then, for the exiles was a theological question: Where is God, and what is he doing? There were, no doubt, Babylonians who mocked the Jews and insisted that Marduk (the god of Babylon) had been stronger than Yahweh. How could this mocking be challenged? One has only to read Psalm 137 to catch some of the bitterness which people nursed in their hearts during this period. Now that God has punished us, the people wondered, will he do anything to restore us? Does he say "Good riddance of bad rubbish" about us? Does he confine his attention simply to Palestine, and if he does, are we not located beyond his horizon altogether now? Or, if he does remember us, why does he allow us to suffer? How many decades have to pass before we have paid for our sins? Why, some of us were not even alive in 587! What will be the shape of our future as a people? And if God does have a future for us, what role will other nations play in that future?[5]

In the summer of 1957, I had occasion to be a guest of one of the German Protestant church organizations at a ten-day conference of pastors from both the west- and east-zones of Germany which took place in Berlin. The first three days of that conference were taken up simply with life-stories;

one by one the participants sketched out the outlines of their careers. Over and over again the narratives were punctuated by the phrases *vor dem Krieg, während des Kriegs, nach dem Krieg* ("before the war," "during the war," "after the war"). For them World War II was a watershed; after the war nothing was as it had been before the war. For the Jews of the sixth century B.C. the fall of Jerusalem was like this. Before the fall Judah had been an intact state, with a foreign policy, an army, borders, government, temple, integrity; after the fall Judah was just one more province in the Babylonian empire. Her temple was gone. Her leaders were refugees in Egypt or interned in Babylon, scattered across the face of the earth. How can Humpty-Dumpty be put together again? was the sort of question they were asking. Do we have anything left but our memories of God's covenanting with us in happier days? "How shall we sing the Lord's song in a foreign land?" (Ps. 137:4). It was within this theological vacuum that Second Isaiah spoke out.

There are two interrelated difficulties we face as we try to come to grips with the message of Second Isaiah. The first difficulty is in understanding the way he interweaves his themes. He touches five or six bases, moving from one to another, relating them in fresh ways. We have already glanced at the contents of chapter 40, but notice now how he weaves back and forth. Verses 21-26 are, in a way, "review" of what was said in earlier verses: the height of God above the nations (vs. 22) is indicated in vs. 18 ("the nations are like a drop from a bucket"), God's stretching out the heavens like a curtain (vs. 22) is hinted at in vs. 12 ("marked off the heavens with a span"), God's bringing princes to nought (vs. 23) is anticipated in vs. 17 ("all the nations are as nothing before him"), and the affirmation that princes are carried off like stubble (vs. 24) is prepared for in the testimony that all flesh is grass (vss. 6-7). Yet these later lines are not simply review, or recollection, or repetition; their images are deepened, they are brought together in fresh ways, they are reinforced by their position in the chapter.

The other difficulty is in understanding the dazzling number of rhetorical and poetic effects the poet creates in his lines. Some of these effects can be seen through a translation, such as the repetition of key words ("comfort, comfort my people," vs. 1) or of phrases ("have you not known, have you not heard?" in both vs. 21 and vs. 28, though it should be pointed out that in the Hebrew text the tense and number of the verbs differ in these two verses). But some of his efforts cannot be seen through a translation. For example, in vs. 22 a verb in Hebrew is repeated three times with different meanings. This verb means "sit" or "dwell"; the root idea evidently was originally "settle down," for one can "settle down" in an armchair or "settle down" in a new town. So here in vs. 22 we have "he who *sits*," "its *inhabitants*" (literally "its dwellers"), and "like a tent to *dwell* in." The poet also loves plays on words: we have "flesh" (Hebrew *bāsār*) twice, vss. 5, 6, echoed by a word with the same sequence of consonants, "herald of good tidings" (*mebasseret*) twice (vs. 9). This word-play suggests a double irony: all flesh shall see the glory of God (vs. 5), though, of course, flesh, alongside God, is transitory and weak (vs. 6). How shall the glory of God be revealed to all *flesh*? Through—how shall we try to say it in English?— "through a *flash* of good news," perhaps! But to try to find an equivalent word-play in English is to fail, simply because we do not weave word-plays into high poetry as the Israelites did. So we must simply affirm that this material weaves together sound and sense into a seamless robe which almost defies analysis.

This is true not only within chapter 40. One has the feeling that one is in touch with large-scale units that span the 16 chapters. To take but one example: the words "comfort, comfort" begin chapter 40. But this Hebrew verb does not appear again until it occurs four times in chapter 51 (51:3 twice, 12, 19). Are we to understand that this grand theme of God's command for his people to be comforted must bracket so wide an expanse of poetry, that we must hold the notion in suspension until then? It is possible.[6] Western classical music may offer an analogy. With the first

Isaiah we were dealing with small units, like movements of the earlier string quartets of Beethoven. Now, suddenly, we are faced with large-scale material like that of Wagner's *Ring* cycle, where the same musical motifs come and go across an enormous span of musical material.

Nevertheless we must come to grips with this material, and we do so in this same chapter 40. The prophet says that God commands a group to comfort his people; we know it is a group because the imperative verbs ("comfort, comfort") are plural in Hebrew. Who makes up the group? Evidently the heavenly assembly, the court audience gathered to hear the command of God.[7] The prophet understands himself to have stood in this heavenly assembly (compare here Jer. 23:22) to hear the awesome command of God. The command is not only to "comfort" (or, perhaps better, to "encourage"—Ronald Knox translates "take heart again"); the command is also to "speak tenderly." But perhaps it is not simply "tenderly," for the Hebrew says literally, "speak onto the heart of Jerusalem." Since the "heart" for the Israelite was not so much the center of the emotions, as it is for us, but more the center of decision-making, of the will, the phrase may then mean "speak reassuringly to Jerusalem."[8]

The word "warfare" (*Revised Standard Version*) is misleading; the alternative rendering "time of service" is more accurate. The term is a general term for "army" (and, incidentally, it occurs again in vs. 26 for the "host" of stars). From being a general term for "army," it shifts to mean "army service," and therefore for any kind of compulsory service; so here. Their time of exile is ended, and by implication, they can go home. The implication is not explicit yet, and though the hints will continue, chapter 40 contains no clear-cut affirmation that the exiles will return. The exiles will have to listen patiently through many lines of poetry to hear clearly the news for which they have been waiting.

Their time of exile is ended, and their wrongdoing has been pardoned. The exile, as always in the Old Testament, was closely related to the idea of punishment (Lam. 4:22a);

but this punishment is over now, God has exacted his penalty. Indeed, in the exuberant language of the prophet, they have taken double what they deserve, as when one punishes a child by forcing him to sit in the corner for fifteen minutes—no, make that a half-hour so he will remember not to misbehave again. If you think you have received more than your share of punishment, so be it, but this is all past now.

Now a voice cries (vs. 3), a voice says (vs. 6). Whose voice? The text does not say. Second Isaiah leaves many things unsaid. It is not God's voice, for the voice speaks about God's activity in vs. 3 and especially in vs. 5. It is not the prophet's voice, for vs. 6a offers a brief exchange between the voice and the prophet. Evidently it is the voice of a spokesman for that heavenly assembly about which we have spoken already.

What is the voice to cry? First, there is a command to the assembly to clear the way through the desert for a road for God—bulldozer work to fill the valleys and cut the hills so that the highway can be straight and level. Then God's glory will be revealed.

We recall from our discussion in Chapter II that the call of the first Isaiah included the hymn of the seraphs which affirmed that the whole earth *is* full of God's glory. But now, if the heavenly assembly is to prepare a highway so that God's glory *is to be* revealed, then evidently the people had not been perceiving God's glory during their years in exile. We also wonder, why does God need a *highway*? Why is God limited to *land* travel? The imagery here is evidently that of preparing a processional road by which a god or king marches in triumph. In the present-day Near East, when a king or president visits a neighboring capital or even a remote hamlet in his own land, the people will erect triumphal arches decorated with inscriptions and pictures and flowers. The prophet proclaims that a road is to be prepared in much the same way for the triumphal march of God himself, the heavenly king. But if God is to lead a procession across the desert, then there is a *procession to be led*, another hint (like "her time of service is ended" in vs. 2) that people are going to go home and that God will

lead the procession of homecomers. It is in this way that
God's glory is to be revealed. The gods of Babylon
manifested their glory in their processions by the marvel of
their images, but God's glory is his action in history.[9]
What the whole world will see ("all flesh," vs. 5) is the quite
unexpected deliverance by God of his people. God's glory
had not been perceived during the years his people had been
in exile because there had been no mighty acts of God;
now, suddenly, there will be.

Most of us have not been understanding vss. 6-8 rightly,
and part of the trouble is that the phrase "surely the people
is grass" at the end of vs. 7 does not belong here. It spoils
the flow of the poem and has been acknowledged as an in-
authentic gloss by almost every scholar. It is true that "the
people" (that is, Israel) is grass, but that is not the point the
prophet is making. The point is that "all flesh" (implication:
"all mankind") is grass (vs. 6), the same "all flesh" which
will witness with surprise the new deliverance of God (vs.
5). It may be pointed out, by the way, that the Hebrew
word translated in vs. 6 as "beauty" would be better translated "constancy" (*New English Bible:* "they last no longer
than a flower of the field").

All flesh is grass, and this grass withers (vss. 7, 8). We
learn from vs. 24 that when "they" wither, the tempest carries "them" off like stubble; in that passage "they" are
evidently the princes and rulers (vs. 23). So "all flesh is
grass" (vss. 6-8) turns out to be a statement about the
powerlessness of the nations, a correlative statement to the
statement that the glory of the Lord shall be revealed (vss.
3-5). We expect the two passages to be correlative, since
they have begun with parallel instructions ("a voice cries,"
vs. 3; "a voice says, 'Cry!'" vs. 6).

So far, the commands have been spoken to an
assembly, presumably that heavenly assembly ("comfort,"
vs. 1; "prepare," vs. 3). Now in vs. 9 the commands are in
the feminine singular, and are given to Zion, to Jerusalem.
In passing we note that the image is somewhat odd in the
address to Zion ("Get you up to a high mountain"),
inasmuch as Zion *is* a mountain, as we learned in Chapter

V. So how can one address Zion as one would address a watchman, commanding him to mount a watchtower? Only by personifying Zion, by telling Zion to accept her position, to be what she is potentially all the time.

Zion-Jerusalem is to tell good news—in New Testament terms, she is to preach the gospel. She is to announce that God has arrived. He comes in power (vs. 10), with a strong right arm as in battle. We have had the impression he was to start leading a procession across the desert (vss. 3-5); now, suddenly, Zion is to announce his *arrival*. Still, nothing is said directly about the arrival of the *exiles*; what we hear instead is that his "reward" is with him—a word meaning "pay" for "work" well done. God has done work and has brought his "pay" with him; this may hint that his *people* are with him, but if so, it is certainly an indirect way of saying it. The parallel to "reward" in the next line is "recompense," and his "recompense" is not parading *after* him, it is *before* him. This curious reversal leads directly to the next image: that the recompense, his people presumably, are his *lambs*, so now he is not the conquering warrior God but a condescending shepherd caring for his sheep. Shepherds walk after their sheep, not in front of them. Everything is topsy-turvy!

Suddenly, by an extraordinary series of rhetorical questions, we are confronted by mystery. Who has measured the waters in the hollow of his hand, and done all the rest? (vs. 12). The answer, plainly, is God the Creator. Then, just as suddenly it is asked: who has directed the Spirit of the Lord? (vss. 13-14). The answer, plainly, is no one. No one has coached God. This is exactly the sequence of a child's questions. "Who made the world?" he asks. *God did.* "Who made God?" *No one.* One looks at creation and affirms the Creator. One looks at the Creator and affirms—no one, beyond or behind him. All this exciting indirectness leads up to the climax-question (vs. 18): "To whom, then, will you compare God?" Again, of course, the answer must be that God is incomparable. From the dizzy height of this affirmation one tumbles down to the farce of an idol-factory, workmen busy hammering away at a dumb, dead image.

God made man in *his* image (Gen. 1:26)—*you* don't make
an image to compare with *him* (vs. 18)! We shall have more
to say on the subject of idols in Chapter VII, but we must
return now to vs. 12 to discuss the matter of God the Creator.

Most of us have assumed that the Old Testament tells
much more about God's creation than it really does. We are
surprised to realize that the Old Testament talks almost ex-
clusively about God's covenanting with his people, about his
rescuing them from Egypt, about his judging and renewing
work with them. When one gets past Genesis 1-2, a few
psalms of creation like Psalm 104, and a few chapters at the
end of Job, there is not really much about creation in the
Old Testament at all. Since the poem of the book of Job
seems to have been taken into Israel's lore at the time of the
exile,[10] commentators affirm that the exile in Babylon
heightened an interest in God's activity as Creator, a pre-
occupation which the book of Job shares with Second
Isaiah.[11] This is very understandable. For a people who
are suddenly transported more than 500 miles from home,
where the landscape is strange, the buildings strange, the
people and language strange, to be able to see familiar
constellations in the sky must have been a striking circumstance. One gains a sense of the scope of the world.

When our children were small we lived for an extended
time in Europe, and when the time came to return to the
United States, one of our children, who was three years old
at the time, asked if there was a moon in Colorado (which
was our destination). This was a natural query. If there
weren't a moon in Colorado, he wanted to get a good, long
look at it in Europe before we had to leave. We reassured him
that he could see the moon in Colorado; and in the same
way the Israelites were reassured to learn that there was a
moon in Babylon, and stars. This awareness led Second
Isaiah to reassure them that since the familiar stars were in
their courses, God was still active and would remember his
promises to his people.

Even more was involved in this talk of creation. A
half-century before the time of Second Isaiah, the prophet

Jeremiah had implied that since the covenant was a dead letter, God might as well tear up creation (Jer. 4:23-26). In that poem Jeremiah had referred to "heavens" and "earth," "mountains" and "hills." Now here (40:12) Second Isaiah touches each of these four items in turn, but now he argues in the other direction: since creation is secure, he says, God must mean business with his covenant. The stability of creation then becomes a powerful validation of God's care for his people. "The word of our God will stand for ever" (vs. 8). A promise is a promise!

We must say another word about "bringing princes to nought" (vs. 23). No one who has not lived under a tyranny can imagine what a blessing human mortality really is. That is, everybody dies eventually, even tyrants. One can live in hope; one may outlive the tyrant. Princes *are* carried off like stubble (vs. 24), though it is certainly hard to believe it when their stem is enrooted in the earth. (We shall return to this theme once more in our analysis of 14:4b-20 in Chapter IX.)

Notice that only in vs. 27 is Israel addressed by name; it is almost as if Israel were being teased up to now by the indirection of all the good news. But now Israel is told how foolish she has been to feel sorry for herself, to complain that her "way" is hidden from the Lord, when all the while the "way" of the Lord, which will become her way, is being prepared in the wilderness (vs. 3). The concern God has for Israel is tied up with the power God has in creation by the parallelism of the questions "Have you not known? Have you not heard?" (vss. 21, 28: compare 22-23 and 29-31).

It is still not said quite directly, even at the end of the chapter, that Israel is going home—not in so many words, but the hints are stronger now. Those who "wait for the Lord" (vs. 31)—literally, who "long for the Lord" (the verb is the same as the "long for" verb in 5:1-7, discussed in Chapter III)—could be none other than Israel. The hint is made stronger by the imagery in vs. 31 of the exodus from Egypt: "they shall mount up with wings like eagles." Compare these words with Exodus 19:4, "You have seen what I did to the Egyptians, and how I bore you on eagles'

wings and brought you to myself," and compare them also
with Deuteronomy 32:10-11. The hint, then, is that if God
could do it before, then God can do it again. He can take
them from an alien land and bring them home.

The chapter then turns out to focus on the surprising
answer to the question, Who really has power anyway?
Israel had assumed that it was the princes who had the
power—how else would Israel have been stuck so long in
Babylon so far from home? But the surprise is that the
princes turn out to have no power at all (vss. 23-24). It is
God, whose glory will be manifest (vs. 5) and who will
come with might (vs. 10), who really has the power and
who will give power to the faint and increase strength to
him who has no might (vs. 29). Most particularly, it is God
who will renew the strength of those who wait for him (vs.
31). All this will happen not to the individual soul in some
way divorced from the events of the day, but in precisely
the same way as the exodus from Egypt happened—within
the events of history.

At the beginning of chapter 41 God himself speaks.
(This is plain from the extraordinary self-identification at
the end of vs. 4.) It was the prophet who spoke all of
chapter 40 ("And I said, 'What shall I cry?'" 40:6). Now,
suddenly, the cry for silence comes from God himself. Why
are the "coastlands" addressed? The answer is clear when
we realize that the Israelites had no first-hand acquaintance
with sea-going trade; there are no inlets or bays on the
coast of Palestine that could serve as ports in Israelite times.
(It took Roman technical skill, centuries later, to build the
breakwater system for the port of Caesarea Maritima.)
"Coastlands," then (and the Hebrew word can equally well
mean "islands"), were simply a reference to other nations
who thrived on their sea-going trade. The prophet is still
talking here about the same "nations" (40:15) and "rulers"
(40:23).

The phrase "renew their strength" (41:1) does not fit
the context and is evidently a textual error based upon the
same phrase in 40:31. The prophet seems to have used a
phrase that looked similar (more word-play!); commentators

guess the phrase to have been "await my presentation."[12]

God is summoning the nations to court. Evidently they are not called as criminals for judgment but are called as parties in a civil case to be adjudicated. The question to be resolved is: Are the gods of the nations divinities, or is Yahweh the true God? It is not clear to the modern reader that when the nations are summoned to court it is actually their gods who are summoned (though that is made clear in vss. 21-24); but to an ancient hearer it would be clear, since, as one commentator states it, the "nerve-center [of the Babylonian empire] was its cult, with its invocation of the gods, its sacrifices and processions."[13] It is assumed that in a civil case, by argument and counter-argument, the matter can be settled: *who may claim divinity?*

God's argumentation begins in vss. 2-4, and he cites evidence from history. In the rhetorical questions of vss. 2 and 4 he asks who it is who has stirred up someone from the east, and answers that he, God, has done this.

But who is this person from the east? Curiously enough we must wait until 44:28 and 45:1 to hear him named. As we have already found out, Second Isaiah's message takes awhile to unroll! The one from the east is Cyrus, king of Persia. If the exiles thought that they had gone a long way east to *Babylon*, now they are told that God is stirring up someone named Cyrus far to the east of *them*, way off on the Persian plateau. It is true, historically, that the Babylonian empire was beginning to fall apart under the pressures of Cyrus, who then did capture Babylon in 538 B.C. (This is why commentators date Second Isaiah to about 540, just before that event.) We learned in 40:24 that the tempest carries off princes like stubble; now we learn (41:2) that the personage from the east is trampling kings like stubble. This figure is then doing what he does under the agency of God. Notice how God's action in Cyrus is accommodated to all the actions of God from the very beginning (vs. 4): "Who has performed and done this, calling the generations from the beginning?" Who is it? "I, Yahweh, the first, and with the last, I am he."

We are accustomed to talking about the biblical faith

as a monotheistic faith. This is true, if by monotheistic we mean that Israel had no loyalty but to Yahweh. But so long as Israel was an independent people in Palestine the reality or unreality of other gods in other nations was hardly such a burning issue. It became one, however, during the exile in Babylon, and Second Isaiah burst upon the scene with these breathtaking affirmations of the absolute uniqueness of God who is first and who is last.

Now that we understand that the court case concerns the reality of the gods of the nations, we understand the sequence of thought. The coastlands are afraid (vs. 5) as they come to court, given their activity of idol-building (vss. 6-7), because Yahweh has stirred up someone from the east and thereby has accomplished something (vss. 2, 4). Meanwhile, the workmen for their part say "it is good" (vs. 7) when the idol is hammered down so it is *immovable*, so it cannot even wiggle.

In contrast to the great "I, I" of God (vs. 4) we have the address to Israel, "you, you" (vss. 8, 9). In contrast to the coastlands who are afraid and the ends of the earth that tremble (vs. 5), God tells Israel, whom he took from the *ends of the earth*, not to be afraid (vss. 9, 10). Now what was implicit in 40:31 ("they who wait for the Lord shall renew their strength") becomes explicit: "I am with *you*, I am your God, I will strengthen you" (vs. 10).

The reassurance to Israel continues through vs. 16. There is only one item here that really cries out for explanation: what does it mean that Israel is called "you worm" (vs. 14)? Is this reassurance? Evidently it is not a term of endearment, as so many commentators have thought,[14] but a reflection of the phrase of lament in Psalm 22:7, "I am a worm and no man." So it becomes an acceptance of Israel's self-image, picking up the mood of self-pity found in 40:27.

God has affirmed himself the God of Israel who will strengthen her to thresh the mountains and the hills (vs. 15). The mountains and hills bar the way to a homeward march (40:4), so the passage implies that Israel will have the strength to go home. But *still*, it is curious that the news is not said straight out. There is still more indirection: the desert (which also bars the way to a homeward march) will bloom with lovely shade-trees, and pools of water will slake the thirst of the poor and needy—again simply a hint. All these marvels God will do so that "men may know," that is, that other nations may know the power of God.

Now a kind of recapitulation is given: God challenges in court the gods of the nations to present proofs from history of their control over events, past and future (vss. 21-23). Verses 25-29 are heavy with allusions and reinforcements of images and lines from both chapter 40 and earlier in chapter 41.

We have said that the hints that the exiles in Babylon are to go home have become a bit clearer as the poems continue; but at the beginning of chapter 42 it appears that another kind of mystery is developing. In 41:8 God addresses Israel as "my servant." However, in 42:1 God continues to speak and refers in the third person to "my servant," but now it is no longer so clear that God's servant is Israel. Israel was to be a threshing sledge to thresh the mountains and hills in 41:15, but now the servant is to tiptoe around the street, not raising his voice. Is *this* still Israel? The New Testament community thought not; the Christian tradition has affirmed that this is a description of Jesus Christ (Matt. 12:18-21). But this may well be another example of the fresh use made by the Christian tradition of material which had had an earlier context; so again we shall lay aside the later interpretation to see if we can understand the meaning of the words for the people of the sixth century B.C.

The word "behold" at the beginning of the chapter must be seen in the light of the two previous "beholds," in 41:24 and 29. There the word introduced the judgment against the nations and their gods: "Behold, you [gods] are nothing" (41:24); "Behold, they [the nations] are all a delusion" (41:29). Now, by contrast, behold *something:* my servant. God invests all of himself in the servant, he puts his Spirit upon him (much as the first Isaiah said of the marvelous king in 11:2, "The Spirit of the Lord shall rest upon him"). What will this servant do for the nations? He will bring out, not so much "justice" (vss. 2, 4, *Revised Standard Version*) as "a judgment" or "a legal decision."[15] The fact is, the same Hebrew word can mean either "justice" or "judgment." and was translated "judgment" in 41:1. Possibly the servant acts as a kind of court official to make known or enforce the decision of the divine king in the court scene.[16]

But this is a strange way for the court official to announce the decision, not by crying it aloud in the streets, but indirectly, by quietness, by gentleness. Notice how his conduct is defined negatively: there are seven "nots" in vss. 2-4. Whatever one would expect from the agent of God will *not* be the case this time. The verbs at the beginning of vs. 4 represent one more bit of genius at word-play, as the *Revised Standard Version* footnotes indicate: the servant will not break the *bruised* reed or quench the *smouldering* wick (vs. 3); but the servant himself will not *smoulder* out or be *bruised* till he confirms judgment in the earth (vs. 4). We must postpone a thorough discussion of the identity of the servant, however, until Chapter VII.

In vss. 5-9 we have familiar imagery. But it is not clear whom God is addressing in vss. 6 and following. Conceivably it could be the servant, though this seems to be a fresh section; conceivably it could be the prophet to whom he is telling his secrets before he broadcasts them (vs. 8). It could be Israel with whom he has covenanted (vs. 6), and, as a matter of fact, it could be Cyrus, whom God has called (46:11, 48:15), whose right hand God has grasped (45:1). As far as that goes, who is to open the eyes that are blind and to bring out the prisoners from the dungeon (vs. 7)—God himself, or the one whom God addresses? There are few passages about which the commentators differ as much as this one, and I myself waver between the assumption that God is here addressing Israel[17] and the assumption that he is here addressing Cyrus.[18] Whoever it is who is a light to the nations, whoever it is who is to liberate those who are in shackles, it will come as a surprise, that is certain. This is something the nations have not expected.

In vss. 10-13 the prophet sings once more of God the

divine warrior. The whole earth will be aware of his work, not only the sea and the coastlands (vs. 10), but locations in the desert. Kedar was an area (and a tribe) somewhere east of the Transjordan area, toward the Arabian desert, and Sela was a name for the later Petra, the city surrounded by rocky cliffs, between present-day Amman and the Gulf of Aqaba. In vss. 14-17 God the divine warrior himself speaks. In a prodigious series of 15 first-person-singular verbs in Hebrew he tells what he is to do. How many unexpected reversals! He speaks of himself with female imagery (vs. 14). And while he had promised in 41:18 to open rivers on the bare heights and make the wilderness a pool of water, now he is doing the opposite, drying up mountains and hills and turning rivers into dry land (vs. 15). The prophet is trying in every possible way to insist that God is not an idler in heaven: God is a God of action. The point is not that God is interested in bringing fertility to the desert; it is that God is interested in effecting change. He brings up and he casts down (compare the poem called the "Magnificat" in Luke 1:46-55, especially vss. 51-53, which strike the same note). God will help the blind whom he will lead (vs. 16), and he will shame those who trust in images (vs. 17).

Since the "blind" and the "deaf" (vs. 18) are identified with God's servant (vs. 19), we are evidently dealing with Israel once more. The material through vs. 22 then deals with the experience of the exile. Verse 23 asks who among the Israelites will pay attention to what is to be announced. But then the announcement itself is postponed and vss. 24-25 deal once more with the terrible events of the exile, which had been set in motion, we hear, by God himself.

Now, finally, in a climactic passage (43:1-7) appears the announcement that can be postponed no longer; now, finally, we hear what is to happen. Fear not, Israel; I, God, have redeemed you—that is, bought your freedom. Here the prophet uses the old word "redeemed" with all its associations with the exodus from Egypt (compare Exod. 6:6). Israel will "pass through," Israel will "walk," more clues for the march homeward, and God will accompany them on the march homeward, whether it be through water or fire (vs. 2). The promise becomes specific within history by the mention of particular nations—Egypt, Ethiopia, Seba (a nation in southwest Arabia). Cyrus of Persia was expected to conquer these nations along with Babylon, so the assurance that God would be willing to give up such rich nations in order to buy Israel's freedom is a measure of his love for her (vss. 3-4). Now listen to the roll-call of the exiles: those from the east, those from the west (vs. 5), those from the north, those from the south (vs. 6), sons and daughters, every one. God will gather them all up because they are called by his name and he owns them (vs. 7).

By now the reader will have a grasp of most of the images and most of the assumptions of the material in chapters 40-55. Thus the image of the courtroom scene continues in 43:8-15, 44:6-8, 45:20-25, and there are reminiscences in still other passages. God promises to break down the bars of Babylon in 43:14, an affirmation that prepares the way for the Cyrus passage in 45:1-7.

There are a few more remarks that may be made on some of these themes, however. One is the matter of the new "exodus" from Babylon to match the old one from Egypt, a theme already discussed in connection with 40:31 and 43:1. This imagery becomes more specific in 43:16-19 and is set forth most strikingly in 51:9-11. The reference in 51:9 to "Rahab" is to the old Canaanite myth of the combat of Baal (the fertility god) with the sea-monster. We discussed this "Rahab" in Chapter IV when we were dealing with 30:7. Here in chapter 51 the old myth has been accommodated to the Israelite faith (now it is *Yahweh* who pierced the dragon) and then the myth has been theologically transformed into *history*, the historical event of the exodus out of Egypt ("didst make the depths of the sea a way for the redeemed to pass over," vs. 10). The God who did mighty acts in the past can be counted on to do mighty acts again.

We took note of the curious feminine imagery for God in 42:14; we find it again in 45:9-10. The pot does not tell the potter how to behave, and one does not argue with either father or mother about the offspring to be produced.

In the same way, one is not to argue with the Creator God. The point I wish to underline here is that the prophet uses both "father" and "mother" in his figure. In 49:14-15 he uses mother-love to describe God's recollection of Zion, employing a kind of argument well known in the Bible, the argument of "how much more" (see Matt. 10:29-31 or Luke 11:11-13 for examples of Jesus' use of this kind of argument). If mothers know how to love their children, *how much more* does God know how to love Zion! Much has been made recently of the preponderance of patriarchal imagery in the Bible in talking about God, and justifiably so; but it is good to recognize that there were spokesmen for God in biblical times who recognized the limitations of male language in describing God and did not feel confined by it.

Finally, we must round off this chapter by taking a closer look at Cyrus, king of Persia, whose advent was anticipated in 41:2, 25, who is named in 44:28 and 45:1, who is addressed in 45:1-7, and who is referred to again, indirectly, in 48:14 ("The Lord loves him, he shall perform his purpose on Babylon"). The way Cyrus functions with Israel is remarkable, for he acts on behalf of God's grace in the same way as Assyria had acted on behalf of God's judgment in 10:5-11 (see Chapter IV). That is, he acts unwittingly. Neither of them knows he is God's instrument. As Assyria "does not so intend, and his mind does not so think" (10:7), so God tells Cyrus, "I surname you, though you do not know me" (45:4). Cyrus has a vocation to do God's work for Israel; he is "called" (vs. 4) by God.

This is an extraordinary notion, and what is even more astonishing, Cyrus is to be God's "anointed" (vs. 1). The Hebrew word for "anointed" here is *mashiah*, the very word "Messiah" which the Bible uses often. It is even more surprising when readers learn what a variety of individuals in the Old Testament were called "anointed." Mostly the term was used for kings in Israel and Judah (see, for example, 1 Sam. 24:6, when David uses it of Saul). Kings in Israel and Judah were anointed (smeared with oil) as a gesture, a symbol, of their vocation. The term was used of the high priest (Lev. 4:3); in Psalm 105:15 the term is evidently used of the patriarchs (Abraham and his descendants). In the Cyrus passage, however, it is used of this king of a foreign empire who might be thought to be far from Israel's ken. It is he, rather than an Israelite now, who is to take on that ancient office of being the agent for God in the smiting of Israel's foes. Of all the surprising reversals of Israel's expectations to be found in the chapters of Second Isaiah, this is perhaps the most surprising. God is innovative beyond all Israel's traditional assumptions.

Earlier in this chapter we took note of the kinds of theological questions with which those in exile had been grappling: Where is God? What is he doing? Does he have any future for us? It goes without saying that the words of Second Isaiah met those questions with a kind of good news which was breathtaking. But it is also clear by now that Second Isaiah did not make everything clear. He, like the first Isaiah, used ambiguity and indirection to point to what cannot be framed in words. One matter in particular must have puzzled his hearers as it has puzzled readers in the centuries that followed, and that is the whole matter of God's servant, his task and his destiny. This question, and the question of the prophet's mockery of idols, need further exploration.

CHAPTER VII

The Folly of Idols, and the Call to Suffer

A T THE BEGINNING OF Chapter VI we took note of the impression of spaciousness which the lines of Second Isaiah make on us—the feeling that we can read on and on without interruption. But for most modern readers there *are* some interruptions—specifically, those passages which mock the making of idols. The problem of idols is a matter so alien to us that we find ourselves blanking out when we meet such lines. There are four extended passages of this sort: 40:18-20, 41:6-7, 44:9-20, and 46:5-7, as well as three other briefer references to idols (42:17, 45:16, and 46:1).

We have discussed the meaning of 40:18-20 and 41:6-7 in their context as we discussed the material of chapters 40-41 in Chapter VI, but we have postponed until now a full-scale inquiry into the whole matter.

To most present-day readers an idol is little more than a stock item in magazine cartoons which concern themselves with missionaries in some jungle clearing, or perhaps at most a curious figure of wood or stone in a quiet room of a museum marked "China," or "Japan," or "Ancient Near East." It is only by an extraordinary act of historical imagination that most of us can begin to grasp the plausibility of idol-worship, the attractiveness of idol-worship. But we must undertake this act of the imagination to make sense out of the words of Second Isaiah. Idol-worship *must* have been plausible and attractive to people, or else Second Isaiah (and others) would not have referred to the matter so often.

For when we think about it, the references to idol-worship are everywhere, from the prohibition in the Ten Commandments and references in the early "Song of Moses" (Deut. 32:21, 38) to later ones in the "classical" prophets—in the first Isaiah (2:8, 20), in Jeremiah (Jer. 2:27, 10:1-16),[1] in Ezekiel (Ezek. 20:32 and often). But the references are sharpest just at the period we are now discussing, when the Israelites came into large-scale contact with Babylonia. (One finds references to idol-worship in the New Testament, too. Paul devotes a whole chapter of First Corinthians to a discussion of whether Christians may eat meat which has been offered to idols [1 Cor. 8].) What, then, we ask, was involved in idol-worship?

Of course there were always small images around for private use. In Palestinian excavations, even in levels dating to times of Israelite occupation, archeologists have found dozens of Astarte figurines (Astarte was the fertility goddess) which are usually no more than a few inches high.[2] These are not of course what Second Isaiah is referring to; he is referring to the large-scale images which had a function in the public cult.

We have no actual example of such a large image surviving from ancient times. This is understandable, for if such images were decorated with as much gold, silver, and jewelry as the prophet indicates, then they obviously would have been a prime target for any ancient conqueror bent on loot. But archeologists have excavated some of the temples in which the images stood. The temple in Babylon devoted to Marduk, the chief god of the city, measured approximately 80 by 85 meters (260 by 280 feet). Its interior had siderooms around a central chamber which was square, measuring approximately 50 meters (165 feet) on a side.[3] Since we do have specimens of immense stone *sculpture* from Mesopotamia—one thinks of the colossal winged lion with the head of a bearded man which guarded the doorway of the palace of the Assyrian king Ashurnasirpal, which is 3.50 meters (11½ feet) in height[4]—we can well imagine that the image of Marduk in his temple would have been an imposing sight.

The very words of mockery in prophets like Second Isaiah help us form an idea of the construction and appearance of images, though of course we have Mesopotamian texts as well. They were made of precious wood plated with gold, their staring eyes were made of precious stones, and they were clad with sumptuous garments that were changed in special ceremonies according to ritual requirements.[5] Various rituals, such as feeding the images sacrificial meals, were carried out within their temples. Sometimes they were carried about, not only within their temples but also in processionals through the city on such occasions as the New Year's festival.[6] Foreign conquerors often carried off images and placed them in their own temples. King Cyrus, when he captured Babylon, sent back to their original home all the images which the Babylonians had captured through the years, evidently as a gesture of magnanimity to the subject peoples of his empire.

But beyond the details of construction and appearance of the images there arises a more basic question: how did their devotees *understand* the images? In other words, what did the images *mean* to the ancient worshiper? And related to this, why was this particular kind of religious observance so universal in ancient times? What we are asking for, really, is a *theology* of idol-worship, strange as such a phrase may seem. Every religious system has a set of assumptions about it, every such system has an internal consistency and meets real human needs, or else it would not persist.

All the gods of any consequence in Assyria and Babylonia were cosmic deities of one sort or another, deities who manifested themselves in astronomical phenomena (the sun, the moon) or in matters connected with weather and fertility (the storm, the soil). The Mesopotamian peoples were well aware how great the powers are that are to be found in the cosmos and how much they needed to be in touch with the seasonal powers of fertility for the sake of the economic undergirding of their culture. Thus they personified these forces and elaborated myths and rituals concerning their interaction with each other.

But what is infinite must be graspable by human understanding; what is beyond understanding must be brought into focus for human need. We might even say that just as Christians affirm that the infinite God has become incarnate in a human being, so more generally, the ancient worshiper was impelled to see his deity particularized. In this way the image of the god became an object which represented the deity, which symbolized the deity. To the image one could give one's attention. The image of the deity, then, for the worshiper, functioned (dare we admit it?) much like the images in a traditional Roman Catholic church or like icons in an Eastern Orthodox church.

But Roman Catholic teaching has been careful to maintain the distinction between *honoring* or *venerating* an image of the saint or of Mary or of Christ, and *worshiping* God.[8] Eastern Orthodoxy likewise has been insistent that an icon is simply a *representation* of a holy personage: "The men who made the icons . . . were decorating a flat surface *and* they were seeking to convey in line and colour an aspect of divine truth" (emphasis mine).[9] And it must be added that almost every Protestant community except the Quakers cherishes some central symbolic object which focuses their apprehension of divine reality, be it an altar, a cross, a pulpit, or a robe.

But this careful distinction between a *reality* and the *representation* of the reality, between an *object* and the *symbol* of that object, was lost on the ancient worshiper, who saw in the representation a real manifestation of the deity. One authority writes, "Fundamentally, the deity was considered present in his image, living in the temple much in the same way as the king resided in his palace."[10] Indeed, there was ritual to endow "life" to images after their construction, a complex ritual of consecration which they had to undergo: their eyes were "opened" so that they could see; their mouths were washed to purify them; minor gods were brought in before the major one for obeisance, just as vassals did obeisance to the king in the etiquette of the palace; and, as I have said, meals were placed before the image, as one served a banquet to the king.

Not only was the image understood to sum up the reality of the god, but the god, in turn, was understood to sum up the whole national enterprise and its ideology. As we would say today, Marduk sponsored the Babylonian way of life. This can best be seen in the relationship between palace and temple, between king and god. We have already noted that the priests treated the image the way courtiers treated the king, but the ancients would have said it the other way around: the courtiers treat the king the way the priests treat the god. The gods are prior; kingship was sponsored by the gods. The king became the "son" of the god on his coronation day (we learned this in Chapter V), indicating that the temple was superior and "prior" to the palace in the assumptions of the culture. All this supports our proposal that the god served to reinforce the ethos, the ideals, of the nation-state and to unite the population of a far-flung empire.[12] Thus, when a nation-state was doomed to fall to a foreign conqueror, the gods were understood to suffer along with the state.

In a way idol-worship was what we would call a "package deal." The whole Babylonian way of life was tied up in the conviction that its gods were its support, and these gods were manifested and represented by their images. We recall the quotation we cited in Chapter VI from a recent commentator: the "nerve-center [of the Babylonian empire] was its cult, with its invocation of the gods, its sacrifices and processions."[13] So when a Jew in exile in Babylon was tempted to look with awe upon a huge image of Marduk, he was not only looking at an imposing statue which we ourselves might covet for our museum, he was being attracted by a total ideology, a total world-view, an angle of vision about the "way things are" which had large consequences.

We may note in passing that Moses offered a contrasting world-view, a contrasting "package deal." The Ten Commandments affirm this: "You shall not make yourself a graven image . . . you shall not bow down to them or serve them; for I the Lord your God am a jealous God . . ." (Exod. 20:4-5). When we hear "jealous God" we must not think that Moses announced a God who was small-minded, petty, and ungenerous. It is simply that one cannot have it both ways. Moses sensed that this God is to be particularized not in an image but in a new and fresh way: not through something that can be *seen* and *pointed* to, as an image is, but through *laws* that can be *heard* ("And God spoke all these words, saying. . . ," Exod. 20:1), through historical *acts* that can be *experienced* ("I am the Lord your God, who brought you out of the land of Egypt, out of the house of bondage," Exod. 20:2). A God who is particularized as speaking and as acting in events is of quite a different sort than a god who is particularized as looking like an image.

Our description of the rationale of idolatry has indicated, then, that it was the tip of an iceberg that betokened a total way of life for its devotees. But Second Isaiah, like other prophets who mocked idol-worship, does not bother with the total theological "package" about which we have been speaking; he zeroes in on the foolishness of thinking one could *make* a god. Here, then, is the *reductio ad absurdum* of idolatry.

Bearing these matters in mind, let us begin with chapter 46. Bel (the same word as the Canaanite "Baal") was another name for Marduk, and Nebo was his son. The verb "bow down" is occasionally used for worship (1 Kings 8:54—in the *Revised Standard Version*, the phrase "had knelt" translates the Hebrew "bowed down to his knees"). People are supposed to *bow down* to a god; how funny that a god would himself bow down! But the verb is ordinarily used of "leaning over." Now why would a deity have to lean over? Literally, in that they are toppled down and loaded flat onto carts to be taken away for loot; and metaphorically, in that the gods are humiliated by Cyrus's victory-to-be in Babylon and are sent off to exile. The beasts "stoop" and "bow down" too (vs. 2) under their burden, and they cannot "save" the burden (when it is the gods who should be doing the saving). In contrast to the gods who *are* a burden, who *cannot* save, Yahweh speaks and says that *he* will carry, *he* will save (vs. 4).

Verse 5 then broaches the question once more (as we heard it in 40:18—see Chapter VI), "To whom will you liken me?" Then the passage returns to idols once more:

how much they cost, all the gold and silver lavished on them (vs. 6)—how one hires a goldsmith and he *makes* a god, and then everybody falls down to worship it. They have to carry it around, they set it down, it stays put (vs. 7), and if they cry to it it cannot answer or save. Then by contrast, the speaking, acting God declares: "I have spoken, and I will bring it to pass; I have purposed, and I will do it" (vs. 11).

Now we turn to the longest passage about idolatry, 44:9-20. Though the *Revised Standard Version* prints the passage as prose, more and more commentators now analyze it as poetry;[15] and though some commentators have judged the passage to be an interpolation, interrupting vss. 6-8 + 21-22, I strongly support its genuineness here.[16] The passage repeats many of the themes we have already met (see vss. 9-11), but the passage is full of details which are really farcical. Watch the blacksmith at work (vs. 12): see his arm forge the image (but do not forget the arm of Yahweh all the while, which both rules, 40:10, and protects, 41:11). However, look now: the blacksmith's getting hungry and his strength fails him, thirsty and he's parched (but do not forget that God promises the returning exiles that they will neither hunger nor thirst, 49:10). Now watch the carpenter at work with all his array of tools (vs. 13): he makes the figure of a man (but do not forget that the craftsmen are but men themselves, vs. 11, and that it is God who created man upon the earth, 45:12). Indeed the carpenter has gone out into the forest to choose a good tree to cut down (vs. 14). But watch what happens to that tree—some of it he uses for the stove-wood to keep warm, some of it he uses in his cook-stove to bake his bread (an echo of the hungry blacksmith in vs. 12), and—oh yes, some of it he makes into a god to fall down in front of to worship (vs. 15)! This is such a joke that the prophet tells it all over again (vss. 16-17): the carpenter roasts meat, he warms himself, and then he makes a god out of the rest of the wood and prays to it and says, "Deliver me, for thou art my god!" That prayer sounds much like a line from a biblical psalm (compare Ps. 143:9-10), but—to use words like that

to something he has just made from cord-wood, imagine!
Just to make sure the point is made, the prophet goes over
the whole matter one more time, pointing out that nobody
has the insight to see that half the chunk of wood went into
the fire and half became an idol (vs. 19). The idolater may
be hungry for spiritual sustenance, but really he feeds on
ashes (vs. 20)—don't forget the wood-ashes in the stove from
the bread-baking and meat-roasting. His twisted mind has
led him astray; nobody should expect deliverance from
something he's made for himself, nobody can deliver himself
(bootstrap salvation!). He does not have the insight to say,
"In my right hand is (not a god but) a lie."

Nowhere in this whole passage is Yahweh mentioned;
but he is just behind the scene, implicit in the words and
phrases used, laughing. The idol-makers are light-years
away from understanding how the real God functions.

This long passage then, I submit, is not an interruption
but belongs here. It is an illustration of "Is there a God
besides me? There is no Rock: I know not any" in vs. 8,
and the affirmation "I have formed you, you are my servant" in vs. 21 is a rebuke to the craftsmen who "fashion"
(the same word in Hebrew as "form") a god in vs. 10. We
saw in Chapter VI what Second Isaiah's perspective is: God
made man, and nobody made God. But the idol-worshiper's
perspective is: a man made the god. Between these proposi-
tions one has to choose.

It would be hard to imagine a more effective presentation of the uniqueness of Israel's God than this sarcastic,
comical peek into the idol-factory. Such a critique might not
encompass the total problem of the attractiveness of the false
gods which Babylon offered, but it does move in for the kill
at the weakest point in the system.

And what of us? Are we really so immune to the
blandishments of idol-worship as we had thought? Can we
afford to sit back looking smugly at those funny people in
ancient times who constructed images to worship? If we
understand idols in Babylon to symbolize where the power is
perceived to reside in society, what people put their ultimate
trust in, what people expect can bring them deliverance,

that which does not *judge* people from the outside but simply undergirds whatever are the cravings and the corporate goals of society—then we ourselves begin to be more uncomfortable. Where is power perceived to reside in our society? (The Computer? The Central Intelligence Agency? The multi-national corporation?) What do people put their ultimate trust in? (An economy of abundance?) What do people expect can bring them deliverance? (Financial security? Children we can be proud of?) What is it to which we give devotion, which undergirds our cravings and our corporate goals without offering any judgment from the outside on the rightness or wrongness of those goals? ("My country, right or wrong!"?) Indeed, are we not more like Babylon than we are like Israel? Is it possible that we are still busy in our idol factories?

At the beginning of chapter 47 we have something new, a long taunt-song over Babylon (vss. 1-15). We may recall the personification of Zion, "daughter of Zion," in 1:8, and the personification "Rahab" for Egypt in 30:7 (see Chapter IV). So "virgin daughter of Babylon" here (vs. 1) is a kind of political cartoon-figure. When Israel is to "pass through the rivers," we remember, God will be with them (43:2), but when Babylon passes through the rivers, they will be shamed and God will take vengeance on them (vss. 2-3).

It is curious that after chapter 48 there is no more mockery of idols, no more talk of Cyrus, no more full-blown courtroom scenes; these themes fade in favor of others. There is no way to know whether the material in chapters 40-55 breaks into two chunks (40-48 and 49-55), suggesting a slightly different historical situation,[17] or whether the prophet is simply moving on to fresh material.[18]

In any event, none of the material in the latter part of Second Isaiah so captures our attention as the material concerned with the "servant" of God. We recall what we determined in Chapter VI: a passage early in Second Isaiah (42:1-4) describes the servant in rather mysterious terms—God has chosen him and has put his Spirit within him. This servant seems to function as a court official, but instead of shouting the judgment of God in the streets he will not raise his voice; yet he will see to it that God's judgment is established in the earth. We also noted that God had identified his servant as Israel in a still earlier passage (41:8) and implies it in another (42:19), but that the identification of the servant as Israel in 42:1-4 is not so clear-cut.

We may go on now to say that God's servant is identified as Israel in several passages (44:1, 2, 21, 45:4), but at the same time there are three more passages like 42:1-4, in which the identification is unclear and in which the task of the servant is quite odd and unexpected. These three passages are 49:1-6 (the word "Israel" in 49:3 will be dealt with below), 50:4-9, and 52:13-53:12. All four passages have become known in the commentaries as the four "Servant Songs." There is an enormous literature on these four passages,[19] passages that raise a whole array of questions. As before, we shall simply try to pick our way as carefully as possible.

The four songs have a certain symmetry: in the first and the last God speaks of the servant in the third person ("Behold my servant, whom I uphold," 42:1; "Behold, my servant shall prosper," 52:13), whereas in the second and third songs the servant himself speaks of God in the third person ("The Lord called me from the womb. . . . And he said to me, 'You are my servant,'" 49:1, 3; "The Lord God has given me the tongue of those who are taught," 50:4).

Since we have examined the first song in Chapter VI, let us turn now to the second (49:1-6). Verse 1 opens as 41:1 did, with an appeal to the coastlands to listen, but now the courtroom imagery fades, and other matters take prominence. It is the servant himself who speaks and who announces his call. The servant has been called from the womb; this wording is modeled on the call of the prophet Jeremiah (Jer. 1:5). The servant is to be like a weapon of Yahweh the divine warrior, except that God is to hide him like a sheathed weapon, at least for the moment. This is another hint, like that of 42:2, that the servant's work is to be secret work. In vs. 3, as we have already noted parenthetically, the servant is identified with "Israel," but there is a suspicion on the part of commentators that this word may here be a later "gloss," added by someone who made too easy an identification of the servant. If the word were genuine here, one would have expected the balancing word "Jacob," as in other such passages (41:8, 44:1, 21). Further, if the servant were Israel/Jacob, how could the servant bring *Jacob* back (vs. 5)? So I think it best to distrust the word here.[20] The great surprise here is that *God* is going to be glorified in his *servant*. This leaves us saying, "How's that again? Don't you mean it the other way around?" Surely it is the servant who should be glorified in God! But no, this is what he means; in fact he has already said it of Israel (44:23).

The nuance in vs. 4 in the *Revised Standard Version* is not quite right; the *New English Bible* has it better: "Once I said, 'I have laboured in vain . . .'; yet in truth my cause is with the Lord. . . ." The "nothing" in the second line of the verse is the expression "without form" of Genesis 1:2, and the "vanity" is the non-gods about which Jeremiah had spoken (Jer. 2:4, RSV—"worthlessness"). Thus the servant had thought his efforts were for nought, for chaos, but now he knows his "recompense" (the same word as in 40:10—see Chapter VI) is with God after all. More paradox!

Verse 5 is a recapitulation, but it does indicate to us that the servant cannot easily be identified with Israel. Then vs. 6 gives us something new and again startling: the servant's relation to God is not an in-house affair but will have fundamental consequences for the whole world. Through the servant God's rescue will be visible to the end of the earth. We remind ourselves that the servant has been speaking to the coastlands and the peoples from afar (vs. 1), so vs. 6 indicates that God's salvage-work is going to be visible to all the peoples in his audience.

The servant continues to speak in the third song (50:4 and following)—at least we *think* it is the servant. It must be admitted, however, that this is the only one of the four songs that does not use the word "servant"; instead, he is likened to *disciples* ("those who are taught," vs. 4). The first Isaiah had made a passing reference to "disciples" (8:16). In the same way the speaker here in 50:4 involves himself in a tradition of learning like that of the prophets. We might be tempted to assume that the speaker here is the prophet Second Isaiah himself (as we assumed for 40:6—see Chapter VI), but his conduct is identical with that to be affirmed of the servant in 53:3-7, who voluntarily accepts shame and mistreatment (50:6, "I gave my back to the smiters"), so that the assumption that the servant speaks must be correct after all.

This conduct is quite unprecedented. We find plenty of laments in the Old Testament in which the worshiper complains of ill treatment and persecution (look at Ps. 143:3-4), but here it is said that the servant deliberately gives his back to the smiters, his cheeks to those who pull out the beard, that he does not hide his face from shame and spitting. The servant knows God is near him to vindicate him (echoes of courtroom language here), so he will outlast his enemies (vss. 7-9). Again, we must ask, what is this astonishing change of conduct all about?

It all comes to a climax in the last song, 52:13-53:12. Now we face the same question as we faced with 7:14, 9:2-7, and 11:1-9, namely that the tradition in the New Testament applies such passages to Jesus (see our discussions in Chapters IV and V). The New Testament applies lines from 52:13-53:12 again and again to Jesus. Thus to cite only three examples, Philip explains 53:7-8 to the Ethiopian eunuch as referring to Jesus (Acts 8:27-35); Paul quotes 52:15 in Romans 15:21; and Matthew quotes 53:4 in Matthew 8:17. But the problem goes deeper, because there is strong indication that Jesus himself took this passage to refer to himself. Thus in several passages of Jesus' anticipation of his coming sufferings, as recorded in Mark's gospel, we find reminiscences of this passage: Mark 8:31, "must suffer many things, and be rejected" (compare Isa. 53:3); Mark 9:12, "that he should suffer many things and be treated with contempt"; Mark 9:31, "will be delivered into the hands of men, and they will kill him" (compare Isa. 53:6, 12); Mark 10:45, "came not to be served but to serve, and to give his life as a ransom for many" (compare Isa. 53:10, 11).[21] Given this array of New Testament affirmation, what becomes of our insistence (Chapter V) that a prophet predicts his near-future, not the far future? Surely nothing could be clearer than this description of Jesus here in Second Isaiah.

Let us see, however, whether our hypothesis will continue to fit here: can we find a meaning for these words spoken in the sixth century B.C. to the hearers of Second Isaiah's own generation?

First we recall that in Chapter I, when we were noting the continuity of themes between Second Isaiah and the first Isaiah, we saw that the "servant" of God is invested with the very characteristics of God himself: the first Isaiah had said that *God* is high and lifted up (2:11, 12, 6:1), but now Second Isaiah says that the *servant* shall be exalted and lifted up and be very high (52:13). This astonishing parity matches the reversal which we met a moment ago, in which God is to be glorified in his *servant* (49:3).

Who are the "many" who are astonished at him (52:14)? Evidently "many nations" and "kings" (vs. 15). They show they are astonished and startled by shutting their mouths. We heard a long time ago that God brings princes to nought (40:23); now we begin to see how the activity of kings is to be canceled. The activity of kings is always to give orders: go here; go there; off with his head! Kings don't shut their mouths. But these kings will. They are struck dumb, for what they now see is unprecedented ("that which has not been told them they shall see," 52:15). The exaltation of one who has been so humiliated—"so disfigured did he look that he no longer seemed human" (vs. 14, *Jerusalem Bible*)—to the kings this makes no sense! (Some commentators wish to take the latter part of vs. 14 and transfer it to come after 53:2—so the *New English Bible*—but the lines make sense where they stand.)

In 53:1-6 we find that the speaker is "we." But who is this "we"? The implied answer is: the kings, the nations (note the close tie between 52:15, "that which they have not heard," and 53:1, "what we have heard"). But this answer is only implied. It is probable that vss. 1-6 constitute the *report which God is making* about the kings, so that God is quoting here what the kings say when they find their tongues again.[22] Verse 1 offers a double rhetorical question such as we have seen before in Second Isaiah (see 40:18): Who would have believed it? Who has understood the prowess of God? The answer is: nobody. We do not forget that the servant is to be weapon of the Lord, but hidden (49:2); so nothing has been revealed plainly yet.

Here begins the great story in all its mystery, with words which echo from many directions in the ear of the hearer. He (the servant) grew up before him (God) like a root out of dry ground (vs. 2); this sounds like some lines from Jeremiah (Jer. 17:6) in which the desert scrub is the figure used for a man that is on the wrong track altogether, who puts his trust in human agencies instead of in God. Here is the paradox: the servant who is really sponsored by God gives every evidence of being a good-for-nothing. Verse 2b picks up the themes of 52:14b: the servant has no beauty. In the Old Testament beauty implied blessing. Both Joseph (Gen. 39:6b) and David (1 Sam. 16:18)— had beauty in both these passages the same Hebrew word for "beauty" is used as in our Isaiah passage—and we know God was with these men. But this servant has no beauty, so how can God be with him?[23]

Not only is the servant unattractive, he is positively rejected by the rest of humankind (vs. 3). The language of the first line is close to that of Psalm 22:6, the situation of someone who calls to God for help in his distress. The second line is better translated "man of pains and no stranger to sickness" rather than the more familiar "man of sorrows and acquainted with grief." The rest of the verse repeats the theme of rejection, for people treat him as if he were a leper (read Lev. 13:45-46 on this matter).

In vs. 4 the kings come to terms with the paradox: they repeat the words "sickness" and "pains" (or "griefs" and "sorrows") from vs. 3 (in reverse order). The Hebrew word translated "surely" in the *Revised Standard Version* is a word for strong contrast; "yet" (*Jerusalem Bible, New English Bible*) is better. The Hebrew sounds like this: "And yet it was our sicknesses that he himself bore, and our pains—he bore them, while it was we who thought him struck, smitten of God, and humiliated." The word order highlights the astonishing reversal; the whole assessment of the situation by the kings was faulty, the conventional understanding of "who deserves what" has been turned upside down. The language up to now has stayed in the area of sickness and hurt, and one wonders, how can somebody else take on "my" sickness? Let me offer a possible parallel. A family is on a hike; they are delayed in getting back to camp; the child forgets his jacket, the mother gives the child her jacket, the mother catches cold while the child stays warm. Something like that, one would suppose.

But in the Old Testament, sickness is closely intertwined with wrongdoing. The psalms, for example, offer sickness-talk that moves to the question, "What did I do wrong? Why does God abandon me?" (Psalm 88 is a good example.) So in vs. 5 the kings make the same transition. It is not just our sickness that the servant has borne, but it is for our *wrongdoing* that he is wounded. "Transgressions" and "iniquities" are accurate translations, but the words sound to us more "holy" than they did to the ancient hearers. Terms that mean more to us are words like "wrongdoing" and "crimes," and that is the kind of impression the lines made on Second Isaiah's audience. The servant is taking the kind of punishment that the kings deserve for their crimes. In fact, the vocabulary here is much the same as the description in 1:5-6 of Israel's pummeling by God for her crimes.

Not only does the servant take the punishment which the kings deserve, but his doing so heals the kings (vs. 5b). The Hebrew poetry here is so compact that it needs unpacking. The half-verse reads: "The discipline (or punishment) for our *shālōm* (welfare, prosperity) is upon him, and by his wounds there is healing for us." Not only do the kings go scot-free when they deserve sickness and punishment, but when the servant takes on the sickness and punishment, this results in healing for the kings. It is not just that the kings escape something negative; they gain something positive. They need what the servant can offer.

Verse 6 presents the surprising image of kings gone astray like sheep without a shepherd, and of kings, who are accustomed to commanding, needing to be chased after and brought back. Indeed the kings say "all of us" are so. And, vs. 6b repeats, it is Yahweh who has stricken him with the iniquity of all of us. The verse ends as it began.

Evidently, vs. 6 rounds off God's report of the kings' speech. Verses 7-9 seem to continue God's speech on his own (though there is no "I" to identify the speaker), and the actions are all vague passives ("he was oppressed," "he was afflicted," and so on), so that the spotlight is on the actions which the servant undergoes rather than on the reactions of the bystanders.

Verse 7 repeats the theme of vs. 4, and then reaches back to 42:2, in the first servant song: the servant will not raise his voice. And then, in a fresh image here which is strongly reminiscent of Jeremiah's own complaint to God (Jer. 11:19), the servant is compared to a sheep led to the slaughter. This is a new note; we have heard of the servant's wounds and pains, but the implication of slaughter is ominous. "Taken away" (vs. 8) is ominous too; the word "oppression" may mean "restraint" or "detention," and "judgment" sounds like a judicial proceeding. The whole phrase is vague, but it indicates that the servant is taken out of circulation. This is reinforced by the tactful "cut off out of the land of the living." He *is* killed, then. The text of the next line seems to be in disarray; it must have read something like "stricken to death because of their sins."

So now he is dead.

And even now that he is dead he suffers humiliation (vs. 9), since his grave is alongside those of criminals; although, as the lines emphasize, the servant had no reason to deserve this fate.

Verse 10 begins something new. If God has been the speaker in vss. 7-9 (and that is the best assumption), the speaker changes in vs. 10 (note the two references to "the Lord" in the third person). But God speaks in vs. 11b ("my servant"). So if God speaks in vss. 7-9 and vss. 11b-12, who speaks in vss. 10-11a? Evidently it is the bystanders, the kings once more (or else God is once more reporting what the kings say, as we suggested for vss. 1-6). They are acknowledging God's purpose in the whole enterprise.[24]

The text appears to be in difficulty in the first half of vs. 10, and one commentator has made the plausible suggestion that it should read, "But Yahweh took pleasure in his humiliated one, he gave him fresh strength." Though the meaning sounds quite different from that in the *Revised Standard Version*, text-critics judge it to be a very plausible reconstruction, and this reading was evidently adopted in the *New English Bible*.[25] By this understanding, the kings acknowledge God's resurrection of his servant from the beginning of their speech. Now we begin to understand how it is that the servant shall prosper, be exalted and lifted up (52:13). It is by God's doing. But it will occur on the far side of the grave. How, it is not said, and we must be content with the indirection of the text.

The lines that follow reinforce the images of resurrection. "He made his life a sin-offering." This is a reference to the old ceremony spelled out in Leviticus 5:1-19 whereby a worshiper brings an offering as a restitution for his misdeed, by way of opening himself to reconciliation with God. "He shall see his offspring, he shall prolong his days." Because the servant gave life up, life is given back to him, and descendants. "The will of the Lord shall prosper in his hand."

Then we have God's final summation (vss. 11b-12): the innocent party, my servant, shall bring a declaration of innocence to many (those kings again). Now we understand what kind of judgment he will bring forth to the nations (42:1). The kings have been guilty (53:5), but now they are pronounced innocent, treated as innocent (this is what the Hebrew verb means). But the phrasing of this summation continues to turn everything Israel had held true upside down. Old laws echoed in their minds: "Keep far from a false charge, and do not slay the innocent and righteous, for I will not acquit [treat as innocent, the same verb] the wicked" (Exod. 23:7). But that which God had forbidden Israelites to do, *he* now does: he allows an innocent servant to be slain, and through this event he treats the guilty as innocent. All Israel's familiar landmarks have fallen by now.

The conclusion of the speech (vs. 12) reinforces the themes we have heard, just to be sure we have them securely in our mind. "Therefore I will divide up for him with the many" (the kings once more, not "the great" as the *Revised Standard Version* has it), "and he will divide the spoil" (yes, loot in war) "with the strong." The servant will be rewarded for his efforts "because he poured out his soul to death." Now in the closing recapitulation, the text reads in Hebrew, "and he was the one who the sin of the many bore," offering one final mention of the kings.

What a story! If it were not so familiar it would hit us with the same thunderclap with which it must have hit its first readers.

The hearers, in their depressed mood of the exile, were waiting for good news, and they heard good news at the beginning ("Comfort, comfort," 40:1); though admittedly they heard more for awhile about God's being in control than they did about going home, as we saw in Chapter VI. But now it turns out that the God who holds power, who will take them home, is at the same time a God whose purpose it is to allow his own servant, in whom God himself finds glory, to be done to death innocently, a happening which is so unprecedented that the very kings of the earth are stunned into silence. Is this *good* news? The question must have been insistent in the minds of the hearers: who, pray tell, could he be talking about? Is he talking about *us?*

But the prophet does not say. He picks up images from Jeremiah's career, his call from the womb (49:2), his innocent suffering (53:2, 7); he gives the impression once or twice that he might be talking about himself (50:4-9 really could be the prophet himself talking, we must admit); he hints that it might be Israel (those identifications outside the servant songs, 41:8 and all the rest); but he never really says.

Second Isaiah has such control over the phrasing of his message that we must conclude his obscurity on this point is deliberate. He intends his hearers to search about for an identification themselves, just as he intends his hearers to wait on tiptoe for the good news of homecoming through all the hints of the earlier chapters. The *task* of the servant is clear even if the identity is not. So we shall pause to see how the *task* laid out for the servant fits into the thinking of the Israelites at this time.

People have always sought an explanation for suffering and pain that makes sense, the Israelites no less than others. The easiest explanation, and the one that was traditional in Israel, was that suffering is punishment for sin. (We saw that identification of suffering with sin in the kings' speech in 53:4-5, but one finds it on every hand. It is the basic assumption of Job's friends, though not of course of Job himself.) A person may find himself with more suffering than he thinks he deserves (sometimes he finds himself with less, though he rarely thinks about that), but any disparity between his sufferings and his deserts can be covered by the notion of family solidarity, that God "visits the iniquity of the fathers upon the children" (Exod. 20:5). One can always blame one's suffering on the conduct of one's forebears.

When this explanation for suffering began to strain, there was a second: suffering is not always punitive, they agreed, sometimes it is pedagogic—it teaches one a lesson. The book of Proverbs has a lot of this: "The rod and reproof give wisdom, but a child left to himself brings shame to his mother" (Prov. 29:15). We got a hint of this in Isaiah 40:2: "She has received from the Lord's hand *double* for all her sins."

But valid though both these explanations may be, they hardly lift the spirit. Furthermore, the effectiveness of these explanations begins to fail after decades of suffering. After all, as we have already noticed, a good many of those hearers of Second Isaiah in 540 B.C. had not even been alive in 587 when Jerusalem fell, before which time the sins had presumably been committed for which people were still being chastised.

It was the steady task of prophets in Israel to bring the news of God's fresh interventions into human affairs, interventions that overturned people's conventional assumptions (as we saw in Chapter V). The fresh news which Second Isaiah brought was that God does not employ double-entry bookkeeping with sin and suffering, and that suffering is not always simply punitive or pedagogic but has another function, a positive part to play in God's new work. He who is to be God's servant must live out a life (and death) of suffering and humiliation, not for any sins he has committed in the past (the past is put far behind—compare 43:18-19), but for the future rescue of others, indeed for the future rescue of the rest of the world. The servant is called to innocent suffering, and when he accepts his calling and is faithful to that calling all the way to the grave, then God will highly exalt him.

We saw in Chapter III that Israel had always had a calling to be God's demonstration community to the world by living out her life in obedience to the covenant God. We now learn that the servant has a calling to be God's specific means to reach that world—not by conquering, not by shouting, not even by teaching; but hiddenly, quietly, willingly, gladly. The world will be reached in that kind of way. Suffering is a vocation when taken on willingly.

Who is the servant, then? It seems clear from the way the servant stands over against the kings, the nations, the many, that the servant is a significant portion of Israel, a significant representative of Israel. Second Isaiah generalized from Jeremiah's innocent suffering, and he saw that Israel's suffering, if and when that suffering is undergone willingly, becomes God's means to change the whole stance of the rest of the world. Second Isaiah uses language which sometimes fits an individual and sometimes fits the group; numbers evidently do not matter.

Who is the servant, then? Second Isaiah is mute; but his very muteness cries out to Israel, "If the shoe fits, put it on." He may have had himself in mind, he may have had Israel in general in mind (though 49:9 would hardly fit), he may have had a representative group within Israel in mind, he may have thought of a single person who would sum up for Israel God's will.

What matters for us is that no subsequent spokesman

within the Old Testament deals with the idea; nobody else took up the insight, or tried it, or worked with it. The hearers of Second Isaiah's time evidently were not so sure it was good news; they were content, so far as our record goes, to stay with the obviously good news which the prophet brought to them, namely: we're going home.

Nobody put on the shoe, not until the time of Jesus of Nazareth, an extraordinary Jew who became overwhelmed by the conviction that he was called by God to gather the lost sheep of the house of Israel, to be the nucleus for a faithful Israel (compare Matt. 9:36, 10:6). The narrative of the temptations he underwent in the wilderness (Matt. 4:1-11) portrays options in his mind for the exercise of his calling, and each of these options had scriptural warrant. Turn stones into bread to feed the hungry? No, not that. Be a wonder-worker and throw yourself from the top of the temple? No, not that. Be a political leader of all the kingdoms of the world? No, not that. But here is another option: "He was despised and rejected by men. . . . He bore the sin of many, and made intercession for the transgressors" (Isa. 53:3, 12). Yes, this.

We might say it this way: Jesus knocked at the door of the shop which had the "Help Wanted" sign in the window. "Is the job still open?" "Yes." "Then here I am, send me."

Or we might say it this way: the shoe fit, and he put it on.

Of course the description of the servant does not fit Jesus in every detail. Jesus was not so scarred, so far as we know (53:2), nor did he have children (53:10). But the pattern of the servant's behavior does fit what we know of Jesus. The description fits him in such an uncanny way, not so much because Second Isaiah was a crystal-ball gazer, as because the description he set forth was for a job which nobody else wanted until Jesus came along and accepted it. Of course it fits; it fits because it became Jesus' own self-understanding of his task. It fits because God's intention was finally demonstrated in Jesus' servanthood.

Was the servant's task bad news, or good news? For Jesus it was good news. For Christians, it is good news. And for Second Isaiah it was good news. Look what raptures he bursts into in chapters 54-55, now that the story has been told. The key word is the very first word in chapter 54, "Sing." Israel, the barren one, is to "break forth into singing" (54:1), indeed the very mountains and hills before you "shall break forth into song" (55:12).

We wish we had some biographical details about this marvelous prophet. But nameless though he must remain, his voice is as clear and marvelous a voice as one could hope for, setting forth in a new historical period the great affirmations of the first Isaiah, of the power, the height, the holiness, and the loving intervention of God. We must be content with this.

"Third Isaiah"

Chapter VIII

The Grandeur and Misery
of those who Returned[1]

W E TURN NOW to the last 11 chapters of the book of Isaiah, chapters 56-66. As we shall see, these chapters are in some ways quite like chapters 40-55 and in some ways quite different. When we first surveyed the book of Isaiah (Chapter I), we concluded that these final chapters are best understood as the work of "Third Isaiah." I shall not attempt to solve the problem of whether Third Isaiah is one individual or several; no one knows for sure. But since I can readily understand these chapters as substantially the expression of one prophet, I shall keep it simple and refer to Third Isaiah as an individual. Scholars believe Third Isaiah mediated the perspective of Second Isaiah in changed circumstances, a generation later, when the Jews had returned to Jerusalem after 538 B.C.

Let us postpone for the moment the historical details, however, and plunge into chapter 56. We shall find there many of the themes which run through all 11 chapters, and we shall realize immediately that this is not quite the kind of thing Second Isaiah would have done.

The abruptness of the first two verses is puzzling. Of course the concern for justice and righteousness in the Israelite prophets was a steady concern, and one we share; we recall meeting it in the very first chapter of Isaiah (compare 1:17, 21). But the word "soon" in vs. 1 strikes us as odd—as if people were getting restless and beginning to ask "when?" and "how long?" It was different in Second Isaiah, where the announcement of God's salvation was immediate and overwhelming (compare 45:8; and note that even 51:5, whose wording is much like that of 56:1, is far

more vivid). Here in Third Isaiah one has the feeling the
prophet is saying, "Just hold on a little longer!"

Furthermore, God's deliverance is linked to people's
perseverance in conduct (both vss. 1 and 2). It is curious
when we think about it: there was little if any concern
in Second Isaiah for the *conduct of the people*. Chapters
40-55 were supremely about *God's* mighty acts. And the one
specific detail of conduct in chapter 56 that is singled out is
sabbath-keeping (vs. 2). Why this, we wonder, rather than
avoidance of stealing or protection of widows (compare
1:17, 21-23 once more)? And what is this about foreigners
and eunuchs (vss. 3-8), and specifically, eunuchs who keep
the sabbath (vs. 4)? It is clear that we are in an unfamiliar
realm of thought and need help to grasp the assumptions of
this prophet.

We can see at once that vss. 3-8 speak of the outcasts of
society, those whom the Jewish community traditionally held
in low esteem. God loves them, we are told; and thus these
verses are an early expression of the same spirit of compassion
which is reflected in Jesus' story of the Good Samaritan (Luke
10:29-37). God draws his circle wider than his covenant
community expects him to. But we need to notice that these
verses are directed toward the specific issue of *worship*. The
Jerusalem temple has just been rebuilt, and the question then
emerges, Who is fit to worship there? The passage is concerned
for "my house" and "my walls" (vs. 5), "my holy mountain"
and "my house of prayer" (vs. 7). Who should have access to
God's temple? Not only those born into the Jewish community,
but also converts to Judaism (vs. 6), and even mutilated
males, who were always the object of contempt and
humiliation (compare the laws of physical fitness for priests,
Lev. 21:17-23—now, even eunuchs are acceptable to God
(vs. 5). The passage turns out then to center not on God's great
act of deliverance, which had been the focus of Second Isaiah's
message, but rather on who is acceptable to God to worship
him in his temple. It is a natural concern for a people who
have just begun temple worship once more, but it is a different
one than Second Isaiah had, who was preaching to a people
without a temple far from home.

Verses 9-12 bring a startling new note: the prophet is scathing in his description of some group who are his enemies. What is this all about? Who are the "watchmen" or "shepherds" who are called "dumb dogs" (vs. 10) with a "mighty appetite" (vs. 12)? Clearly the prophet is speaking against the leaders of his community. He insults them by calling them "dogs" and wants to see them devoured by wild animals (vs. 9). True, the first Isaiah had spoken out against the leaders of his day (1:23), but not in such insulting terms; and in Second Isaiah one finds no trace of any rivalry or split within the community.

We had best try to gain our historical bearings and understand the pressures which this community was undergoing after its return from Jerusalem. (It is unfortunate that the evidence we have for reconstructing this period is to be found in Old Testament books we do not ordinarily use so much, books like Ezra and Haggai; readers of this study may be excused from following out all the clues of the next few pages!)

In our study of Second Isaiah we learned that Cyrus did come in and capture Babylon in 538 B.C. Almost immediately after that he announced what so many of the Jews had been waiting for: a proclamation that they could return to Jerusalem. (He also freed other captive peoples to return to *their* homelands, but we cannot linger over the details.)[2] He gave back to the Jews all the gold and silver plate which Nebuchadnezzar of Babylon had looted from the Jerusalem temple in 598 and 587 (Ezra 1:1-7) and encouraged the organization of an expedition back to Jerusalem. A Jewish official named Sheshbazzar was appointed governor over the group returning, and they set off for Jerusalem (Ezra 1:8-11). Thus the Jews really did go off to home; Second Isaiah's words really did come true.

The group did not include all the Jews in Babylon, however—far from it. We must not forget that the time was now almost a half century after Nebuchadnezzar had destroyed Jerusalem. Two generations had passed. Young people who had never seen Jerusalem were by now well settled in Babylon. Not everyone wanted to leave the security of his residence for the dubious privilege of reclaiming his grandfather's inheritance far to the west. So Sheshbazzar's expedition took only some of the exiles; those who stayed behind were content to lend financial support to the colonists (Ezra 1:4, 6).[3]

When they arrived, the colonists did not find it easy. After all, Jerusalem had been thoroughly destroyed by Nebuchadnezzar. After the Babylonians had captured the city, those left in Judah had to establish the capital of their province outside the city, at Mizpah, some miles north (Jer. 40:5-6). Later on, the looting done by Edomite tribes from across the Jordan (Obad. 8-14) surely did not improve living conditions in the Jerusalem area. Accordingly, the colonists had all they could do to survive. A beginning was made in rebuilding the temple, but it is clear that nothing substantial was accomplished on this project in Sheshbazzar's time (Ezra 4:24).

Though the evidence is indirect, apparently another group of colonists set out from Babylon to return to Jerusalem some time before 522 B.C. under the leadership of Sheshbazzar's nephew Zerubbabel.[4] Zerubbabel was evidently of royal descent, since there was later a movement to declare him Messiah-king (Hag. 2:20-23). He shared leadership of the community with a Joshua (or Jeshua), the high priest (compare Ezra 3:2 and Hag. 2:2). The fresh leadership offered by Zerubbabel and Joshua at this time was no doubt a consequence of an act of Darius king of Persia, a successor to Cyrus, for Darius had reinforced Cyrus's proclamation of aid to Jewish colonists early in his reign (Ezra 6:1-12).

Two prophets arose at just this time, Haggai and Zechariah. They rallied the people to set to work again on the rebuilding of the temple. Haggai offered to his listeners (and thus offers to us) a vivid description of the economic difficulties the community faced (Hag. 1:4-6). It is not hard for us today to identify with people who can say, "He who earns wages earns wages to put them into a bag with holes" (or, even better, with the *Jerusalem Bible*, "the wage earner gets his wages only to put them in a purse riddled with holes"). The solution for their perennial poverty, said Haggai, is simple: don't concentrate on your private well-being—get going on that temple rebuilding project (Hag. 1:2-3, 7-11). The community responded to his appeal (Hag. 1:12), but the fact that they had to begin by setting the altar of the temple in its place (Ezra 3:2-3) indicates that they had virtually to start from scratch. Even this new effort, however, was greeted with mixed emotion by those who could remember back to the glories of the earlier temple destroyed in 587 (Ezra 3:12-13). One has the impression that this new building was to be a much more modest affair. But the building was finally completed and dedicated in 516 (this is the information given in Ezra 6:15)— a full 22 years after the first settlers had started out under the sponsorship of Cyrus. This is the temple, then, and this is the community reflected in Isaiah 56.

It is clear that the contrast between Second Isaiah's words in chapters 40-55 and the words of Third Isaiah in chapters 56-66 is a contrast between high anticipation on the one hand and inadequate fulfillment on the other. Second Isaiah and his community in 540 B.C. could dream their glorious dreams, for if God were to enter history once more as he had in times of old, then *no* words were adequate to describe his work:

> The mountains and the hills before you
>   shall break forth into singing,
>   and all the trees of the field shall clap their hands.
> Instead of the thorn shall come up the cypress;
>   instead of the brier shall come up the myrtle . . .
> (55:12-13).

Those metaphors and images dazzled our eyes and our ears! Those were the words of a visionary far from home, spinning his lines into the soaring stratosphere, lines anchored to the ground by one specific historical item only—the coming of Cyrus king of Persia. And, marvel of marvels, it came true: Cyrus did beat Babylon, he did spring us free. But now that we are home again, it is still the same old world—there are children to feed and bills to pay and committees to organize, and the thorns (alas) are still thorns and the briers still briers. The contrast between dream and reality is hopelessly severe. So, when will the marvel of God's salvation be evident? "Soon" (56:1). And what do we do in the meantime? "Keep the sabbath" (56:2), accept foreign converts and castrated males into the blessed community (56:3-7)—and a curse on our corrupt leaders who do nothing but eat, drink, and be merry (56:9-12). It is all quite understandable, and sad.

The attack on the corrupt leaders continues in the first 13 verses of chapter 57. The passage plays on two uses of the word "bed": the "beds" of the righteous are, sadly enough, their graves, into which they slip unnoticed and forgotten (vss. 1-2); at the same time the leaders are accused of sharing in illicit fertility rites in their "bed" (vss. 7-8).

Our attention in 56:9-12 was on the "dumb dogs"; now at the beginning of chapter 57 the emphasis is on the righteous man—"But it is the righteous man who perishes" (this is the emphasis in the Hebrew of 57:1). Then in vs. 3 the prophet suddenly addresses the leaders directly: "But you, you sons of a witch, come here, offspring of the adulterer and the whore" (*Jerusalem Bible*). Their parentage is impugned on both the fathers' and the mothers' side—strong language—after which the prophet describes various forbidden religious practices of which they stand accused: sexual acts in the worship of pagan fertility gods, child sacrifice.

In vss. 3-5 the prophet has been addressing the leaders with masculine plural pronouns and verbs, but suddenly he switches to the feminine singular in vs. 6 (and the feminine singular forms continue to the end of vs. 13). The change cannot be signaled in English translation but is immediately significant in Hebrew. What he has done is to personify the leadership as a whore.[5] This is a device which Jeremiah had used (in Jer. 2:16, 25, for example), but it is new here to the Isaianic tradition. Not only is the gender change here unexpected, but the whole vocabulary is quite raw. Thus the word "symbol" early in vs. 8 may well indicate a phallic symbol (*New American Bible:* "indecent symbol"), and the end of the verse, marked in the *Revised Standard Version* by the note "The meaning of the Hebrew is uncertain," may originally have offered a text whose wording was toned down and blunted by later copyists.[6]

How literally should we take all this? Were the leaders of the community really guilty of fertility cult practices? I think not, for reasons which will soon become clear. Later in this chapter we will clarify the nature of the leadership he is addressing, but for now we must simply affirm that he has found highly abusive language to level at these leaders.

Verse 11 begins the climax to the passage as God speaks; in the third line the "me" is emphatic. The Hebrew can be rendered:

> *Whom did you dread and fear,*
> *that you played false,*
> *while me you did not remember,*
> *nor pay attention?*

Israel had belonged to God at one time, but she had forgotten her obligations and was playing around with other gods—it is the same old, sad story. The first line in vs. 13 is much more clipped in Hebrew: "At your cry let your bunch save"—"your bunch" implying "your crowd of gods." Gods, of course, should embody supernatural "spirit." But these gods are picked up by the "wind" (the same word in Hebrew) and blown off like so much dust.

Bitterness at the leadership in his community is a noteworthy feature of Third Isaiah's utterances, and the passage we have just examined is by no means the only one to manifest it. As we examine other similar passages, we shall find clues to clarify the prophet's situation.

We turn first to a long passage, 63:7-64:12, which reads smoothly and is not hard to understand. It is a moving account of God's great act of rescuing his people from Egypt (63:7-9) and his people's consequent disobedience (63:10). The prophet is troubled by the terrible contrast between the love that God and Israel had for each other in the early days and the rebellion that Israel has offered God more recently (63:11-13).

There follows a long lament (63:15-64:12) addressed to God in plaintive tone. Where are you, God?

> *Look down from heaven and see,*
> *from thy holy and glorious habitation.*
> *Where are thy zeal and thy might?*
> *The yearning of thy heart and thy compassion*
> *are withheld from me* (63:15).

> *O that thou wouldst rend the heavens and come*
> *down,*
> *that the mountains might quake at thy presence—*
> *as when fire kindles brushwood*
> *and the fire causes water to boil—*
> *to make thy name known to thy adversaries,*
> *and that the nations might tremble at thy presence!*
> (64:1-2).

How far we are from both the first and Second Isaiah—the first Isaiah, who "saw the Lord, high and lifted up" (6:1), who proclaimed that "the Lord will rise up as on Mount Perazim, will be wroth as in the valley of Gibeon, to do his deed" (28:21); and Second Isaiah, who announced that "the glory of the Lord shall be revealed, and all flesh shall see it together" (40:5), that God has "stirred up one from the east whom victory meets at every step" (41:2). How is it, we continue to wonder, that the prophet who is commissioned to speak for almighty God is reduced here to this hand-wringing: "Oh, if you would only show yourself!"?

The prophet's agony continues unabated through the whole of chapter 64. Verse 3 implies that God used to show himself all the time when Israel on her part had no reason to expect him, while at present, when the people want him, he is nowhere to be found. (In passing we may note that the *Revised Standard Version* for the first line of vs. 3 is somewhat misleading: "terrible things which we looked not for" sounds as if it means "bad news we don't need." The Hebrew text simply means "awesome deeds we could not hope for" [*New American Bible*] or "unexpected miracles" [*Jerusalem Bible*].) The whole of chapter 64 communicates a deep sense of the unworthiness of Israel's past conduct and a desperate hope for some signal from God to indicate that he knows, that he understands, that he will respond to the needs of his people.

At the beginning of 64:8 we have the words "Yet, O Lord, thou art our Father." The transition here is striking in Hebrew and carries great emotional weight. The same phraseology appears earlier in the passage (63:16), "For thou art our Father," followed there by the extraordinary and puzzling statement "though Abraham does not know us and Israel does not acknowledge us," and then a repetition of the affirmation, "thou, O Lord, art our Father, our Redeemer from of old is thy name." Plainly more is going on here than meets the eye. We can understand that God is father, but we cannot grasp why "Abraham does not know us and Israel does not acknowledge us." Are "Abraham" and "Israel" code-words here? Who are "we" who are not included in "Abraham" and "Israel"? The answer to these questions takes us to the heart of the passage and helps illuminate the split within the community which we have already witnessed in 56:9-57:13.

The key to the matter is something we would hardly notice, namely the double reference to Moses in 63:11, 12. Surprisingly, these occurrences of Moses' name are virtually unique in the prophets. "Moses" does not occur anywhere else from beginning to end in the book of Isaiah. Neither Amos nor Hosea mentions him. Micah and Jeremiah mention him once each (Mic. 6:4; Jer. 15:1). Otherwise we have to wait until the late books of Malachi and Daniel for any other references to him. I am not sure why Moses should be mentioned so sparsely in the prophets, unless it is because the prophets had their eye more on the acts of God than on his servant Moses who mediated God's will. But we can be sure that the double mention here in chapter 63 has quite a specific purpose.

A recent study of Third Isaiah[7] makes a convincing suggestion. Once again, however, we need a little background to understand it. Evidently in the earliest days of Israel the priesthood was largely if not entirely confined to the tribe of Levi. To take only one example, in the time of the judges a northerner named Micah set up a private shrine and appointed his son to be priest at the shrine (Judg. 18:5); but soon thereafter he replaced his son with a Levitical priest (Judg. 18:7-13).

Then during David's kingship a priest named Zadok emerges (2 Sam. 15:24-37), who became chief priest at the Jerusalem sanctuary after David's death (1 Kings 2:35). Zadok's ancestry is unclear, although at a later period he was assumed to be a Levite.[8] It is clear, however, that by the time of the Babylonian exile only the Zadokite priests had a claim to be the legitimate priests for the Jerusalem temple, and that they attempted to demote the Levites into a subordinate role (like Christian deacons rather than priests, let us say). This is the program for the future which the prophet Ezekiel set forth (Ezek. 40:46, 48:11). The author of 1 and 2 Chronicles, writing in the fifth century B.C., also reflected this changed situation in his own description of the early days of David. Look at the subsidiary tasks given the Levites according to 1 Chronicles 23:2-5, and notice the fact that the priests are distinguished from Levites in vs. 2 there.[9]

Now when the Jews returned from Babylon it was evidently the Zadokites who laid claim to the administration of the temple area; it was they who insisted they were the legitimate spokesmen for Israel, the inheritors of Abraham and Jacob (=Israel).

But the Levites were a repository of some of the most sensitive spirits in Israel. For example, it is likely that they were the ones who had preserved the traditions that gave rise to the book of Deuteronomy.[10] No doubt some Levites had remained in Palestine during the time of the Babylonian exile, for one notes that there were attempts to continue offering sacrifices in Jerusalem even after its destruction by Nebuchadnezzar (compare Jer. 41:5). Also, there surely must have been Levites among those who returned from Babylon (compare Ezra 1:5).

A scenario then that would fit the evidence of conflict in 63:7-64:12 is this. The Zadokite priests got hold of the administration of the temple and claimed authority and exclusive rights, as those in religious power are wont to do.

They claimed, "We have Abraham, we have Israel for our father" to those who were excluded from power, to those specifically outside the power structure who nevertheless claimed to be spokesmen for God (including Levites, and including our Third Isaiah). Third Isaiah affirms that those who boast of "Abraham" and "Israel" do not know "us" (63:16), and he makes the counterclaim that it is *God* who is *our* father (63:16, 64:8). He further makes elaborate mention of Moses and what God did through Moses (63:11, 12)—but Moses was a *Levite* (Exod. 2:1), indeed the Levite through whom God brought the people into existence. Third Isaiah is fighting here against the exclusiveness of a priestly party that had reserved to itself the rights and privileges of a religious aristocracy. God's heritage, he affirms, is wider than the confines of some priestly in-group: it consists of his "servant," the "tribes" (plural) of his heritage (63:17). Now we can begin to comprehend some of the emotion behind the affirmation that even foreigners and eunuchs (who could *never* qualify to be priests—we recall Lev. 21:17-23 once more) are welcome in God's temple. We can imagine how the priestly party would react to that.

This is an example of a common phenomenon, namely, that when a group is systematically excluded from power and responsibility, the out-group compensates for its powerlessness by affirming that "they may have the power, but we have God on our side." Sometimes, of course, this makes religious sense. Since power corrupts, God is more likely to be on the side of the powerless. But sometimes one suspects the claim to be purely a defense mechanism. I recall once seeing a crudely lettered sign on a small frame church in the midst of the great farms in the San Joaquin Valley in California: "Jesus' Only True Church." The claim was theoretically possible, but did seem to me unlikely.

In any event, this is the process evidently at work in Third Isaiah. The priests may hold the temple area, but God speaks through his excluded prophets, who insist that there is more to God's work with his people than the power group would allow.

Chapters 58 and 59 also betray tension between these

factions in the community. In 58:1-12 we find the controversy circling around the question of fasting. It is fascinating
how the questions of the religious life in this period began to
center on matters of cultic obligation—who should enter the
temple, how one should observe the sabbath, how one
should fast.

Who are "they" in vs. 2, which reads, "They seek me
daily"? The Hebrew verb "seek" here is a frequent technical
term for getting a yes-or-no answer from God through cultic
means (compare the first Isaiah in 31:1: "But [they] do not
look to the Holy One of Israel or *consult* [the same verb] the
Lord"). In the same way here the Hebrew says, "And me
day by day they consult," and the next line mimics it: "and
knowledge of my ways they delight in." The rest of the
verse describes people who claim to speak for God, who
follow meticulously the Standard Operating Procedure. In
short, the verse describes the priestly party once more.

The first half of vs. 3 is the prophet's quotation of the
priests' perplexity: they cannot figure out why their routine
doesn't pay off. The prophet's answer begins in the last half
of vs. 3 and continues through the first half of vs. 9. Soon
it appears that the prophet's answer is really *God's* answer
(vss. 5, 6, "I choose"), and God's answer is that though you
thought your delight was in God's ways (vs. 2), you are
really only pursuing your own gratification (vs. 3b). Fasting
that means something will mean sharing your food, your
shelter, your clothing with the destitute who need it (vs. 7).
Then the light you look for will dawn (vs. 8)—words that
echo Second Isaiah, "For a law will go forth from me, and
my justice for a light to the peoples" (51:4). *Then* the glory of
the Lord will be your rear guard (58:8)—again echoing Second Isaiah, "the glory of the Lord shall be revealed"
(40:5), "the God of Israel will be your rear guard" (52:12).
The rest of the passage, vss. 9b-12, summarizes most
movingly what we have already heard: take away the yoke
(of oppression to your fellows in the community), take away
the pointing of the finger (of scorn—compare Prov. 6:13),
take away the speaking of wickedness (of slander), and then
your light will rise in the darkness (vss. 9-10).

This passage suggests how the themes of Second Isaiah were being grappled with in the give and take of the restored community. God's glowing promises announced by Second Isaiah are true *if* (and it is a big "if") you who lead the community only manifest the compassion of heart which God expects.

Chapter 59 begins with a declaration based on a rhetorical question of Second Isaiah, who had announced God's asking, "Is my hand shortened, that it cannot redeem?" (50:2). Third Isaiah, still evidently addressing the careless leadership of the community, affirms the negative: "Behold, the Lord's hand is not shortened, that it cannot save, or his ear dull, that it cannot hear; but your iniquities have made a separation between you and your God" (59:1-2). That is, don't keep wondering when God is going to manifest himself: you have only yourselves to blame. This sort of message—that God has not helped the people because they are wicked—is the same kind of message we heard Haggai making to explain the poverty of the community. Haggai had said: you are poor because you have not pressed to rebuild the temple (Hag. 1:2-11—we discussed this material earlier in the chapter). It is an understandable religious response, and there is no doubt an element of truth in it; but one does miss the spacious sense of God's grace and the thankful response of the community in faith which one gains from the first Isaiah and from Second Isaiah.

What an accusation it is which the prophet levels! "Your hands are defiled with blood . . . your lips have spoken lies" (vs. 3). And his accusation continues with "they"—he is not even speaking to them directly any more: "they conceive mischief" (vs. 4), "they hatch adders' eggs" (vs. 5). No question about it, in vss. 4-8 the prophet finds vivid language to express his bitter contempt for those leaders. Notice, at the same time, how carefully he shapes his poetic lines: vs. 5a mentions both adders' eggs and the spider's web, vs. 5b elaborates on the adders' eggs (they are no good for food, and snakes come forth from them), and vs. 6a elaborates on the spider's web (it is no good for clothing).

It is striking that the indictment in vss. 1-8 is not followed by any announcement of God's judgment in vss. 9 and following, as we might expect (look back at 5:8-30 and see how closely the announcement of God's judgment follows the "woes"). By this period of time the prophetic word came in a different mood, a mood of realism shaped by the difficulties of the religious life. Our leaders have misled us: this is why justice is far from us (vs. 9). We looked for that light (vs. 9) for which Second Isaiah had prepared us (51:4 once more), but find nothing but darkness; we grope for the wall like the blind (vs. 10), we moan and moan like doves (vs. 11). The community finds itself slipping farther and farther from the shining promises of Second Isaiah.

The announcement of God's judgment which we did not get in vss. 9-15a does come, after all, in vss. 15b-20. God is "astonished" or "appalled" (vs. 16—not "he wondered," as the *Revised Standard Version* has it) that there was no human agency to intervene. We cannot help wondering whether Third Isaiah was wishing for another Cyrus to deliver them as the historical Cyrus had delivered the community from oppression a generation before. So God himself must intervene personally, God himself must be the warrior. The image of God as the divine warrior was of course an old theme in Israel: the first Isaiah and Second Isaiah both drew on it (see 31:4-5 and 42:13), but Third Isaiah goes at it much more elaborately than his predecessors in the Isaianic tradition did. His words recall the elaborateness of the early hymns from Israel's tradition (see, for a good example, Exod. 15:1-18). Third Isaiah mentions God's arm that brings victory (59:16) as the Exodus poem did (Exod. 15:16). But there is this great difference: Third Isaiah uses symbolic and almost mythical language to describe the activities of the warrior (metaphors for his breastplate, his helmet, his clothing, his mantle, vs. 17), while the old poem in Exodus gives the specifics of history (Pharaoh's chariots in the sea, Exod. 15:4; the dismay of the chiefs of Moab, Exod. 15:15, and all the rest). Third Isaiah is attempting to give stability to his faith by reference to the ancient images for God among his people, but he is losing his grip on the specificities of God's dealings with real people (the reference to "enemies" and "coastlands" in vs. 18 seems only an echo of Second Isaiah).

There is one more passage of conflict literature which we must touch on now, and that is 66:1-6. This passage is scathing in its denunciation of the whole apparatus of temple and sacrifice. "What is this house which you would build for me?" (vs. 1). Why a temple at all? "Heaven is my throne and the earth is my footstool." The idea of trying to centralize me in Jerusalem is ridiculous. And as for sacrifice, one who offers an ox is no better than a murderer; one who offers a lamb is no better than someone who gets rid of a stray dog; one who makes a cereal offering is no better than someone who messes around with pig's blood; one who offers incense at the altar is no better than an idolater (vs. 3). We have already met words that try to put the sacrificial system into perspective (we recall our discussion of 1:12-15 in Chapter III), but there is no parallel to this blast of Third Isaiah's anywhere else in the Old Testament. If we take this word seriously, then what becomes of the careful directions in Leviticus (Lev. 1-7), what becomes of the great dreams of Ezekiel to restore the temple system (Ezek. 43:18-27)? They are dismissed by Third Isaiah with a contemptuous wave of the hand. Those of us who see no place in the religious life ourselves for sacrifice will no doubt applaud him, but we must see how unprecedented his words were in his day— only so can we grasp how bitter must have been the split between the priestly party and the prophetic party in his community. The last part of vss. 3b-4 turn on the word "choose": if they for their part chose what made them happy, then I for my part choose to afflict them, because they chose what does not make me happy at all.

Conflict we find within the lines of Third Isaiah, but not all of his chapters are so. If there was misery for those who returned from Babylon, there was also grandeur, and chapters 60-62 sing with some of the old excitement of Second Isaiah. Of all the material of Third Isaiah, it is these chapters that are most familiar to us. The words "Arise, shine, for your light has come" (60:1) echo in our minds from Handel's *Messiah* or from the readings in Christian liturgies for Epiphany. "The spirit of the Lord God is upon me . . . to bring good tidings to the afflicted" (61:1) is familiar to us as the portion from Isaiah which Jesus read in his synagogue at Nazareth to proclaim his own mission (Luke 4:16-20; see our reference to this event in Chapter I). But though these chapters are "easier to read" than some others in Third Isaiah, close attention to the historical circumstances of his time may aid our understanding of these chapters too.

The whole of chapter 60 is addressed to Jerusalem, since all the second person references are feminine singular. We have already noticed the same phenomenon in 57:6-13, where the prophet addressed the leadership collectively as a whore. But here the reference is not contemptuous at all, as 57:6-13 was; it is tender and joyful. Though the object of the address is not made plain till vs. 10 (by implication— "your walls"), or vs. 14 (specifically—"they shall call you . . . the Zion of the Holy One of Israel"), cities are feminine in gender in Hebrew, and the reference is clear. This long address to a female makes a striking effect, since a society that reserves a subservient place for women is very alert to sex-tags in grammatical features. Feminine singular address to Jerusalem was found in Second Isaiah, too ("Rouse yourself, stand up, O Jerusalem," 51:17; "Awake, awake, put on your strength, O Zion," 52:1); but the elaborate length of the address, which continues for the whole of chapter 60, is impressive indeed.

In content as well as in form we sense that we are back with Second Isaiah: the glory of the Lord is upon you (vs. 1; compare 40:5); the scattered exiles shall come home (vs. 4; compare 43:5-7); the wealth of the nations shall flow to Jerusalem (vs. 10; compare 49:23). Plainly, God will pardon and restore his people, and Third Isaiah uses the same glowing terms for God as Second Isaiah used: "Savior, Redeemer, the Mighty One of Jacob" (vs. 16; compare the same series in 49:26).

Yet for all the resemblances to Second Isaiah in these verses there is a difference. Second Isaiah was speaking to a scattered people far from home and attempting by his words to gather a community. Chapter 60, by contrast, is focused on a city, indeed on Zion, the place of the temple (vs. 14). We are concerned no longer about the road home (compare 40:30) but about the walls and gates of Jerusalem (60:18). What we see here, in short, is the attempt to make the vision of Second Isaiah *concrete*, to make it a *program* for the re-creation of life in Jerusalem. Even though we find here no bitter words of conflict such as we found in other chapters of Third Isaiah, still, beneath the surface, one can detect some special pleading.

Thus in contrast to the program for the future found at the end of the book of Ezekiel, which included a delimitation for the various tasks appropriate in the new temple (compare Ezek. 44:11), Third Isaiah insists that the overseers will not be a particular rank of personnel, but abstractions, the very characteristics of God himself, "peace" and "righteousness" (vs. 17). The walls and gates to be built will not be defined by measurement, by the number of cubits in their dimensions (compare Ezek. 40-42), but again by "salvation" and "praise" (vs. 18), words commonly associated with God.

When we move to chapter 61 we find at the beginning an announcement in the first person (vss. 1-3). This announcement is in contrast to the first-person declarations in chapter 60, which in form were words from God (60:16). Here in chapter 61 they are not (compare vs. 1), and scholars have understandably looked here for as clear a picture of Third Isaiah's own self-understanding as we are likely to get.[11] Whether this attempt is justifiable or not, the announcement is a remarkable one. God has anointed the spokesman to bring good news to the afflicted. The verb "anoint" is rare in the book of Isaiah; we have seen (Chapter VI) that Second Isaiah called *Cyrus* God's anointed (45:1), but the verb does not otherwise appear except in a late passage where the command is given to "anoint" (that is, smear oil on) leather shields (21:5). Since it was kings who were anointed (1 Sam. 16:3) and priests (Lev. 6:20), and since the anointing of a *prophet* is rare, spoken of only otherwise in the case of Elisha (1 Kings 19:16), we must assume that the word here, although used in a figurative sense, has a quite deliberate intent to underline the legitimacy of Third Isaiah's words.

And what good news he brings! Second Isaiah had used the term "good tidings" (40:9, 41:27, 52:7), but he used the term in the context of all of Zion/Jerusalem: "How beautiful upon the mountains are the feet of him who brings good tidings . . . who says to Zion, 'Your God reigns'" (52:7). But here it is not Zion that is being addressed, but the afflicted (or poor), the brokenhearted, the captives, the prisoners, the mourners—all the faceless, forgotten ones who have lost hope, if indeed they ever had any. It is to *them* that God has directed his prophetic word. No wonder Jesus picked out this passage to read; no wonder he made it his own!

A word is needed about "vengeance" in vs. 2. It has become clear in recent years that this Hebrew word means "legitimate sovereignty," not "vengeance"; a good translation here is "restitution" (*New English Bible*) or "vindication" (*New Jewish Version*).[12] The outcasts will no longer be nobodies, but will be called "oaks of righteousness," "the planting of the Lord" (vs. 3).

In vss. 5-7 the outcasts are addressed directly. Along with the reassurance which they are given that foreigners will no longer exploit them but rather be their servants (vs. 5), there comes another explosive item of special pleading: you (the outcasts) are the ones who shall be called "priests of the Lord," "ministers of our God" (vs. 6). The "you" in vs. 6 is emphatic; the prophet knows exactly what he is saying. He is deliberately undermining the pretensions to exclusiveness upon which the priestly clique in the temple area were insisting.

The remainder of the chapter does not bring any surprises. We find a pronouncement from God in vss. 8-9 of his faithfulness to his forgotten people, and a pronouncement from the prophet in vss. 10-11 to match the opening words of good news in vss. 1-3.

Chapter 62 continues the attempt to put Second Isaiah's program to work, now by repeated suggestions of new names which the nation shall gain, not names of contempt like "forsaken" or "desolate," but rather "my delight is in her" and "married" (vss. 4-5). These are motifs upon which Second Isaiah had touched (54:1), but what was poetry for Second Isaiah has now become a programmatic scheme. The marriage image had been used by Hosea, Jeremiah, and Ezekiel in the past as a metaphor for God's relation to Israel (Hos. 1-3; Jer. 2-3; Ezek. 16, 23), but it has not appeared previously in the Isaianic tradition. Incidentally, the traditional Hebrew text has evidently been copied wrongly in vs. 5 in reading "your sons." A slight change yields a better reading, "your Builder" (=God; so the *New American Bible*, and similarly the *Jerusalem Bible* and the *New English Bible*). The people have felt cast off by the God who first made a covenant with them, but he will be re-united in covenant with them once more. The end of the chapter brings still more reassuring names: "the holy people," "redeemed of the Lord," "sought out," "city not forsaken" (vs. 12). Curiously enough, I cannot find this phrase "holy people"[13] anywhere else in the Old Testament, certainly not in the book of Isaiah. The word "holy" in Third Isaiah refers mostly to God's mountain, that is, Zion (five times)—so the word is again a priestly concern. Here, quietly, comes the reassurance to the whole people that they, and not simply the priests and their affairs, are dear to God.

The last chapter with which we must deal is chapter 65. God speaks through the entire chapter. We hear words of judgment against the wicked in alternation with words of promise to God's faithful. The question "Where are you, God?" echoes through the pages of Third Isaiah, but listen to God's answer: I've been here all the while, but you were not really asking for me (vs. 1). Indeed I spread out my hands the whole day to a rebellious people (vs. 2). What irony this is! To "spread out one's hands" is to be in prayer (so, we learned, the meaning of 1:15). But the first Isaiah had insisted in that verse that God will hide his eyes from his people when they try to communicate with him; now Third Isaiah is saying that God is trying all day long to communicate with his people, but they do not respond to him.

Once again we find that bitterness against the leaders: a

people who involve themselves in fertility cult worship (vs. 3), who seek to traffic with the spirits of the dead (vs. 4a), who eat pork (vs. 4b). We wonder as we wondered earlier: are we really to take these accusations literally, or are they simply an insulting way of addressing the leaders? The earlier accusation of fertility cult worship (57:5-9) was in a passage in which the leadership was addressed as a whore, so the accusation there could have been symbolic (that is, Third Isaiah could have been accusing the leaders in an especially vivid way that they were religiously "prostituting" themselves and being disloyal). But now that we have a clearer understanding of who it is whom Third Isaiah is addressing—a party of meticulous Zadokite priests—we do wonder. Did these priests *really* sneak off to worship Baal and Astarte, did they really attempt to consult ghosts (a forbidden practice, of course; see Lev. 19:31), did they really eat pork? Or is the prophet not resorting here to the most emotionally charged language he can muster to put these priests in their place? Evidently, it is the latter. We recall that 66:3 says that he who offers an ox is like a murderer, and all the rest. He does not say there that the priests are murderers, only that they are no better than murderers. The intent is the same here in chapter 65 where the accusations of fertility practices, trafficking with the dead, and eating pork are in the context of vs. 5: "Who say, 'Keep to yourself, do not come near me, for I am set apart from you.'" The expression "I am set apart from you" in Hebrew is literally "I am too holy for you" (the *New English Bible* and the *New American Bible* have "I am too sacred for you"). Here is the nub of it: "Keep your distance; we are holy." The elite leaders of the cult in the temple regard themselves as having an exclusive claim on holiness,[14] and that claim is as disgusting in God's sight as would be the resort to pagan practices. God will punish this kind of thing (vss. 6-7).

Verses 8-12 continue the contrast between God's faithful people and his unfaithful priesthood. Look at the chasm between "you" (the priesthood) and "my servants" in vss. 13-15: my servants shall eat, but you shall be hungry. It reminds one of the blessings and woes which Jesus pronounced, according to Luke 6:20-26.

The chapter ends (vss. 17-25) with a new theme—a new heaven and a new earth (vs. 17). Second Isaiah had implied something like this, for in 51:6 we read that "the heavens will vanish like smoke, the earth will wear out like a garment . . . but my salvation will be for ever, and my deliverance will never be ended." But Second Isaiah's imagery was intended to emphasize the stability of God's care for his people—the destruction of heaven and earth were expressions to highlight that stability. Now Third Isaiah begins to examine the specifics involved in a destruction of heaven and earth, and what will replace them.

If, as we have affirmed, Second Isaiah's visions became a basis for a program in Third Isaiah's word to the community, then we see him here taking the vivid metaphors of a transformed nature which Second Isaiah implied ("instead of the thorn shall come up the cypress," 55:13, and all the rest), and making a predictive program out of it. A new heaven and a new earth, he says. What will this imply? No more distress, nothing but rejoicing (vss. 18-19); and, wonder of wonders, no more infant mortality (vs. 20). After the prophet has proclaimed this good news, he is back once more to general reassurance: those who build and plant will enjoy the fruits of their labor (vss. 21-22), and in general people will live as long as the trees. Finally, to climax this wonderful announcement, in vs. 25 he summarizes 11:6-9: the wolf and the lamb shall feed together.

When we first met this passage of the first Isaiah, we puzzled over it (see Chapter V), and our tentative conclusion at that time was that in that context it voiced Isaiah's expectation of international peace. But the imagery obviously lends itself to the use of those who would envision "a new heaven and a new earth," so that what had evidently been a poetic image for a new era in international relations for the first Isaiah becomes an altered biology for the world in Third Isaiah's vision of a new creation.

At this point we are on the edge of what we call "apocalyptic": a religious outlook that affirms God at work not in the here and now of present historical events—since those

present events are seen to offer no hope, no clues to God at
all—but affirms him at work only in a future transformed
creation where the givens of this world no longer operate.
Third Isaiah does not quite arrive there, but is tending in
this direction. We shall see material in the book of Isaiah
that is fully apocalyptic in Chapter IX.

If we look back over what we have covered in the book
of Isaiah so far, we shall recognize that the first Isaiah sees
God revealing himself in the events of the eighth century
B.C.—God judges his people through the military expansionism of Assyria, and God refines and restores his people
after Assyria has come and gone. God's restoration may
change the face of his people, but they are still recognizably
of this world. In Second Isaiah the contrast between God's
seeming neglect of his people and his coming restoration is
great, so great in fact that the prophet in his imagery
reaches far beyond the expected, and the whole world will
have a different look ("instead of the thorn shall come up
the cypress," 55:13). But his description appears to be the
metaphor of a poet rather than the blueprint of the physics
and chemistry of a new creation, and his whole message is
tied to one great historical event, the coming of Cyrus. But
Third Isaiah has two problems: first, that he tries to apply
this metaphorical language to his real world, and second,
that he sees no deliverer coming like Cyrus. As a result, he
is tempted to envision a new physics and a new chemistry.
This is new, and what becomes of this urge in the expression
of his successors we shall see in the following chapter.

Before we take leave of Third Isaiah, however, we must
notice an instance of feminine imagery for God to match the
words of Second Isaiah in 49:14-15. The verse in Third
Isaiah is a brief one, 66:13: "As one whom his mother
comforts, so I will comfort you; you shall be comforted in
Jerusalem." Second Isaiah was more indirect in his affirmation: a mother may forget, but I will not forget—that is, I
am like a mother, but more dependable than a mother.
Third Isaiah no longer hesitates to make the direct comparison: I am like a mother, period. He has said several times
that God is our Father (63:16, 64:8), but here he says God

is like a mother. Those in our day, then, who insist that calling God "Father" is symbolic language and that sometimes comparing God to "Mother" is appropriate have good biblical precedent.

Other "Isaiahs"

CHAPTER IX

Visions for a People Forgotten

OUR STUDY OF Third Isaiah took us through the last chapter of the long book of Isaiah; yet, if the conclusions we reached in Chapter I are sound, there are still more "Isaiahs"—a good deal of the material within chapters 1-39 is to be attributed to anonymous spokesmen for God who helped shape the Isaiah tradition in later centuries. Our study of the book of Isaiah is not complete, then, without an attempt to examine some of these later additions.

At first, these passages seem quite miscellaneous. But if we view them simply as one random addition after another, we miss the point: these passages represent the efforts of many people to keep the Isaiah tradition alive, to keep old affirmations relevant to new situations, to say, "Look at these old words: they really refer to us in our day!" They are evidence of the process by which the Jewish people kept up their listening to the old, time-bound words of earlier prophets in the tradition of Isaiah and kept those words relevant in new times and new circumstances.

We recall the collection of pronouncements against foreign nations in chapters 13-23 (see again Chapter I). A good number of these are genuine to the first Isaiah, as we learned in Chapter IV. Thus 17:1-6 was a word against Syria and Israel at the time of the Syro-Ephraimite war. And, though we did not take note of 17:12-14, if we now compare that passage with 29:5-8, which we did examine in Chapter IV, we see how similar the two passages are: they no doubt belong to the same phase of the Assyrian crisis. We looked, too, at 18:1-6 and 19:1-5, pronouncements against Egypt, and at 20:1-6 (Isaiah's going barefoot and naked) when we studied Isaiah's insistence that Egypt was to no avail against Assyria.

But Isaiah's subtle message—that God is sovereign over all nations and that Judah should rely on God and his promises rather than on playing power politics—triggered a whole array of pronouncements against various enemies of Judah in later generations. It is always easy to work oneself up against the wickedness of some foreign power; and traditional phrasing came easily to tongue, therefore, for any prophet who felt impelled to produce such oracles. For example, chapters 15-16 offer a pronouncement against Moab, a people living to the east of the Jordan River northeast of the Dead Sea; but many phrases in these chapters are identical with a similar passage against Moab in Jeremiah 48. Furthermore, the text in Isaiah gives clear evidence itself of having been expanded—note 16:13. No doubt prophets in both the Isaiah and Jeremiah traditions drew on common phraseology, and there is no way to date such material with any precision. One commentator, for example, suggests the mid-seventh century B.C. for chapter 16, a half-century after the first Isaiah.[1] There are two separate passages against Babylon (13:1-22 and 21:1-10) which can hardly be credited to the first Isaiah—Babylon became a problem nearly a hundred years after his time. (For 14:4b-20, see the discussion at the end of this chapter.)

So, while it is important to try to date such passages, or at least to try to determine which of all of them are conceivably genuine to Isaiah and which of them must be placed at a later period, we must constantly remind ourselves that the motive for these later anonymous oracles was not pious fraud. The anonymous spokesmen were not trying to palm off their words as those of Isaiah to lend those words a credibility they would not otherwise have had. Rather they were attempting to think Isaiah's thoughts after him, they were undertaking to view their world as Isaiah had his, convinced that God was continuing to work in their decades as he had worked in Isaiah's. Of course their outlook was not totally congruent with Isaiah's. How could it be? They were different people and the circumstances of their world had shifted. Never mind; if God reveals himself through words in history, then though the words may be time-bound, God's activity and purpose is not, and all the array of anonymous material is a monument to that paradox.

Let us turn now to a famous problem, 2:2-4, which is duplicated almost word-for-word in Micah 4:1-3 (+ vs. 4, which sounds like a logical end to the passage, missing in the version in Isaiah). We glanced at the poem in Chapter I, but we must now take a closer look. What does it have to say? It is a prediction that the time will come when the "mountain of the house of the Lord," which is of course Zion, the location of the temple in Jerusalem, shall be preeminent among all the mountains of the world, and all the nations shall stream there to learn the words of God in his law. At that time God will make a permanent judgment among the nations and all weaponry will be recycled to the tools of peace.

It is a marvelous passage; it not only occurs in both Isaiah and Micah—its image of "swords into plowshares" turns up, in reversed order, in the later book of Joel (Joel 3:10, "plowshares into swords"!). Its message of universal peace has touched many hearts since—one thinks of the Black spiritual "Ain't Gonna Study War No More."

The passage clearly bears many of the marks of Isaiah's own interests: the centrality of Zion as the "cosmic mountain" (see Chapter V), the "word of the Lord" in parallelism with "law" (compare 1:10, "word of the Lord" and "teaching," the same Hebrew pair), God acting as judge of the nations (compare Chapter IV). But is the poem genuine to the first Isaiah? Commentators split their vote.[2] One can find indications within the poem to make a judgment in either direction. As for myself, I must confess that I cannot envision the passage as an expression of a time any earlier than that of the rebuilding of the temple. The theme of the pilgrimage of all nations to Jerusalem was a feature of the sixth century and thereafter; for example, look at Zechariah 8:20-23. The prophets Zechariah and Haggai, we recall, emerged at the time of the rebuilding of the temple in 520-518 B.C. (see Chapter VIII). Here then, I suggest, is an unforgettable reshaping of the concerns which the first Isaiah had for universal peace and the centrality of God's judging and saving word: the temple in Jerusalem is to become the pulsating heart of God's work for all nations and peoples of the world.

The prophet affirmed that all this would take place "in the latter days" (2:2). There is another passage focusing on Zion (4:2-6) which begins in similar fashion: "in that day." But while "swords into plowshares" is a passage which is easy to grasp, this one is not. The first thing we take note of is that vs. 2 is evidently poetry. It reads, literally,

> *On that day shall be*
> *the sprouting of the Lord*
> *for beauty and for glory*
> *and the fruit of the land*
> *for pride and for adornment*
> *for those spared of Israel.*

Laid out in this way, the poem reveals its parallels—"beauty," "glory," "pride," "adornment"; and again, "sprouting of the Lord" and "fruit of the land." There will be, then, a restoration of the fertility of the land for "those spared"—a vague term meaning "whatever (or whoever) escapes" in Israel.

To this poetic verse someone else has added four verses of prose commentary. There is no way vss. 3-6 can be construed as anything but prose. Verse 3 says that anyone who remains in Zion shall be called "holy"—everyone, that is, who is "written" (or "recorded") "for life" (rather than for death) in Jerusalem. We saw in Chapter VIII, in our study of 65:5, that one of the concerns people had, both those within the temple establishment and those outside, was where "holiness" resides. To be "written for life" evidently is to be recorded in God's book as destined for survival. There are similar expressions in Psalm 139:16 and Exodus 32:32. Anyone in Jerusalem who survives, then, will be holy.

But the commentary continues (vs. 4), "when the Lord shall have washed away the filth of the daughters of Zion and cleansed the bloodstains of Jerusalem from its midst by a spirit of judgment and a spirit of burning." The word "filth" is a strong one, meaning "excrement"; it is the word that occurs in 28:8 (see Chapter III). "Spirit" here might be "wind" as well: all the nastiness of the women of Jerusalem will be cleaned away by the blowing of God's purifying spirit. And then what will God do? He will create over Zion and her assembly the very same cloud by day and smoke and fire by night (vs. 5) which had been the sign over the Israelites of the mysterious presence of God after they had left Egypt and were wandering in the wilderness (Exod. 14:24). That is, God will be present in and over the temple as surely as he had been over the marching Israelites of old. He will no longer be separate from his people. But that protecting cloud and that signal fire now take on a new meaning. They not only signal God's presence, but also protect Jerusalem from summer heat and winter cloudbursts. The old symbol now begins to take on an apocalyptic function (compare the "new heaven and new earth" of 65:17-25, discussed in Chapter VIII).

What we have in 4:2-6, then, is a bit of poetry which might or might not be genuine to the first Isaiah,[3] followed by a later commentary on the poetry. This commentary reflects priestly concerns—holiness, cleanness, and the centrality of the temple. In fact, both the poem about "swords into plowshares" in chapter 2 and this passage in chapter 4 betray the same focus on the temple. Third Isaiah, we learned, had a bias against the group that controlled the temple, but he remained a lonely voice; after all, the temple was the only visible symbol of the unity claimed by the scattered Jewish communities after the exile of Babylon.

We now turn to a major collection within the book of Isaiah, chapters 24-27. In our preliminary survey in Chapter I these four chapters were described as a "collection on doom and triumph for the whole world," which is simply a way of saying that they exhibit the themes of apocalyptic thinking toward which Third Isaiah was tending. The first Isaiah understood God to be working most specifically

through the historical events of his day—the behavior of the
covenant people, the march of the Assyrian army, and all
the rest. Now we are dealing with the "new heaven and
new earth" on which Third Isaiah had touched. Look at
24:21-23: "On that day the Lord will punish the host of
heaven, in heaven." Who are the host of heaven? "They will
be gathered together as prisoners in a pit"; "then the moon
will be confounded, and the sun ashamed." Clearly this
apocalyptic mentality, though familiar to us from other
parts of the Bible, is new in our survey of the *Isaiah* tradition, and we must explore now what kind of circumstance
in history would render such affirmations plausible and necessary for faith.

Let us begin by reading all of chapter 24. We not only
have here the kind of cosmic changes described in the last
three verses; we not only have here the kind of thorough-
going destruction of the world described in as many ways as
possible ("the earth lies polluted under its inhabitants," vs.
5; "a curse devours the earth," vs. 6)—we also have something else, and that is a sudden veering from the darkest descriptions of destruction (vss. 1-12) to sudden outbursts of
joy (vss. 14-15) and then back to terror and destruction (vss.
17-23). These sudden alternations of mood continue through
the next three chapters. It all seems rather hysterical. We
ask ourselves, Is a single prophet responsible for all four
chapters? Is it one prophet's mood which swings so wildly,
in a kind of manic-depressive way? Or do we have here prophetic fragments from various people which have been
woven together in this emotional checkerboard by some
editor for his own purposes—a liturgy perhaps? What kind
of liturgy would it be?[4]

The first section, vss. 1-12 (or perhaps 1-13), offers
gloom; but there is a curious problem here which the English translations cover over, namely, that the same Hebrew
word *'ereṣ* can mean both "land" (=territory of a given people, like "the land of Israel") and "earth" (as opposed to the
heavens). The *Revised Standard Version* has translated the
word as "the earth" from vss. 1 to 13, but not all commentators agree that this is justified.[5] Let us feel our way. In

vs. 4 the word is in parallelism with "world" and "heavens" and is almost surely to be understood as "the earth"; similarly in vs. 13, where "in the midst of the *'ereṣ*" is in parallelism with "among the nations," and therefore again is almost surely to be translated "earth."

But vss. 1-3 are different. Here the word could well be translated "the land"—for example, "the Lord will lay waste *the land* and make it desolate, and he will twist its surface and scatter its inhabitants," and similarly with vs. 3. The first Isaiah offered descriptions of the destruction of the land—look back to 1:7 (where "your country" is the same Hebrew word "your land") and 5:25. Could 24:1-3 have been spoken by the first Isaiah? I think so. The long list of opposites in vs. 2 is in the style of Isaiah. (In passing we may note that the first line, "And it shall be, as with the people, so with the priest," has been borrowed from Hosea 4:9; but Hosea was a contemporary of Isaiah's, and there is no reason why Isaiah could not have borrowed the phrase and extended it.) We recall Isaiah's list of the ranks of leadership in 3:2-3, his list of all the high things in 2:13-16, his list of the cities conquered by the Assyrian kings in 10:9, his list of animals living peacefully side by side in 11:6-7. My suggestion, then, is that we have here a genuine fragment of Isaiah's prophecy, triggered perhaps by an earthquake experienced or envisioned ("he will twist its surface," vs. 1).

Verse 4 begins in the same way as does Jeremiah's description of a drought (Jer. 14:2-6), but where Jeremiah said that "Judah mourns, and her gates languish," this prophet says, "the earth mourns, and the world languishes." Jeremiah lived a century after Isaiah, so this line of vs. 4 is unlikely to be due to Isaiah. Since the phrasing takes what I assume to be local destruction in vss. 1-3 and moves it in the direction of the whole cosmos, I think here in vs. 4 we find the beginning of the words of an apocalyptic prophet. He has used the words of the first Isaiah as a launching-pad, but has taken the word "land" in the words of the first Isaiah in the more extended meaning of "earth." And off he goes, bringing us a vision of cosmic destruction.

Verse 5 states that "the earth lies polluted under its inhabitants." This phrase refers specifically to Numbers 35:33. There it is stated that the blood shed by a murderer pollutes the land. So Isaiah 24:5 implies that the earth is polluted because of the heavy toll of murder it has sustained. This image is reinforced by the phrase "everlasting covenant," a reminiscence of Genesis 9:16 in which God made an eternal covenant with all the sons of Noah—with all mankind, that is—after he forbade the shedding of blood (Gen. 9:4-6).

Verse 6 reinforces the images of drought from vs. 4. The "curse" is evidently conceived of as a kind of creeping bane that destroys everything in its path. "Curse" is also associated with drought in Jeremiah 23:10, a good passage for comparison. Verses 7-9 pick up the words "mourn" and "languish" from vs. 4 and move them in a different direction—to the wine and the vine; and the images of these verses interlock nicely—"wine" matches "vine," "merry-hearted" matches "jubilant" (vs. 8), "timbrel" and "lyre" (two musical instruments) match each other, and "wine" in vs. 9 (not the same as "wine" in vs. 7, but a synonym) matches "strong drink" (really "barley beer"; see the discussion on 5:11 in Chapter III). These last two items pick up the images of vs. 7 once more.

What is this "city of chaos" in vs. 10? With the continued local images of "house" (vs. 10) and "streets" (vs. 11), of "city" and "gates" (vs. 12), are we no longer in the realm of cosmic images? Have we gone astray in our understanding of vss. 4-12? Should we understand the references to be local land rather than the cosmic earth? No, I think we are still on the right track. It is true, there is no way to be sure what the prophet meant by "city of chaos." "Chaos" is a word used in Genesis 1:2 ("without form" there) and it therefore reminds the hearer of all the formless evil in the universe which stands over against God. So the "city of chaos" is a phrase that refers not necessarily to any particular city but to any and all cities which embody the corruption of the present age. The images of "wine" and "joy" from vss. 7-9 are now combined with images of cosmic destruction.

Then, suddenly, vs. 13. Is this joy or desolation? Some

commentators take it as joy (it is, after all, harvest time);[6] but this is evidently not the case. The image is borrowed from 17:6, part of a passage genuine to Isaiah, and that verse describes a harvest as an image of destruction: only a few olives will be left on the tree. To sum up, our apocalyptic prophet has taken an utterance from the first Isaiah of the land left desolate by an earthquake (vss. 1-3) and has extended it (in vss. 4-13) by images of drought to describe a cosmic destruction by God.

The next few verses are hard to interpret, for the Hebrew text is uncertain at several points. Verse 14 begins with the emphatic pronoun "they"—"they for their part lift up their voices," and continues with the words "over the majesty of the Lord." The references to "west" and "east" are not clear—readers of the *Jerusalem Bible* or the *New American Bible* will find quite different translations here; but the reference to "coastlands" (or "islands") of the "sea" in vs. 15 is clear, and the general context is of wide distances across the world (compare "ends of the earth," vs. 16). But who are "they," referred to in vs. 14? Plainly those who know of the majesty of the Lord, the glory of the Lord, the name of the Lord, the God of Israel, as the text indicates. They may be the faithful Jews, or they may in addition be inhabitants of other nations who now acknowledge the God of Israel—we recall Second Isaiah's vision that other nations would acknowledge the God of Israel (41:1 and often).

We might well ask how anyone could be left to sing the praises of God if there is as universal a destruction on earth as we have heard in the material up through vs. 13. The answer must be that the prophet is not thinking logically; rather he is giving voice to one religious impulse after another. He is a part of a people crushed by circumstances and forgotten by the world who are caught up by the conviction that only on the basis of the utter destruction of the present world-order can God move in to triumph. There is no contradiction in his mind, then, for when the present world is destroyed, God will show himself in all his power and glory, and all his faithful people will rejoice in that triumph of God.

The end of vs. 16 is so difficult and uncertain in Hebrew that we had best pass it by. With vs. 17, of course, we are back in the world of destruction. The first line in the Hebrew of that verse offers a remarkable triple pun: *paḥad wāpaḥat wāpāḥ*. The Zurich Bible in German offers something similar: *Grauen und Grube und Garn*; but I know of no English translation which offers anything but the bare meaning, "terror and pit and snare" (or the like), without the powerful sound-play of the Hebrew. Verse 18 enlarges on these images, and the rest of the passage through vs. 20 piles up the synonyms of cosmic collapse.

Verses 21-23 bring something still different. It must be said first of all that the Hebrew does not actually say "the moon" and "the sun" in vs. 23, but rather "the pale one" and "the hot one." But clearly the moon and sun are meant. (The same terms are used in 30:26.) Now in what way will the moon and sun be "confounded" or "ashamed"? Clearly by the shining of God in his glory, since he will outshine the sun and moon. Then what does the "host of heaven" in vs. 21 refer to? Is it the stars (since we hear of the sun and moon in vs. 23)? Or is it some group of angelic beings? We note that the "host of heaven" is in parallelism with "kings of the earth." Evidently our prophet shares the belief of his time that God gave the stars to pagan nations to worship (see Deut. 4:19), that the stars are really some kind of angelic beings,[7] that each nation had its guardian angel (compare Dan. 10:12-13). Our prophet here mingles these notions together and foresees a time when God will punish the host of heaven (=the guardian angels of the nations) just as he will punish the kings of those nations. He will shut up in a prison the host of heaven (=the stars) so that their light is extinguished, so that what will happen to the stars is quite parallel to what will happen to the moon and the sun.

One wonders why we have euphemisms in vs. 23—why "the pale one" and "the hot one" rather than simply "the moon" and "the sun"? Is it to avoid any suggestion that these are astrological deities that a Jew might be tempted to worship? It may be helpful to notice that Genesis 1:14-16 uses euphemisms too—there the sun and the moon are called simply "lights" instead of being named. So, we are told, God is superior to *any* heavenly body whom anyone might want to worship: he will outshine them all.

Then, suddenly, in 25:1-5, we have a psalm of thanksgiving, beginning much as Psalm 145:1 does. In the last half of vs. 4 we find mentioned the storm and the heat, and it looks as if we have here an expansion of phrases found in 4:6, a passage we studied earlier in this chapter. The word "aliens" (vss. 2, 5) is not what we expect in a psalm; it is, however, common in the prophets—it occurred twice in 1:7. The singer here in 25:1-5 affirms that aliens have ruled Israel too long, and that their defeat is near.

This psalm is followed by a remarkable description of a final banquet for all nations which God will provide "on this mountain" (vs. 6). The passage continues from vs. 6 to vs. 10a (ending, as it began, with "on this mountain").

Both vss. 6-8, the description of the feast, and vss. 9-10a, the response of the people to the feast, are in poetic form (in spite of the prose format of the material in the *Revised Standard Version*), and it is repetitive poetry of the kind the Israelites took over from their Canaanite predecessors.[8] Note the interlocking repetition of the last part of vs. 6. The Hebrew is quite clipped and striking:

> *mishtēh shemānīm*
> *mishtēh shemārīm*
> *shemānīm memuḥāyim*
> *shemārīm mezuqqāqīm.*

The *Jerusalem Bible* renders the lines with good repetition, though it is not so concise as the original:

> *a banquet of rich food,*
> *a banquet of fine wines,*
> *a food rich and juicy,*
> *of fine strained wines.*

It is not only the poetic form which resembles old Canaanite models, but the content offers Canaanite reminiscences too. We recall the Canaanite idea of the cosmic mountain, the mountain which the Israelites later understood as Jerusalem (see Chapter V). The present passage describes a banquet on the cosmic mountain, just as the old Canaanite myths had described the banquet of the high god 'Ēl on the divine mountain.[9] The affirmation that God will swallow up death (Hebrew *māwet*) forever is a reflection of the myth of the victory of Baal over *Mot*, the Canaanite god of death and the underworld.[10]

We are not sure of the meaning of the phrases "the covering that is cast over all peoples, the veil that is spread over all nations" (vs. 7). But since the face or head was covered at the time of mourning (see 2 Sam. 19:5, Jer. 14:3-4), and since the context of this passage is of God's swallowing up death and wiping tears from all faces, it is best to see this gesture of God as a means to rid the peoples of the earth of all anguish and mourning forever.

So the prophet envisages a final culminating banquet at the end of days. We may remark here that the descriptions of this banquet became more and more elaborate as Jewish apocalyptic thinking developed in later centuries: for example, it was said that God has saved the two primeval monsters, Leviathan and Behemoth, from the foundation of the world, to be food for the final banquet.[11] The Dead Sea Scroll community later seems to have practiced dress-rehearsals of that banquet in preparation for the end-time.[12] The idea was clearly central to Jesus—he not only referred to it directly (Luke 13:29), but he presupposed it in his parables (Luke 14:15-24), and it was no doubt part of the background of his thinking in his feeding of the multitude and in his celebration of the Last Supper. It certainly was the backdrop for the disciples' understanding of the Last Supper as they continued to observe it.[13]

Our passage offers a nice bit of irony in that "death," which has always swallowed up everyone (we remember the gaping mouth of Sheol in 5:14, discussed in Chapter III), will itself be swallowed up (vs. 8). As the people of the earth swallow the marvelous food and drink, so God will swallow up death. This line also became part of St. Paul's great pronouncement in 1 Corinthians 15:54-55.

As one might imagine, the people respond with joy (vss. 9-10a). But vss. 10b-12 are something else again, for we move from the sublime to the coarse (as well as to the ridiculous). Here is a crude word of judgment against Moab which depends on a play on the name of a Moabite town, "Madmēn." The name sounds like the Hebrew word for dung-pit (*madmēnā*), hence the passage before us. But why insert it here? Did some Moab-hater offer it, believing that Moab stands for all the enemies of God's people?

The next passage, 26:1-6, insists that God will keep the "strong city" (vs. 1)—Jerusalem, whether the earthly Jerusalem or some future transfigured one—against the inhabitants of the "lofty city" (vs. 6), which represents the enemy. There are echoes here of old psalms, but there is vindictiveness here which might well trouble us. God not only lays low the lofty city, but the humble poor trample it themselves and appear to take great pleasure in doing so.

The following section, 26:7-19, is central for our understanding of apocalyptic mentality, so we shall work through it with special care. Unfortunately, some phrases in it are not at all clear. It is a poignant passage; the suffering of God's people is manifest in almost every line. It is also a passage whose poetry is densely interlocked, where almost every line suggests words and images for subsequent lines.

Verse 7 begins with a conventional affirmation—the way is smooth for the righteous (or innocent) person. The Old Testament is full of such expressions—one thinks of Psalm 1:6. Psalm 1, however, is quite calm about it all—good people get rewarded, and bad people get punished. But our prophet in Isaiah 26 has a sizeable head of steam behind his words. He is like a man drowning in the sea who, clinging to a timber, repeats "The-Lord-is-my-shepherd-I-shall-not-want." By the time we get to vss. 8-9a we hear of "waiting" and "yearning"—the word "wait" in vs. 8 is the same verb "to long" which is discussed in 5:1-7 (Chapter III). The prophet and his community *long* for God, so that what is true in theory ("the way of the righteous is level") will turn out to be true in experience.

"The inhabitants of the world" (vs. 9b) learn

righteousness only when God's judgments are manifest. These are the outsiders, the enemy, the people who can be expected to shape up only when forced to. Verse 7 had spoken of the innocent; now in vs. 10 we hear of the guilty. Even if the guilty one is shown favor, he does not learn righteousness. By implication, then, the "inhabitants of the world" are in the camp of the guilty; and the rest of vs. 10 fills out the picture—"in the land of uprightness," where things are straight or level (vs. 7), where the speaker is, he (the guilty one) is not aware of the majesty of the Lord. Clearly we see that the covenant community has been pushed around by foreign bullies until they are tempted to wonder where the eternal verities are, verities that reassure them that God will reward his faithful people.

Verse 11 continues this line of thinking: "Yahweh, your hand is raised, but they do not see it" (*Jerusalem Bible*). We know you are active, God, but they don't. How can we get them to know it? Show them who you are, Lord. Let them know who is in charge. Destroy them.

That is what God should give *them*; but what about us? "O Lord, thou wilt bestow prosperity on us, for in truth all our works are thy doing" (vs. 12—*New English Bible*). The word "prosperity" or "peace" (*Revised Standard Version*) is the Hebrew *shālōm* which we discussed in Chapter V when we dealt with 9:6, "Prince of Peace."

Verse 13 continues to calm the mood. Here is the sad truth: "Other lords besides thee have ruled over us." Literally, this means "have been our Baals," with all the innuendo of pagan cults which that word implies. "But thy name alone we acknowledge," literally, "memorialize," with a reminiscence back to vs. 8, "thy memorial name."

Verse 14 turns to a new direction, and the Hebrew of 14a is more clipped than the *Revised Standard Version* implies, since the twice-repeated "they are" is not in the Hebrew. It is something like "Dead, they will not live; ghosts, they will not rise." There will be no remembrance of the pagan lords, in contrast to the steady remembrance of God's name with his faithful (vss. 9 and 13 once more). What reassurance it is to know that pagan lords die too: finally they fall, never to rise again.

Again by contrast, vs. 15 picks up the "prosperity" motif of vs. 12. But it is only potential prosperity. One has the impression that by now the prophet is living in a dream world. When has God recently enlarged the borders of the land? Not for a long time. By the logic of faith he must do it some day, but the vividness of the phrase is matched by the hopelessness of the hope.

In vs. 16 the pronouns must almost surely be "we" and "us" rather than "they" and "them." There is textual evidence in this direction (so *Jerusalem Bible*, *New English Bible*, and *New American Bible*), and note "we" again at the end of vs. 17. Verses 16-18 increase the emotional pressure again, in a kind of spasm of despair. The verb "sought" in vs. 16 is literally "visit"—the same verb as "visit" in vs. 14. But really, it is *God's* job to visit *mankind*—by rewarding or punishing. Verse 16 is the only occurrence in the Old Testament where the verb is used of *Israel's* visiting *God*. It is in desperation that Israel tries to deal with God as God ordinarily deals with them. The word "chastening" at the end of vs. 16 carries the emotional freight of all the tragedies of the people that by conventional reckoning can be understood in no other way than as God's pedagogy, his discipline for his people.

Desperate people indeed, they are exactly like a woman in childbirth (vss. 17-18a), except that a woman's agony is crowned by a new life, while Israel's agony is crowned by—nothing at all, wind. It is an ugly phrase, a measure of the nihilistic mood of the prophet. (Admittedly the Hebrew words may be grouped differently, as the *Jerusalem Bible* has it: "we writhe, as if we were giving birth; we have not given the spirit of salvation to the earth. . . ." Here "wind" is taken with the next line and translated "spirit," to go with "salvation." This reading softens the image of giving birth to wind, but the general mood is still pessimistic. The traditional Jewish reading of the Hebrew lines, however, is as the *Revised Standard Version* has it.)

Verse 18b rounds off the pessimism of the earlier lines:

"We have wrought no deliverance in the earth, and the inhabitants of the world have not fallen." The "inhabitants of
the world" (compare vs. 9) are the rulers, the pagans, the
others—and they still stand there, doing their oppressive
work. There is a subtle alternation in this passage between
the verbs "rise" and "fall." The verb "(a)rise" occurs in vs.
14—the dead lords of the earth will not arise; but, alas, the
live lords of the earth have not fallen. (I see no warrant, by
the way, for the translation "are not born" or the like for
"have not fallen," as the *Jerusalem Bible*, the *New English
Bible*, and the *New Jewish Version* have it, nor for "bring it
forth," as the *New American Bible* has it. There is a nice
ambiguity between "let it fall" and "give birth" in the last line
of vs. *19*, but not *here* in vs. 18, I am convinced.)[14]

But the bitterest pessimism gives rise to the overwhelming optimism of vs. 19.[15] By a change of one letter, the
Dead Sea Scroll of Isaiah reads the second line of this verse
a bit differently: "Let the dwellers in the dust awake and
sing for joy!" It is also quite possible that the first line
should be translated, "Let thy dead live, let their bodies
rise." Whatever the exact shade of meaning may be, the
message is clear: God's faithful will be raised from the
dead; there will be a resurrection. The phrase "dew of
light" is a bit uncertain. If it is so understood, it means that
God's dew is a dew not of the night only, but of his permanent heavenly light. We would then have a symbol of the
life which he will give his revived dead; compare the phrase
"light of life" at the end of Psalm 46. (The translation "dew
of herbs" in the *American Standard Version*, and similarly
in the *New Jewish Version*, is less likely.)[16]

The last line of vs. 19 seems clearly to be ambiguous by
design; it can well mean "and on the land of the shades
thou wilt let it [that is, the dew] fall," as the *Revised
Standard Version* has it. But it can also mean "and the land
of the shades will give birth," or possibly "and the Land
[that is, Sheol] will bring forth the shades [in new birth]."
Ambiguity is a central feature of much poetry,[17] and it is
plain that both images coalesce here—of God's dew falling
(the same words occur in 2 Sam. 17:12) and of God's suc-

cessful bringing to birth in contrast to his people's failure to bring to birth (vs. 18). The conclusion is a brilliant stroke.

Thus, the lords of the world are dead, they are shades, they will not live (vs. 14); but God's faithful dead *will* live, the dust will bring them forth. Now what of this affirmation of resurrection? If we think for a moment, we shall realize that by and large resurrection is not an Old Testament idea. People die (Job 14:7-19); the continuity of life is in one's descendants, through whom one continues on in history. Thus "Jacob" is not only the ancestor but all the descendants as well. This continuity between the generations is well symbolized by the notion that the iniquity of the fathers will be visited upon the children to the third and fourth generation (Deut. 5:9); that is, responsibility persists beyond the span of an individual human life. So if, in early Israel, someone did not seem to get what he deserved— either by way of rewards or punishments—then the assumption was that his descendants would receive the rewards or punishments on his behalf.

But when the fabric of society was torn apart as it was so profoundly in the Babylonian exile in 587 B.C. and thereafter, the idea of individual responsibility before God became more prominent (compare Jer. 31:29-30 and Ezek. 18). By this understanding, one paid for one's own sins. So at this point new explanations needed to be found if someone did not get what he deserved. How can one explain such terrible disparities as one sees? Several solutions were proposed. Some people tried to deny that there was any problem (see Ps. 37:25). Others were tempted to curse God and be done with it, as Job's wife recommended (Job 2:9). Others, like Job himself, struggled over the riddle of a just God who rules over a world so full of injustice. But ultimately the belief in resurrection—another chance, a further opportunity to receive the reward which a just God will surely grant to his faithful people—became a plausible and convincing solution to many theologically sensitive people. The belief is reflected not only here in 26:19, but in the late book of Daniel (Dan. 12:1-2). It is also expressed in various intertestamental works[18] and became normative for Pharisaism and in the orthodox Judaism of the second century A.D. and thereafter (compare Acts 23:6-8). Christians, for their part, center their hope in the resurrection on the basis of the testimony of the apostles that Jesus Christ was raised from the dead. Here, then, in 26:7-19, we find a crucial affirmation about God's work with his people, an affirmation which grew out of a theological problem which had been heated to the boiling point.

There follow three verses (26:20-27:1) which describe a coming judgment from God: he is to punish the oppressor for all the blood shed on earth—and we recall our discussion of 24:5 ("the earth lies polluted" because of all the bloodshed upon it). Then, curiously, that final punishment of the unjust is linked with the punishment of "Leviathan," the cosmic dragon representing the chaos of the sea. It is the same dragon called "Rahab" in other passages (compare our discussion of 30:7 in Chapter IV and of 51:9-10 in Chapter VI) whom the Canaanite god Baal was said to have defeated. This old myth, we know, was incorporated in various ways into Israelite proclamation. So now we see it as a controlling image of the apocalyptic program for the last days: God will defeat not only his historical enemies but his cosmic enemy as well.

The rest of chapter 27 consists of various additions to this basic apocalyptic collection. Verses 2-6 appear to be an abrogation of the song of the vineyard in 5:1-7 (see Chapter III). Now, it seems, God will *not* destroy his vineyard but will guard it day and night against all enemies; there will be no more punishment of Israel. Verses 7-11 are quite obscure. Apparently, the author is struggling with the guilt and innocence of his people, how God has treated them in the past and will treat them in the future, but we must confess our uncertainty of the direction of the passage. Finally, in vss. 12-13, we are told there will be a last threshing of the grain of the world, and the Israelites will be picked out one by one, from wherever they may have been exiled, whether in Assyria or in Egypt, and brought home to worship in Jerusalem once more.

How do we react to a series of visions such as chapters

24-27 offer us? In various ways, no doubt. Few of us, I suppose, really crave to read phrases like "the earth lies polluted under its inhabitants" (24:5), no matter how much we may fear the possibility of just such a reality in mankind's future because of the carelessness or stupidity of generations like the present one. To be reassured that God is in control of the destiny of his people beyond such horrors is not likely to seem too cogent to those of us who become excited by the words of the first Isaiah, that God acts primarily through the here-and-now events of history to bring his sovereign will to pass. In addition, the crudeness and vindictiveness, the self-pity and the sense of helplessness which some of these passages exhibit do not render them appealing.

On the other hand, not too many readers of this book, I dare say, have served long prison terms, or been prisoners of war for many years, or watched their friends and neighbors being wiped out by the genocidal fury of some tyrant. Within the border of our own nation, most of us can locate a lawyer when we get into trouble. And if any one of us is abroad, an American, Canadian, or British passport will reassure its bearer that he or she will hardly be forgotten for long, even if the bearer is in difficulty with the authorities. But Blacks in the inner cities of the United States understand. Armenians from the Middle East understand. Jews from Europe understand. There are times in history when whole populations stand helpless before the swirl of events; and to these people the words of chapters 24-27 take on meaning. Couched in crude language though these assurances may be, still they are timbers to which drowning people can cling. God is not thwarted by the worst the world can do, we hear; he does not forget his people.

It is certainly curious that early Israel moved bravely away from the kind of cosmic, mythic language offered by Canaanite culture to view the specific *historical* events from God's viewpoint (we saw this with the first Isaiah); and then, as historical events seemed more and more to pass Israel by, the visionaries went back again to use some of the images of those old Canaanite myths with renewed power. Still, there are crucial differences. No longer do we assume a

polytheistic interaction among the divine powers, no longer
are we fixated on fertility and prosperity. Instead we have
one God, a God of justice and of grace, who guides his
people both through and beyond history to get his goals accomplished.

Now that we understand by our work with chapters
24-27 what some of the marks of apocalyptic vision are, we
can spot such passages elsewhere in the Isaianic collection:
thus 30:18-26 speaks of a time when "you shall weep no
more" (vs. 19), when "the light of the moon will be as the
light of the sun, and the light of the sun will be sevenfold,
as the light of seven days, in the day when the Lord binds
up the hurt of his people, and heals the wounds inflicted by
his blow" (vs. 26). Chapters 33 and 34 offer similar
visions—for example, 33:17-24 speaks of the king back on
his throne (vs. 17), the disappearance of insolent conquerors
whose speech is incomprehensible (vs. 19), a time when "no
inhabitant will say, 'I am sick'" (vs. 24).

One curious passage may be mentioned here, a passage
which foresees a time when Egypt will be converted to the
faith of Israel, and when Israel will be the bridge in a tri-
partite peace with Egypt and Assyria (19:19-25). Egypt, of
course, was the original oppressor in Moses' day, and Assyria
was the more recent oppressor in Isaiah's day. But in God's
good time these monstrous powers will be transmuted into
peers of Israel, and Israel will be the catalyst for peace. In
this way Israel is envisaged as fulfilling the old call to Abraham, that his descendants shall be a blessing to all the families of the earth (Gen. 12:2-3).

It is appropriate to round off this study of visions of the
future by a look at one of the most powerful poems in the
whole book of Isaiah, 14:4b-20. The poem carries its own
message, but still we wish we had a better grip on the
background of the poem. We wonder whether it is genuine
to Isaiah, and we wonder whether it really does refer to the
king of Babylon, as vs. 4a indicates. If the poem is genuine
to Isaiah, its application to the king of Babylon is unlikely,
for it was Assyria, we recall, which was the great threat
from the east in Isaiah's time, and it was only in the fol-

lowing century that Babylon replaced Assyria as the great threat. Further, there is nothing in the poem itself, in vss. 4b-20, which associates the lines with Babylon. It is altogether likely, then, that the poem was applied to the king of Babylon only secondarily.

The question whether it is genuine to the original Isaiah is more difficult to answer. The compactness and boldness of language render it worthy of Isaiah of Jerusalem, and I have hoped for a long time that I could persuade myself of its authenticity, but recent close analyses of its vocabulary by scholars[19] have convinced me that it is an anonymous poem of the exilic or early post-exile period. Our study of it will make a fitting conclusion to our survey of the anonymous poems in the tradition of Isaiah.

In form, the poem is a dirge. Dirges in Hebrew had a particular form, namely, three words plus two, three plus two:

> *How the oppressor has ceased,*
>   *the fury ceased!*
> *He has broken*[20] *the staff of the wicked,*
>   *the scepter of rulers. . .*

It is ironic in the extreme that the prophet should propose to sing a dirge for a hated tyrant of whom he and the whole world is glad to be rid. Besides its dirge-form, the poem is united by an alternation of words suggesting downward motion and words suggesting upward motion.[21] Further, the poem also echoes with alliteration. We cannot pause to explore every example, but we can cite one example, vss. 4b-5, which offers the repeated word "ceased," *shābat*, followed by "broken," *shābar*, and "staff," *shēbeṭ*.

The poem says the oppressor is quiet, his military power stilled. What a relief! The whole earth is at peace for a change, and the world breaks into song (vs. 7). The tall trees of Lebanon are glad—they have peace and quiet too, because since the tyrant is laid *low* no woodsman makes the hike *up* into the mountains to hew them down for the construction of new palaces or siegeworks or whatever. Here is an example, then, of the contrast between "down" and "up" which recurs in the poem.

Verses 9-11 bring something new: Sheol is preparing to receive you, your majesty! (For Sheol, see the discussion in Chapter III of 5:14-17.) Sheol is beneath, way "down," but look at its "up" verbs: it is stirred up, it rouses, it raises. Look at the welcoming committee: all your fellow-rulers are on hand to make you feel at home. And what is their welcoming word? "You, too, have become as weak as we!" (vs. 10). A fine welcome indeed for a tyrant who wielded all power. "Your pomp" in vs. 11 is literally "your pride"— another "up" word; and it is "brought down" to Sheol. And here is your bed, fit for a king—maggots below you, worms your blanket above (again, "down" and "up"). We began with the tyrant at rest (vs. 4b); now we find him preparing to rest in his permanent bed.

In vss. 4b-8 we have looked at nature—the earth, trees; in vss. 9-11 we have looked in on Sheol below. Now (vss. 12-15) we turn to heaven above: "How you are fallen ['down'] from heaven ['up'], O Day Star, son of Dawn!" We wonder, of course, who this "Day Star, son of Dawn" is. "Dawn" was a goddess in Canaanite mythology, and the "Day Star" was evidently a minor god who, in a myth now lost to us, tried to gain leadership over the gods and fell from eminence as a result.[22, 23] So here the earthly tyrant has overreached himself as foolishly as did the god in the myth, and down he comes to the ground, he who laid the nations low (vs. 12). Listen to him boast how high he will be (vss. 13-14), consorting with the high gods in their assembly. He even wants to make himself like the "Most High"—the Canaanite title for the highest god of all, 'Ēl. But down he comes (vs. 15), all the way to Sheol.

Verses 16-17 turn the searchlight on the bystanders who stand gawking at the downfall of the tyrant, who ask, "Is this the man who made all earth tremble. . . ?" The bystanders describe the tyrant four ways: he made the earth tremble, he shook kingdoms, he made the world like a desert, and he overthrew its cities. In vs. 17 something seems to be wrong with the last line, since "who did not let

his prisoners go home" has no parallel. One recent commentator emends the last line of vs. 17 (and the first word of vs.
18) this way: "For his prisoners he did not open the house
where he held them fast";[24] the *New Jewish Version* mentions another possible emendation of these words: "Who
chained to his palace gate all the kings of the nations? Yet they
were all laid in glory. . . ."

Verses 18-20 then contrast the impressive burial of other
kings with the humiliating non-burial of the tyrant. Unfortunately, the key word translated "like an untimely birth" in
vs. 19 is uncertain. This translation (which of course means
"miscarriage") is only a guess, but it is a plausible one. The
ancient Greek translation reads "like a carcass," which is
another possibility. In any event, the fate of the tyrant's
body is not in keeping with the pomp and circumstance of
his life.

And suddenly, at the end of vs. 20, a concluding line
that looks to the future—nobody who is like *that* should go
down in history!

So who is the tyrant? Nebuchadnezzar? His son? Some
Persian king? Some local autocrat lost to history? It does not
matter: the tyrant, whoever he is, is mortal like the rest of
us (as 40:23 implied, and as 26:14 has reminded us), and
the world can take heart that he finally does fall.

Those of us who were alert to the headlines in 1953 will
never forget the day we learned of Stalin's death. Stalin,
really dead! Stalin, nevermore to send millions off to Siberia,
there to die without a trace! He really has died, himself, and
we have outlasted him! So, as we can see, the dirge in 14:4b-20
is an all-purpose dirge; it fits equally any tyrant at all.

Although God is not mentioned as the one who brings
the tyrant down (if one excepts the doubtful mention of "the
Lord" in vs. 5)[25] we know from the prophetic tradition that
this event, too, is in the providence of God.

We have titled this chapter "Visions for a People
Forgotten," for these passages were framed when the Jewish
community did feel forgotten by the world. But the title is
not quite accurate, for these visions reassured them that
though the world might forget them, *God* had not forgotten

them. If the visions are valid, if God can transmute in these ways the raw material of their life and of their death, if he can transmute it past the comprehension of anyone in the community, then they surely can take heart, and rejoice, and be glad.

Summation

CHAPTER **X**

Prophets for the Centuries

WE HAVE COME a long way in listening to the voices within the 66 chapters of Isaiah, voices which are both united and diverse: united in the common prophetic tradition they share, and diverse as they embody that tradition over the varied historical circumstances of several centuries.

There remain three questions to face, simple to pose, complex to answer. (1) How can we characterize that long prophetic tradition? (2) What has that tradition meant to later generations? (3) What can that tradition mean to us?

Let us first try to characterize the Isaianic tradition. At the beginning of our inquiry, in Chapter I, we took note that the phrase "the Holy One of Israel" recurs throughout the book of Isaiah.[1] The phrase may have originated in priestly circles in Jerusalem centered around the Davidic monarchy (it appears in Ps. 89:18—for the Davidic interest see vss. 3-4 there).[2] Isaiah, we learned in Chapter II, had an overwhelming experience of the transcendent specialness of God; he heard the seraphim singing "Holy, holy, holy is the Lord God of hosts." The phrase "Holy One of Israel," then, became for Isaiah a perfect affirmation of the transcendent specialness of God, and he made it a watchword in his oracles. Second Isaiah took it up (11 times in chapters 40-55), and so did Third Isaiah (twice in chapters 56-66). The phrase is splendid evidence for the existence of a particular prophetic tradition.

The tradition is united in the use it made of the image of God as king. The first Isaiah saw God the heavenly king looming far above the brutal power of the Assyrian king. Then Second Isaiah was able in his day to reassure Zion that

215

"your God reigns" (52:7—"reigns" and "king" are related words in Hebrew). The apocalyptic prophet of chapters 24-27 used the image of kingship once more when he anticipated a time when God would truly reign in Jerusalem after sun, moon, and stars are dimmed (24:23). (By contrast, one finds little or no use of this image in Jeremiah; there a controlling image is of God as husband, Jeremiah 3 and often, an image hardly found in the book of Isaiah.)

We have already noticed how Second Isaiah used the descriptions "high" and "lifted up" to refer to God's *servant*, using terms which the first Isaiah had reserved for God himself (compare 52:13 with 2:12 and 6:1; see Chapters I and VII). We may go on to observe that Third Isaiah balanced an affirmation that God is high and lofty in heaven with another that is at home with people of lowly and humble spirit (57:15).

We need not take time to document the concern of the whole of the book of Isaiah for Jerusalem and Zion, a concern found from the earliest (1:21-27) to the latest strata (26:1-6) of the book.

We know of the first Isaiah's concern for the Davidic monarch in Judah (chapter 7; 9:2-7, 11:1-9), but after the monarchy was gone, the tradition broadened out the images of human kingship in many ways. Thus Second Isaiah saw all Israel embodying God's covenant with David of old (55:3-5), but he called Cyrus of Persia God's "anointed" as well (45:1). Finally, Third Isaiah understood *himself* to be "anointed" to preach the good news (61:1).

But there is diversity within the tradition as well, most notably perhaps in the extent to which a prophet in the tradition understands the *current historical arena* to be the major stage on which God does his work. It was most so with the first Isaiah and the least so with the apocalyptic seers. We have taken note of this contrast at several points along the way, notably toward the end of Chapter VIII, but it will be helpful to summarize the matter here.

When we studied the first Isaiah, we were concerned with the headlines of his day so that we could make sense out of his words. But we observe that for Isaiah God was in no way *trapped* by the headlines; rather, God paradoxically weaves his own pattern and purpose *on the basis* of the headlines. Thus Assyria might do her best to terrorize the world and think that is that; but beyond her terrorizing and unbeknownst to her, God uses that terror to accomplish his own will (10:5-15).

By contrast, Second Isaiah's words do not speak often of the headlines. His words convince the hearer that the hills and valleys of this world are now to be transfigured by God's fresh presence. But there *is*, of course, one firm tie in his words to a headline, and that is Cyrus of Persia. It is that reference which anchors Second Isaiah's words to this world.

For Third Isaiah Cyrus has come and gone. The exiled people are home again all right, but home to the same old Jerusalem, and the priestly clique has taken over the same old temple area. Third Isaiah was thus torn between the marvel of Second Isaiah's visions on the one hand and the untransfigured reality of the Jerusalem before him on the other. Thus, he turned to glimpse a new heaven and a new earth in which Second Isaiah's words could be fulfilled. Third Isaiah was followed by others who depicted the new heaven and new earth with a variety of baroque details.

The successive prophets in the tradition vary, too, in their attention to their people's sins. The first Isaiah spoke steady words of judgment against the unjust people of his day: those who exploit the poor, those who corrupt the law courts, leaders who are drunk and disorderly. Then Second Isaiah is suddenly quiet on this issue: his focus is on God's coming act of deliverance of his people. Even his word against idolatry is not a word about people but about God. He mocks the building of idols as spurious divinities rather than uttering any judgment against Jews who might have been tempted to worship them.

Third Isaiah is concerned once more with obedience, but he perceives the community to be divided between the faithful like himself and his circle, and the unfaithful in the temple establishment. One hears from the apocalypticists no talk of social injustice, since they take it for granted that

God's people obey his law and that the problem is their need to be delivered from cruel oppressors.

These various voices within the book of Isaiah do not really *contradict* each other, for after all, the earlier words were kept even after later words were spoken. Even though Second Isaiah at some points suggests that the old is past and gone and to be replaced by the new (43:18), one has the impression that later generations heard the older words as carefully as they could even while giving fresh voice to their perception of God's ways with his people. Clearly, the tradition expressed in the book of Isaiah has offered a variety of perceptions in a richness that defies easy systematizing. We shall return to this matter at the end of the chapter.

A crucial turning-point came, perhaps in the latter half of the fifth century B.C.,[3] when the community ceased adding substantial material to the collection of Isaianic prophecy (though small editorial additions no doubt continued to be made). There was a basic shift of focus in the Jewish community. Ezra the scribe came west from Babylon to Jerusalem (Ezra 7:1-6) and gathered the community around the norms of the written tradition they had compiled, so that the emphasis was now no longer on a search for *fresh* revelation but rather on the meaning of the written deposits of revelation which were *already on hand*.[4] When the time came again for seers to proclaim apocalyptic visions, in the course of the second century B.C., such visions were circulated in fresh literary works rather than being incorporated into books already in circulation. The tradition of prophetic utterance associated with the name of Isaiah came to an end. Thus the question ceased to be "What would Isaiah say today?" and became instead "What do the lines of the book of Isaiah really mean?"—"what do they mean?" that is, in whatever circle of believers, in whatever century, the question was raised.

It is our question, too, of course; but an answer that deals only with the New Testament and with our modern perception would not be an adequate answer for us. Too many communities in too many centuries have listened to the lines of Isaiah and been sustained by them to limit their meaning to New Testament or modern times. Most notably, two separate streams of interpretation have existed, the Jewish and the Christian streams, and for almost all the last 20 centuries these communities have been foes over issues crystalized by the book of Isaiah. In our own day, thankfully, Jewish and Christian interpreters are sharing in biblical scholarship and are not at sword's point with each other, but the streams have been separate and both need attention. When we turn to look at the commentaries which both streams have produced, however, we find the number is immense, so that only the merest sample can be touched on here.

We begin with the Jewish tradition. From the pre-Christian era we have no full Jewish commentaries on Isaiah, but we do have hints of how the book was being interpreted by various circles within the Jewish community at that time.

In the last few centuries B.C. the Jews lost their fluency in Hebrew and began to use Aramaic, a sister language. As a result, there grew up a tradition of oral translations of Jewish scripture into Aramaic, which later became fixed in writing. For Isaiah it was not a word-for-word translation but more of a paraphrase, a paraphrase which offers us a window into Jewish understandings of the lines.[5] We have already taken note in Chapter II how this translation softened "I saw the Lord" in 6:1 to "I saw the glory of the Lord."

This Aramaic translation certainly does tone down the stark style of the first Isaiah. Thus the first two verses of the Song of the Vineyard (5:1-2) read this way:

> (1) The prophet said, I will now sing unto Israel—which is likened to a vineyard—the seed of Abraham my friend—a song of my friend touching his vineyard. My people—my beloved one is Israel—I gave them an inheritance in a lofty mountain, in a fat land. (2) And I sanctified them and honored them, and established them like the plant of a chosen vine; and I built my sanctuary among them; yea, I gave them my altar to make atonement for their sins; I said that they would do good deeds, but they did evil deeds.

We see that the suspense which Isaiah contrived, of saving till the last verse of the song the clue what the vineyard represents, is lost—now we learn the secret in the first verse. Isaiah's metaphor (Isaiah: "The vineyard of the Lord of hosts *is* the house of Israel," vs. 7) has now become a simile (translation: "Israel, which *is likened to* a vineyard," vs. 1). Then the translation confuses the simile: not only is Israel *like* a vineyard, Israel has also *been given* an inheritance on good land. Further, the details of Isaiah's metaphor are now identified allegorically: the watchtower has become the sanctuary, that is, the temple in Jerusalem; the wine vat is now the altar of the temple; the good grapes are good deeds and the wild grapes evil deeds. Isaiah's stunning poem is now pious uplift.

Chapter 53, in this translation, is equally diffuse. It refers the descriptions of the suffering servant of God, willy-nilly, to the kingdoms of the world *and* to Israel, leaving us disoriented. Thus "He was despised and rejected by men" in vs. 3 becomes "Then shall the glory of *all the kingdoms* be despised and come to an end," while "by oppression and judgment he has taken away" in vs. 8 becomes "out of chastisements and out of punishment shall he bring *our exiles* near." One can only imagine the enormous loss the Jewish community sustained when the old words of Isaiah were so weakened; yet we must bear in mind that the Jewish interpreters of that day *were* trying to make sense of the old words, in however inadequate a fashion.

In the last two centuries B.C. the community which produced the Dead Sea Scrolls, including the great Isaiah scroll described at the beginning of Chapter I, produced real commentary material for the passages of scripture which interested them the most. The so-called Caves 3 and 4 in that Dead Sea area have preserved a few scraps of a commentary (or commentaries) of theirs on passages of chapters 1, 5, 10, 11, 30, and 54 of Isaiah.[6]

Thus the commentary quotes the phrase in 54:11, "And I will lay your foundations with sapphires," and follows it with, "Interpreted, this concerns the priests and the people who laid the foundations of the Council of the Community . . . the congregation of his elect [shall sparkle] like a sapphire among stones." The "Community," of course, is a term for the membership of the Dead Sea sect itself.

After 30:15-18 is quoted, this interpretation appears: "Referring to the last days, this saying concerns the congregation of those who seek smooth things in Jerusalem." The phrase "those who seek smooth things in Jerusalem," an adaptation of 30:10, was evidently used by the sect to designate its enemies, the priestly class in Jerusalem in the second century B.C.

The sect interpreted 11:1-4 to refer to the Messiah to come: "Its interpretation concerns the shoot of David, who will arise at the end of days. . . ."

We see, then, that the Dead Sea sect used selected passages of Isaiah (and other biblical material, of course) to say, in effect: "These passages are talking about *our* group, or about *our* enemies, or about *our* future." This, of course, is what the New Testament community did too. But before we turn to the New Testament, let us pursue the Jewish use of Isaiah since the time of Jesus.

There was an enormous amount of commentary work on the Scriptures done by Jews in the medieval period.[7] Of the Jewish scholars in this period, three are outstanding: Rabbi Solomon ben Isaac, familiarly called "Rashi" from his initials, of Troyes (France), whose dates are 1040-1105; Abraham ben Meir Ibn Ezra, of Toledo (Spain), ca. 1090-1167; and Rabbi David Qimḥi (Kimchi), of Provence (southern France), 1160-1235. These scholars and their successors wrote verse-by-verse commentaries on large sections of the Old Testament, and these commentaries, written in Hebrew, are gathered together in great "Rabbinic Bibles,"[8] such as the Warsaw Bible (1874-77), a work of over four thousand pages.

We have already taken note of Ibn Ezra's hint that chapters 40-66 of Isaiah might not be attributed to the original Isaiah (see Chapter I, and note 9 there). But most of the material in these Jewish commentaries is not concerned with larger problems of theology or authenticity; instead, it deals verse by verse, often word by word, with difficult Hebrew expressions. With these matters we cannot linger, but we can at least see samples of their work on passages which Christians have assumed to refer to Jesus Christ.[9]

In dealing with 9:6-7, Rashi evidently believed the passage refers to King Hezekiah, but he also quotes another opinion that contradicts this. Here is the relevant portion of his discussion.

> *To us a child is born.* Though Ahaz [Hezekiah's father] is wicked, nevertheless his son, who is born to him many years later, shall be righteous, so that he may be king for us in his place. . . . *He shall call his name.* [This is the traditional Jewish reading, not "his name shall be called," as the *Revised Standard Version* has it.] The Holy One, blessed be He [the commentators' pious phrase for "God"], who is wonderful in counsel, and a strong God, and father for ever, shall call his name, that is, Hezekiah's name, "prince of peace," for peace and truth shall be in his days [39:8]. [Here Rashi takes the first three throne names as applying to God, and the fourth throne name to be the king's new name—and the Hebrew text can sustain this translation; and "prince of peace" he compares to the remark on Hezekiah in 39:8.]. . . *From this time forth and for evermore.* His future, that is, Hezekiah's, all his days; and in the same way we have found that Hannah said about Samuel: "And let him stay there for ever" [1 Sam. 1:22]. [Rashi argues that if "for ever" can be used for Samuel, who was not eternal, it could be used of the king in 9:7 as well, and therefore could refer to Hezekiah.]. . . *Will do this.* Ahaz was not worthy for such a purpose, and above all, the protecting influence of the Patriarchs had ceased. (There is a) Tosephta [a set of traditions of rabbis of the early centuries of the Christian era]: and our rabbis have said, the Holy One, blessed be He, sought to make Hezekiah Messiah, and make Sennacherib Gog and Magog [Ezek. 38-39]; but then the ministering angels before the Holy One, blessed be He, said, "Shall he who cut down the doors of the temple and sent them to the king of Assyria [2 Kings 18:16] be made Messiah?"

Rashi thus defends the identification of the king in 9:6-7 as Hezekiah, but still he quotes a contrary opinion that he was not worthy of the office, leaving us uncertain of his own decision on the matter.

Ibn Ezra and David Qimḥi both affirmed that the passage refers to Hezekiah. Qimḥi agreed with Rashi that only the fourth throne name refers to the king; Ibn Ezra, however, argues that all four names refer to Hezekiah.

In regard to 11:1-9, Ibn Ezra nicely balances two views:

> The majority of commentators apply this chapter to the Messiah, as if the prophet said, "The Assyrian army, which is now attacking Jerusalem, will perish"; but besides this partial deliverance, a time of complete redemption will come for Jerusalem. Rabbi Moses Hakkohen [Moses ibn Gikatilla, of Cordova, who lived in the latter part of the 11th century] refers the chapter to Hezekiah, on account of its being the continuation of the prophecy recorded in the preceding chapter.

In regard to 52:13-53:12, there is an old Jewish tradition that understands this passage to refer to the coming Messiah: indeed the (pre-Christian) Aramaic tradition, already discussed, renders "Behold, my servant shall prosper" (52:13) as "Behold, my servant Messiah shall prosper"; and many later Jewish commentators took his route.[10]

But the three commentators whom we have singled out saw themselves responding to Christian arguments, and all of them insisted that the passage describes Israel. Let Ibn Ezra speak for them all:

> The passage which follows offers great difficulties. The erring in spirit [his term for Christians] say that this alludes to their God [i.e. Jesus] and explain "my servant" to indicate his body. This is wrong; the body cannot "have understanding" [the Hebrew word "shall prosper," 52:13, may also mean "have understanding"] even during a person's lifetime. Again, what is the meaning of "he shall see his offspring, he shall prolong his days" [53:10]? He did not have a son, and he did not prolong his days. Again, "and he shall divide the spoil with the strong" [53:12]. But the best proof is in the preceding passage, "And the Lord will go forth before you" [52:12], where they are Israel; and afterward similarly, "Sing, O barren one" [54:1], where she is the congregation of Israel.

Ibn Ezra thus argues that both the preceding and following

passages refer to Israel, and that this indicates that 52:13-53:12 likewise refers to Israel.

We must not, however, assume that these three commentators had no place for a future Messiah; on the contrary, passage after passage in Isaiah is given just such a reference. For example, on 1:26, "And I will restore your judges as at first," David Qimḥi remarks, "This is like 'she that was full of justice' [vs. 21]. This will be in the days of the Messiah, when the wicked will be finished, all of them, and the remnant of Israel shall not do wrong nor speak lies."

It is not fair to sample these scholars on the basis of how they treat passages in Isaiah that have been called "Messianic." Their concern was not really with the *person* of the Messiah anyway, but rather with the nature of the marvelous *new age* which the Messiah would inaugurate, an age in which Israel would live at peace and the Messiah would rule as king.[11] One can affirm, then, that the book of Isaiah is beloved by the Jewish community because of the rich series of descriptions of the restoration of Israel as God's people which the book offers, to live and thrive in peace in a world which will know God's law and acknowledge him the ruler of all things.

We have noted the joining of Jewish and Christian work on the Old Testament in the modern period, so we must point out that current Jewish commentaries on Isaiah avail themselves of the kind of historical approach represented by this study guide.[12] Indeed Christians have benefited profoundly from Jewish teachers on the prophets. Listen to Abraham Heschel speak of Second Isaiah:

> In contrast to the books of the earlier prophets where the word of God speaks of Israel in the third person, now the Voice speaks to Israel directly in the second person. It is not a prophet speaking in His name; it is predominantly God addressing Himself to the people; it is I, not He. Prophetic receptivity is shared by all. Meaning is manifest, insight is common. It is as if in fulfillment of Moses' prayer, "Would that all the Lord's people were prophets, that the Lord would put His spirit upon them!" (Num. 11:29), Israel is declared to be God's spokesman, or prophet (49:2). Just as

the Lord said to Jeremiah, "I appointed you a prophet to the nations" (Jer. 1:5), He said to Israel, "I appointed you a light to the nations" (49:6).[13]

Now we must turn to the use Christians have made of the book of Isaiah. Instead of beginning our discussion with the New Testament, however, it is best to begin with the casual impressions Christians have. When I indicated recently to an acquaintance that I was writing a study guide on Isaiah, she asked, "Isn't that the prophet that predicted Jesus?" This impression, which is compounded by the use made of Isaiah in churches during Advent and Christmas, during Lent and Easter, and summarized by a line we have already quoted from the Christmas hymn "Lo, How a Rose E'er Blooming"—"Isaiah 'twas foretold it," is something we must explore.

Many Christians have been nurtured on Isaiah from the stated readings in their lectionaries, or from sermons preached on texts from Isaiah from time to time. But I suggest that for a majority of English-speaking Christians in our day, the message of Isaiah has been mediated most profoundly through Handel's *Messiah*. Several times in the course of this study we have mentioned having to turn our backs temporarily on that oratorio, but now it is time to turn and examine it.

Handel's *Messiah* consists of three parts: the Christmas section (selections 1-21, ending "His yoke is easy and his burthen is light"), concerned with Christ's birth; and the Easter section, in two parts—Part II, concerned with his passion (selections 22-44, ending with the "Hallelujah" chorus), and Part III, concerned with his resurrection (selections 45-53, ending with "Worthy is the Lamb," and the great "Amen" chorus).

The text of the work consists of verses from the Old and New Testaments. About 25 percent of the text is from the book of Isaiah, more than from any other biblical book. (The Psalms account for about 20 percent, 1 Corinthians 14 percent, and all other books less than 10 percent apiece.) The Isaiah material appears in the first two parts but not in the third.[14] Beyond the *quantity* of citations, however, it is clear on examination of the work that Part I is *structured* around Isaiah 40:1-11 (the verses stretch from selections 2 through 20), with the insertion of Isaiah 60:1-3 and 9:2-6 in the middle of that structure (selections 9 through 12) and other miscellaneous verses added. Part II, though more varied in its sources, *draws essentially from a sequence from Isaiah*—53:3-8 (selections 23-31) as well as a sequence from Psalm 2 (selections 40-43). The *Messiah*, then, draws the listener powerfully to four passages of Isaiah—9:2-6, 40:1-11, 53:3-8, and 60:1-3, in its presentation of the Christian message (as well as drawing on other single verses from Isaiah as well, such as 7:14).

It is crucial to understand the role of Handel's music in the explication of these verses. A live performance of the work is normally before an *audience*, and members of the audience are touched in all sorts of mutual ways by the music as the work progresses. Those who sing the work are to an even greater degree participants in an experience which far transcends the verbal "meaning" or "meanings" which a commentator provides a reader of the passages. Indeed, the music and one's memories of performances shared in are so built in to the text for many of us as to lead to that caution offered repeatedly in the course of this study to lay aside for the time being the musical lines of the *Messiah*.

What can be said about the meaning of the musical experience? At least three things. First, the weaving of texts together from the Old Testament and the New Testament, and the unity of Handel's style and musical conception, suggest to the listener the unity of God's work for us. Whatever God has done for us, he has done with a single purpose. The music moves on with steady beat and with that sense of order that is the great gift of the eighteenth century to us. The conductor is in control. The composer is in control. God is in control. God has always been in control, and he works his will from the wordless Overture (selection 1) through the reassurance of 40:1, "Comfort ye, my people" (selection 2), all the way to the vision of the culmination of all things enunciated in Revelation 5:12-13, "Worthy is the Lamb" (selection 53).

Second, one senses that the texts from Isaiah and elsewhere are not musically "dressed up," are not elaborated beyond their due; on the contrary they are given a musical setting appropriate to them, almost (by now) intrinsic to them. Thus selection 4, "And the Glory of the Lord," from 40:5, begins, after an instrumental introduction, with the alto section lining out the phrase, and is joined by the other three voices of the chorus. The parts now interweave the theme in various sequences to indicate musically the complexity and richness of God's "glory"; and then the same treatment is given to the phrase "and all flesh shall see it together, for the mouth of the Lord hath spoken it." The chorus ends, finally, in the last four measures, unanimously, in slow tempo: "hath spoken it"—for God is affirmed to have spoken once and for all.

Third, the total experience, though ostensibly a performance, an *esthetic, musical* experience, has become for its listeners a profoundly *religious* experience. It is performed in churches as well as in concert halls. The tradition is that at its first London performance in 1743, King George II spontaneously rose to his feet at the beginning of the "Hallelujah" chorus, and this custom has been followed by audiences ever since. The text of that chorus, though taken from Revelation 19:6, is most profoundly in consonance with the great call-vision of Isaiah in chapter 6. "Hallelujah: for the Lord God omnipotent reigneth!" It would take a heart of stone to remain unmoved by these words, by this music. One responds with wonder and adoration. In short, Handel's *Messiah* is a *liturgy* for Christians— not a liturgy which has evolved in the traditions of the church, but a liturgy from the creative impulse of a layperson, which has shaped more Christian hearts and minds than many an "official" liturgy has. This is a crucial matter, for the words of the book of Isaiah are not just words, and they are not intended simply to be a text deciphered by the scholar, a text explained in the classroom, a text argued over by the believer (important and necessary as these activities have become). The words are intended to be heard, experienced, and shared by the believing community as that com-

munity worships God and seeks his will for them. We have
indicated that this has been the case with the Jewish community, and now we see that for English-speaking
Christians it is true too—pre-eminently as set forth in
Handel's *Messiah.*

The *Messiah* uses 7:14, 9:2-6, 40:1-11, 53:3-8, and 60:1-3
as Christian proclamation, interweaving these texts with
New Testament ones like the infancy narrative from Luke 2
and the resurrection passage from 1 Corinthians 15:51-57.
What can we say about such use of Isaiah, given what we
have learned about the original thrust of such passages in
the course of this study?

Our first answer must be that we do this because the
New Testament does it. True enough; but when we turn to
the New Testament we find a surprising fact: the New
Testament cites not only the "favorite" texts from chapters
7, 9, 40, 53, and 60—it quotes quite massively from nearly
all parts of Isaiah. Of the 66 chapters of Isaiah, 53 are represented in New Testament quotations or reminiscences. I
count 298 quotations or reminiscences of material from
Isaiah in the New Testament. Only the book of Psalms edges
out the book of Isaiah in quantity of quotations in the New
Testament.[15] The New Testament, then, draws more richly
from Isaiah than we had realized; and so we ask, What does
the New Testament do with these *other* passages which we
would *not* consider "Messianic"?

St. Paul quotes 10:22, and then 1:9, in Romans 9:27,
29. Isaiah 10:22 reads, "For though your people Israel be
as the sand of the sea, only a remnant of them will return,"
and 1:9 reads, "If the Lord of hosts had not left us a few
survivors, we should have been like Sodom, and become like
Gomorrah." Paul uses these passages to remind his readers
that God never intended to include *all* Israelites in his rescue
operation, and this helps him understand what is behind
Israel's rejection of his gospel message in his own day.

Jesus uses phrases from the dirge over the fallen tyrant
(Isa. 14) to apply to the pride of the village of Capernaum
(Matt. 11:22, Luke 10:15), and the Revelation of St. John
(Rev. 8:10-11) uses another phrase from that dirge to

describe the fall of a star from heaven, though that star is evidently a fallen angel (compare the discussion of Isa. 24:21 in Chapter IX).

In short, the speakers and writers in the New Testament used passages from Isaiah quite freely in all sorts of ways, some of which seem appropriate to us who are familiar with the historical context of the passages (like Paul's use of "remnant" passages) and some of which seem more remote to us (like the use in Revelation of the fallen tyrant passage). But even this latter use of the fallen tyrant passage for a fallen angel makes sense if one believes absolutely in the reality of angels and believes furthermore that a fallen angel is a rebel against God.

The New Testament community, then, was so galvanized by the great news of God's deliverance of them through Jesus Christ that they insisted (in the same way as the Dead Sea sect had done earlier), "Now we *really* understand what the scriptures are talking about—they are talking about *us!*" And, among the scriptures, pre-eminently Isaiah.

Indeed, what the New Testament did with Isaiah is quite parallel to what Second Isaiah did with the first Isaiah. Second Isaiah was so galvanized by what God was about to do to liberate his people from the Babylonians through his anointed one Cyrus, that he could scarcely contain himself. The earlier Christians were so galvanized by what God had done to liberate his people from sin and death through his anointed one Jesus, that they could scarcely contain themselves. Both Second Isaiah and the New Testament confirm that God works in unprecedented ways to get his work done. Second Isaiah "piggy-backed" on the first Isaiah, and the New Testament "piggy-backed" on the book of Isaiah. We shall return to this matter in a moment.

A curious questions arises: why did the New Testament pay so much more attention to the book of Isaiah than, say, to the book of Jeremiah? There are no quotations of Jeremiah in Handel's *Messiah*. Though the book of Jeremiah is not much shorter than the book of Isaiah (52 chapters against 66), there are only about 60 citations of Jeremiah in

the New Testament (as against 298, we recall, for Isaiah).
Why?

For many reasons. For one thing, the bulk of the book
of Jeremiah is either biographical narrative about Jeremiah
or judgment oracles from Jeremiah; the New Testament
community could not use the details of Jeremiah's biography, and Jeremiah's words of judgment were not of prime
use in its proclamation of the gospel. The book of Isaiah
contains more material of "comfort," more material about
God's restoration of his people (most of chapters 40-66), and
this material was what became useful for preaching the
good news. Again, Isaiah's concern for kingship and for cult
is reflected in the New Testament transposition of these
themes into Christian categories.

We have traced Jewish commentaries on Isaiah; so likewise we must now take a sample of Christian commentary
work on the book. But where shall we begin?[16] No one
can master all the languages to compass all the Christian
commentaries on Isaiah—even for the ancient period there
are too many for us. For that period we must be content to
name a few and look at one, and then we must hurry on
and look at one only from the period of the Protestant
Reformation.

For the Greek fathers there is a commentary by Eusebius
of Caesarea (ca. 260-340) which survives.[17] For the Latin
fathers, there is a commentary by St. Jerome (ca. 340-420),[18]
who translated the whole Bible into Latin, the translation
(called the "Vulgate") which became standard for Roman
Catholics until the modern period.

For an example of Jerome's work, let us choose 11:10.
This verse has had a curious history. Its Hebrew text is
much as the *Revised Standard Version* gives it: "In that day
the root of Jesse shall stand as an ensign to the peoples; him
shall the nations seek, and his dwellings [literally 'his rest'
or 'his resting-place'] shall be glorious." The ancient Greek
translation gave a different meaning to "stand as an
ensign"—and it was in that Greek form that St. Paul had
quoted it in Romans 15:12, applying it to Jesus Christ.
Jerome rightly turned his back on the Greek rendering and

returned to the original Hebrew text; but, convinced along with Paul that the verse refers to Christ (as he and other Christians assumed 11:1-9 did also), he saw the "ensign" as the Cross. Therefore, Jerome translated "his rest" in the last line as "his tomb": "In that day the root of Jesse, who stands as [or 'in respect to'] a sign of the peoples, him the Gentiles shall beseech, and *his tomb* shall be glorious."

In his commentary on this passage Jerome remarks, "The sense is: his death shall be glorious, so that what he prayed in the gospel might be fulfilled, 'Father, glorify me with the glory which I had with thee before the world was made' [John 17:5]."

On the other hand, Jerome was quite capable of applying prophetic words of woe to the situation in his own day. On 5:11, "Woe to those who rise early in the morning, that they may run after strong drink, who tarry late into the evening till wine inflames them!" he writes, "Those who do these things do not look at the work of the Lord nor consider what is to come. Let us apply this testimony to the princes of the Church, who rise early in the morning to run after strong drink and to drink until the evening."[19]

There are other commentaries in the farther reaches of the church—for example, the commentary on Isaiah in Syriac by Ishodad of Merv (a bishop in the middle of the ninth century in the eastern part of Iran),[20] and the commentary on Isaiah in Armenian by Mekhitar Kosh (an authority on civil and canon law, who lived in what is now southern Turkey in the last part of the 12th century)[21]—which no doubt hold great riches if we could master them.

In the period of the Protestant Reformation John Calvin (1509-64) wrote commentaries on almost every book of the Bible, and they are still used extensively, and rightly so. Again one quotation must suffice from the almost 1900 published pages of his commentary on Isaiah.[22] Let this comment be from the other end of the book of Isaiah, namely, on 61:1: "The Spirit of the Lord God is upon me, because the Lord has anointed me to bring good tidings to the afflicted. . . ." Calvin writes:

As Christ explains this passage with reference to himself
(Luke 4:18), so commentators limit it to him without hesi-
tation, and lay down this principle, that Christ is introduced
as speaking, as if the whole passage related to him alone. The
Jews laugh at this, as an ill-advised application to Christ of
that which is equally applicable to other prophets. My opinion
is, that this chapter is added as a seal to the former [i.e.
chapter 60], to confirm what had hitherto been said about
restoring the Church of Christ; and that for this purpose
Christ testifies that he has been anointed by God, in consequence of which he justly applies this prophecy to himself,
for he has exhibited clearly and openly what others have laid
down in an obscure manner. But *this is not inconsistent with
the application* of this statement *to other prophets*, whom the
Lord has anointed; for they did not speak in their own name as
individuals, or claim this authority for themselves, but were
chiefly employed in pointing out the *office* of Christ, to whom
belongs not only the publication of these things, but likewise
the accomplishment of them. This chapter ought, therefore, to
be understood in such a sense that Christ, who is the Head of
the prophets, holds the chief place, and alone makes all those
revelations; but that *Isaiah and the other prophets*, and the
apostles, *contribute their services to Christ*, and each performs
his part in making known Christ's benefits. And thus we see
that those things which Isaiah said would be accomplished by
Christ have now been actually accomplished [emphasis mine].

It is a subtle argument: *both* Isaiah *and* Christ; not at all
the kind of "either/or" position which too many Christians
have taken.[23]

Since the New Testament uses Isaiah extensively to proclaim the Christian message, and Christian commentators
have done likewise, how are *we* to understand the material
of the book of Isaiah? What does it mean to us?

Many years ago I was teaching an introductory course
in the Old Testament to first-year college students, and I
dealt with Isaiah 9:2-7 in much the same way presented in
this study guide in Chapter V: that "to us a child is born" is
most likely to have been a coronation ode for a king of
Judah. But then, a couple of weeks before Christmas, I
shared in a pre-Christmas candlelight service in the chapel,
and I read that passage in the context of the Christmas

story. The next morning several students cornered me and said, "You're a traitor! That was a cop-out last night." My self-defense, I recall, was again along the lines suggested in Chapter V: that the passage is about a new king, indeed a new king described in ideal terms, and that Christians, whose testimony is among other things about the ideal king whom we know as Lord, are justified in using the passage in Isaiah to resonate with Christian proclamation, indeed as an integral part of Christian proclamation.

I would maintain that the old easy answer, namely, that the prophets predicted the coming of Jesus Christ, is not adequate; we explored this matter at the beginning of Chapter V. But I also affirm the relevance of texts from Isaiah to Christian proclamation. How is this possible? The answer I can give here is not a thorough one, but may at least be suggestive. I suggest that no *one* overall formula is possible, but that actually Christians use different texts in many different (if related) ways. Jews have done so, too, of course. Most of what I am about to say is applicable only to Christians, but some of it is applicable to Jews as well.

(1) *Jesus used a few passages* from Isaiah himself, according to our record, *to talk about his own mission*, or to understand his own mission. Among these, we have seen, are 61:1-2a, according to Luke 4:18-19 (compare our discussion of the passage in Chapter VIII). Third Isaiah saw himself bringing good news to the outcasts, but Jesus took up the task and did it far better than Third Isaiah could, so that he becomes for us the embodiment of God's mission to those outcasts. Calvin is right in saying that the passage is *both* a reference to the prophet who enunciated it *and* to Christ. The prophet proclaimed Christ in the sense that he set forth God's will to announce good news to the poor. Jesus chose this task for himself, and we honor it, as Jesus did, by a word from Third Isaiah. In much the same way Jesus seems to have used 52:13-53:12 as a description of his mission (compare Chapter VII). Not every detail fits, as Ibn Ezra pointed out, for Jesus did not have children. But the general description of a servant who suffers and dies vicariously for the sins of the world was one which Jesus

voluntarily undertook. So again, what Second Isaiah announced as a job to be done Jesus lived out deliberately. Of
course these passages describe him; he saw to it that they
did.

(2) Occasionally an *early Christian translator translated
some word or other* in Isaiah to betoken the gospel story: so
Jerome with "his tomb" in 11:10. This translation was carried over into English Roman Catholic Bibles such as the
Douay Version (1609), and even Ronald Knox's translation
(1950) hints at this interpretation ("where he rests in glory,"
with a footnote on Jerome), but more recent Roman
Catholic versions (the *Jerusalem Bible,* the *New American
Bible*) have translated the Hebrew correctly. Such translations are part of the Christian past but are not relevant to
the Christian present.

(3) The New Testament writers, particularly the gospel
writers, know Isaiah in the ancient Greek translation, not in
Hebrew, and the Greek is not always as close to the Hebrew
as one could wish. Thus, one is faced with a dilemma when
the New Testament uses a Greek rendering *which is not
close to Isaiah's Hebrew.* The most signal example, of
course, is 7:14, where the Hebrew "young woman" has
become "virgin" in the Greek translation, which Matthew
then used. We discussed the matter thoroughly in Chapter
IV. One can assign credit (or blame) on this matter in a
variety of ways. We could say, The Greek translation, and
therefore Matthew, misunderstood Isaiah; or we could say,
God intended the shift in translation to lend resonance to
the Christian witness to the virgin birth. Whatever we say,
we must affirm, I believe, that Matthew found a meaning
in the verse which we can relate only with difficulty to the
rest of the context of chapter 7 of Isaiah which describes
Isaiah's meeting with King Ahaz.

(4) Both Jesus and the various New Testament writers
used phrases and ideas from the book of Isaiah to lend
images and metaphors to their own discourse. Jesus said,
"Behold I saw Satan fall like lightning from heaven." There
is no way of course to know whether he used Isaiah 14 only

as an analogy ("I saw Satan fall the way the prophet saw the tyrant fall") or as a real interpretation ("the prophet really means that Satan's rule is finished"). But it is not surprising that a community so saturated with the words of scripture would weave them in all kinds of ways into its discourse.

(5) There are *general theological themes* which recur in both Isaiah and in the New Testament, so it is not surprising that the words of Isaiah would be used to reinforce the gospel story. Thus Second Isaiah begins with *"Comfort, comfort* my people," with the news of the people's liberation from Babylon; but since, as we know, the New Testament word is likewise a word of liberation from sin and death, Handel's *Messiah* uses the passage justifiably to begin its array of texts. Again, Jesus, in describing the coming kingdom, says, "Many will come from east and west and sit at table with Abraham. . ." (Matt. 8:11). It is likely that this is a reminiscence of Isaiah 49:12, "Lo, these shall come from afar, and lo, these from the north and from the west." Second Isaiah had anticipated a general return of exiles from all points of the compass when Cyrus came. In the minds of later prophets and seers, that general return was postponed and became part of the expectation for the new age, an expectation in which Jesus shared.

There are other theological themes common to both Isaiah and the New Testament. Isaiah has words of *judgment*, and we have seen how Paul used two "remnant" passages (10:22 and 1:9) to speak of Jews who had rejected the gospel message (Rom. 9:27, 29). Again, there is much in the first Isaiah about *kingship*, and his words in 9:2-7 and 11:1-9, disencumbered of their military and administrative overtones, have been used to proclaim the lordship of Christ.

(6) Words either of comfort or of judgment in Isaiah are always *applicable within Jewish and Christian communities*. The words of Isaiah are not simply appropriate to the task of setting forth the meaning of Jesus' coming on the lips of members of Christian communities—they are applicable

by both Jews and Christians to their own various needs. "Mister Dooley," the creation of the nineteenth-century American humorist Finley Peter Dunne, once asserted that the task of a newspaper was to "comfort the afflicted and to afflict the comfortable." It would be hard to find a more succinct definition of the prophet's task. Thus, Jerome found Isaiah's words about drunken leaders applicable to the princes of the church of his day. The temptation to idolatry is always with us (compare the remarks on modern idolatries in Chapter VII). On the other hand, how many lonely Jewish or Christian congregations have heard the good news that their own desert will be pools of water (41:18), that their own thorns will be replaced by cypresses (55:13)? And for those communities who take seriously God's word that there will come a time of summing-up, a righting of wrongs, a last judgment, a new heaven and new earth—however perceived—then words from the book of Isaiah which depict such a summing-up will build up the community of faith which looks to that future with hope.

We may go on to say that the descriptions in the book of Isaiah of God's restoration of his people (whether heard in the present tense or the future tense) will always be more vivid to Jews, whose heritage includes the Hebrew language and Hebrew thought-forms, than they will be to Christians, who must find ways to translate "Israel" into "church" (compare Paul, in Gal. 6:16, who calls the church "the Israel of God"). In his letter to the Romans, Paul uses the metaphor of an olive tree, whose root and branch are Israel; onto this olive tree a wild olive shoot (the Gentiles) has been grafted (Rom. 11:17-24). Gentile Christians are an alien branch, nothing more.

(7) *Everybody has been selective* in his or her use of Isaiah. This is part of the difficulty between Jews and Christians, for both communities have been selective, but have to some degree selected different texts for their own self-understanding and their understanding of God and his work. Handel's *Messiah* uses 9:2 and 6, but not vss. 3-5. Most Christians who use the passage at Christmas time are a

bit startled at vss. 3-5, and students are even more surprised at the whole passage when they read it line by line for total meaning instead of listening with Christmas audio-filters. The New Testament is selective, for although it may have quoted from 298 verses and groups of verses in Isaiah, Isaiah contains 1292 verses. So if we are to do any more with the book of Isaiah than to use it simply as a source for verses for the New Testament, then we must see it whole, see it as a work in itself. That is what we have attempted to do in this study.

(8) *Jews and Christians have had an immense advantage* in recent years that no scripture reader of earlier times had: *the chance to hear these words in* something like *their original historical setting.* The disciplines of history, archeology, and language study have helped us reconstruct the world of Isaiah and his successors so that we can begin to hear the old words in their original context. In this way many more verses in Isaiah come alive than the New Testament was able to use.

I am convinced that it is part of the providence of God that we are able in our own day to avail ourselves of these historical reconstructions of the scholars. People who are shaped by the biblical faith, whether Jewish or Christian, have always been convinced that God has revealed himself through history. The more history we can learn, then, the more we may understand the God who revealed himself through that history. By learning some of the history of those far-off days we can begin to hear the old words in the way they were first heard.

The meanings of the old texts are not exhausted by this kind of historical inquiry into their original context. We have just affirmed this by our exploration of later translations, commentaries, and meditations on the words. Many of the words are so luminous with meaning that fresh luster is seen in them by later generations. But the fact that God has spoken in Jesus Christ must not blind us to his earlier speaking. We began our quest when we saw Isaiah's lips being purified so that he might speak for God (6:5-8). We end as we began, seeking to understand the process of God's speaking.

We ended Chapter I by citing the first verse of the letter to the Hebrews: "In many and various ways God spoke of old to our fathers by the prophets"; but the phrase continues in vs. 2: "but in these last days he has spoken to us by a Son." The whole mystery of old words lasting through history in fresh contexts for new communities is perfectly summed up by these words. God spoke; he has spoken. It is the same God who speaks through both the Old Testament and the New. Handel's *Messiah* portrays this witness most powerfully in its interweaving of Old and New Testament texts. "The mouth of the Lord has spoken" (40:5). Although it is the same God, and the same kind of self-disclosure—speaking—the channels for his speaking are distinctive in the two testaments: God spoke *of old to our fathers through the prophets; but now* he has spoken *to us by a Son*. It is appropriate, then, that we understand the book of Isaiah as a book preserved by ancient Israel, to be read on its own terms. But even more, *in many and various ways* God spoke of old to our fathers through the prophets. This is true, we have discovered, not only for the Old Testament as a whole, but for the book of Isaiah itself. Within the single book God spoke in many and various ways through several prophets.

These prophets were prophets not for their centuries alone, but for the centuries that came after them, and even for our own century, if we will but listen. They have spoken for God, whose will it is to speak to us—the God whose will is accomplished within history, and beyond history—the God in whose grasp the past, the present, and the future cohere.

Further Reading

*I*T IS CLEAR TO the reader by now that the book of
Isaiah has produced an enormous literature, but much
of it is by now out of date, or is uncritical in its approach—
or both; or else it is forbiddingly technical. Here are some
suggestions, however, which may be helpful to the reader
who would like to go further.

In the realm of commentaries, verse by verse and
chapter by chapter, the most thorough and balanced work,
up to the minute, for Isaiah 1-39, is in German and is not
yet complete: Hans Wildberger, *Jesaja* (Biblischer Kommentar, Altes Testament 10; Neukirchen-Vluyn: Neukirchener
Verlag, 1972-). At the time of this writing (early 1977),
Wildberger's work has reached 19:25. For chapters 40-66,
the corresponding commentary is equally good but even less
complete: Karl Elliger, *Jesaja II* (Biblischer Kommentar,
Altes Testament 11; Neukirchen-Vluyn: Neukirchener Verlag,
1970-). At the time of this writing, Elliger's work has reached
44:8.

Focusing less on the minute details of the Hebrew text
and more on general meaning are two German commentaries which fortunately have been translated into English:
Otto Kaiser, *Isaiah 1-12* (Philadelphia: Westminster, 1972)
and *Isaiah 13-39* (Philadelphia: Westminster, 1974); and
Claus Westermann, *Isaiah 40-66* (Philadelphia: Westminster, 1969). For someone without advanced training who
reads only English, these works give by far the most well-
rounded guidance to the book of Isaiah now available. It
must be stated, however, that Kaiser's theories (in his *Isaiah
13-39*) of multiple redactors and his dating of various passages

is not always convincing, at least to me.

The most detailed work in English on matters of the text of Isaiah is now out of date, but still contains much useful material. It is in the International Critical Commentary series: George B. Gray, *The Book of Isaiah*, Vol. I (New York: Scribner, 1912). This volume covers only chapters 1-27; unfortunately, Gray's work on chapters 28-39, and the work projected by A.S. Peake on chapters 40-66, never appeared.

The introduction and commentary material in *The Interpreter's Bible* 5 (New York: Abingdon, 1956), by R.B.Y. Scott for chapters 1-39 (pp. 149-381) is excellent, though not as full as one might wish, and also now to some degree out of date. The material in that volume by James Muilenburg for chapters 40-66 (pp. 381-773) is superb, particularly in his sensitivity to poetic and rhetorical features.

There are many other good treatments, chapter by chapter, which are more concise and less detailed. I shall mention three: Frederick L. Moriarty, S.J., and Carroll Stuhlmueller, C.P., in *The Jerome Biblical Commentary* (Englewood Cliffs, NJ: Prentice-Hall, 1968), I, pp. 265-82 and 366-86; Peter R. Ackroyd, "The Book of Isaiah" in *The Interpreter's One-Volume Commentary on the Bible* (New York: Abingdon, 1971), pp. 329-71; and two little volumes in the Cambridge Bible Commentary on the New English Bible (New York: Cambridge University Press), both by A.S. Herbert: *The Book of the Prophet Isaiah, Chapters 1-39* (1973), and *The Book of the Prophet Isaiah 40-66* (1975).

Two thorough and accessible background articles on the book of Isaiah may be mentioned: C.R. North, "Isaiah," in *The Interpreter's Dictionary of the Bible* (New York: Abingdon, 1962), 2, pp. 731-44, with full bibliography; and an up-date on this material, James M. Ward, "Isaiah," in *The Interpreter's Dictionary of the Bible, Supplementary Volume* (New York: Abingdon, 1976), pp. 456-61, again with bibliography.

There are many works on the Old Testament prophets in general; one in particular is well worth perusing:

Abraham Heschel, *The Prophets* (New York: Harper & Row, 1962; paper: Vol. I, 1969; Vol. II, 1975). More demanding is Gerhard von Rad, *The Message of the Prophets* (New York: Harper and Row, 1972 [paper]). This book is a translation from German and is a revision of the second volume of his *Old Testament Theology;* that second volume appeared in English from New York (Harper and Row, 1965). Von Rad has a chapter on each of the prophets: chapter 12 is "Isaiah and Micah," chapter 17 is "Deutero-Isaiah" (Second Isaiah), and chapter 19 is "The Prophets of the Later Persian Period," including "Trito-Isaiah" (Third Isaiah).

But of course "of making many books there is no end" (Eccl. 12:12), so the student should be guided by the bibliographies found in works such as those cited here for still further investigation.

Notes

Foreword

1. *Jeremiah: Spokesman Out of Time* (New York: The Pilgrim Press, 1974).
2. *Acta Sanctae Sedis* XLI (1908), pp. 613-14; compare Thomas Aquinas Collins, O.P., and Raymond E. Brown, S.S., in *The Jerome Biblical Commentary* (Englewood Cliffs, NJ: Prentice-Hall, 1968), II, pp. 629-30.
3. See Collins and Brown in *The Jerome Biblical Commentary*, II, pp. 624-32; and Carroll Stuhlmueller, C.P., in *The Jerome Biblical Commentary*, I, pp. 366-86.
4. *The Book of Isaiah* (Philadelphia: Jewish Publication Society, 1973).

Chapter I

1. Now renamed the Albright Institute of Archaeological Research.
2. Frank M. Cross, Jr., "The Development of the Jewish Scripts," in G. Ernest Wright (ed.), *The Bible and the Ancient Near East* (New York: Doubleday, 1961), p. 167.
3. New York: Abingdon, 1957.
4. Bleddyn J. Roberts, *The Old Testament Text and Versions* (Cardiff: University of Wales Press, 1951), p. 80.
5. Otto Eissfeldt, *The Old Testament, An Introduction* (Oxford: Blackwell, 1965), p. 641; James A. Sanders, "The Dead Sea Scrolls — A Quarter Century of Study," *The Biblical Archaeologist* 36 (1973), p. 136.
6. For a discussion of the matter, see C.H. Roberts, "Books in the Graeco-Roman World and in the New Testament," in *The Cambridge History of the Bible*, I (Cambridge University Press, 1970), pp. 55-58.

7. Some of the following analysis can be found in R.B.Y. Scott, in *The Interpreter's Bible* 5 (New York: Abingdon, 1956), p. 158.

8. Otto Kaiser, *Isaiah 1-12* (Philadelphia: Westminster, 1972); Hans Wildberger, *Jesaja* (Biblischer Kommentar, Altes Testament 10; Neukirchen-Vluyn, Germany: Neukirchener Verlag, 1972-).

9. The relevant passage occurs in his commentary on Isaiah at the head of his remarks on chapter 40: "About the last section [or 'half'] of the book there is no doubt that it refers to a period yet to come, as I shall explain. [He nowhere expands on this point.] It must be borne in mind that the opinion of the orthodox, that the book of Samuel [i.e. 1 and 2 Samuel] was written by Samuel, is correct as regards the first part, till the words 'and Samuel died' [1 Sam. 25:1]." The implication of course is that the same pattern of "half-way" authorship which he discerned in 1 and 2 Samuel prevails for the book of Isaiah. For the English translation of Ibn Ezra, see M. Friedländer, *The Commentary of Ibn Ezra on Isaiah: Translation* (London, 1873): see p. 170.

10. See James Muilenburg, in *Interpreter's Bible* 5, p. 382.

11. This is implied by his description of a paper he had submitted to a biblical journal on the authorship of Isaiah, in his *The Unity of Isaiah in the Light of Statistical Linguistics* (Hildesheim, Germany: Gerstenberg, 1973), p. 20.

12. See repeated indications in his *Unity*, especially pp. 21-22.

13. More technically, nouns with possessive suffixes.

14. The data are set forth most conveniently in Y.T. Radday, "Two Computerized Statistical-Linguistic Tests Concerning the Unity of Isaiah," *Journal of Biblical Literature*, 1970, p. 322. The same material is found in his *Unity*, pp. 132-34.

15. See his "Two Computerized . . . Tests," p. 324.

16. In fairness it should be recorded that another student has recently challenged Radday's results: L.L. Adams, *A Statistical Analysis of the Book of Isaiah*, an unpublished dissertation submitted at Brigham Young University, 1971. From the published summary, it would appear that Adams confined himself to such linguistic tests as were not contrastive for the different sections of the book of Isaiah. See *Dissertation Abstracts* XXXII A (1972) 4701-A. Adams had access to Radday's preliminary publications, including "Two Computerized . . . Tests," but not his complete study (*Unity*), published in 1973.

17. In Isaiah 1-39: 1:4, 5:19, 24, 10:20, 12:6, 17:7, 29:19, 30:11, 12, 15, 31:1, 37:23. In Isaiah 40-55: 41:14, 16, 20, 43:3, 14, 45:11, 47:4, 48:17, 49:7, 51:5, 54:5, 55:5. In Isaiah 56-66: 60:9, 14. Elsewhere: 2 Kings 19:22; Psalms 71:22, 78:41, 89:18; Jer. 51:5.

18. For example, James D. Smart, *History and Theology in Second Isaiah* (Philadelphia: Westminster, 1965).

19. To return to Radday's work with the computer once more, it is only fair to record that he sees the first Isaiah as writing all or most of chapters 1-35, a second prophet writing chapters 40-48, and a third prophet writing chapters 49-66 (*Unity*, pp. 274-77). He evidently worked with various groupings of chapters within 40-66—(1) 40-48, 49-57, and 58-66; (2) 49-55 and 56-66; (3) 40-55 and 56-66; (4) 57-66 (*Unity*, p. 77), and he finally settled on grouping (1). His statistical analyses are cogent for this grouping, but he does not publish his analyses for contrary groupings in most of his tests (sentence-length is the only test for which he offers comparable data for contrary groupings: *Unity*, pp. 77-88). He concludes his whole study: "Chaps. 49-57 and 58-66 display so many affinities with each other and so few with the rest of the book that one has to attribute them to yet another prophet" (*Unity*, p. 277). Those who are inclined to follow Radday's division should read the discussion of the first half of Chapter VII of the present study as the thinking of *Second* Isaiah (the passages which mock idols are found within the compass of chapters 40-48 only), and the discussion of the second half of Chapter VII as the thinking of *Third* Isaiah (only the first "Servant Song" comes before chapter 49, and this Song is discussed in Chapter VI). But I am not convinced by Radday's grouping of his data; the *contents* of chapters 49-57 divide best into 49-55, attributed to Second Isaiah, and 56-57, attributed to Third Isaiah, as most scholars agree.

20. Scholars disagree on this one. Wildberger defends its authenticity, while Kaiser challenges it. For bibliography both for and against, see Kaiser, *Isaiah 1-12*, p. 25, note a. For a good summary of arguments against authenticity, see E. Cannawurf, "The Authenticity of Micah IV 1-4," *Vetus Testamentum*, 1963, pp. 26-33.

Chapter II

1. I follow John Bright, *A History of Israel* (Philadelphia: Westminster, 1972), p. 254. The data given in 2 Kings 15:1-2 need some adjustment. Kaiser, *Isaiah 1-12*, gives slightly different dates. For a thorough discussion of this chronological problem, see John Gray, *I & II Kings* (Philadelphia: Westminster, 1970), pp. 65-66, 75.

2. See J.F. Stenning, *The Targum of Isaiah* (Oxford University Press, 1949). For further discussion of this Aramaic trans-

lation of Isaiah, see Chapter X.

3. Frank M. Cross, Jr., *Canaanite Myth and Hebrew Epic* (Cambridge, MA: Harvard University Press, 1973), p. 16.

4. This was first pointed out by George Mendenhall, *Law and Covenant in Israel and in the Ancient Near East* (Pittsburgh: The Biblical Colloquium, 1955); see also, most conveniently, his "Covenant," *Interpreter's Dictionary of the Bible* (New York: Abingdon, 1962), I, pp. 716-21.

5. New York: Macmillan, 1953.

6. For a reproduction, see James B. Pritchard, *The Ancient Near East in Pictures Relating to the Old Testament* (Princeton: Princeton University Press, 1954), p. 214, No. 655.

7. Helmer Ringgren, *Israelite Religion* (Philadelphia: Fortress Press, 1966), pp. 68-69.

8. So Walter Baumgartner, *Hebräisches und Aramäisches Lexikon zum Alten Testament* (Leiden: Brill, 1967-), p. 60; Wildberger, *Jesaja;* Kaiser, *Isaiah 1-12.*

9. So Baumgartner, *Lexikon*, p. 216.

10. The basic work on the matter for the Amorites is in German, Friedrich Ellermeier, *Prophetie in Mari und Israel* (Herzberg, Germany: Erwin Jungfer, 1968); there is an extensive review of this work by Stanley D. Walters in *Journal of Biblical Literature*, 1970, pp. 78-81. More convenient is Herbert Huffmon, "Prophecy in the Mari Letters," *Biblical Archaeologist*, 1968, pp. 101-24, reprinted in Edward F. Campbell, Jr., and David N. Freedman (eds.), *The Biblical Archaeologist Reader 3* (Garden City, NY: Doubleday Anchor, 1970), pp. 199-224. For the Canaanites, see the amusing incident in the Egyptian Wen-Amun narrative, most accessible in James Pritchard, *Ancient Near Eastern Tests Relating to the Old Testament* (Princeton: Princeton University Press, 1955), p. 26 (lines 35-41); and see commentary on this passage in Johannes Lindblom, *Prophecy in Ancient Israel* (Oxford: Blackwell, 1963), pp. 29-30.

11. See Hermann L. Strack and Paul Billerbeck, *Kommentar zum Neuen Testament aus Talmud und Midrasch* (Munich: C.H. Beck, 1956), I, pp. 662-63; compare Charles E. Carlston, *The Parables of the Triple Tradition* (Philadelphia: Fortress Press, 1975), pp. 106, 107, and notes 29 and 30 there.

12. So Abraham Heschel, *The Prophets* (New York: Harper and Row, 1962), p. 90; so also, earlier, H. Hackmann, *Die Zukunftserwartung des Jesaja*, 1883, cited in George Buchanan Gray, *The Book of Isaiah*, International Critical Commentary (New York: Scribner, 1912), p. 110.

13. So H. Ewald, *Die Propheten des Alten Bundes*, 1867-68, cited in G.B. Gray, *The Book of Isaiah*, p. 110.

14. So Edwin M. Good, *Irony in the Old Testament* (London: S.P.C.K., 1965), pp. 136-37.

15. For a sensible approach to the passage, see James M. Ward, *Amos and Isaiah* (New York: Abingdon, 1969), pp. 154-58.

16. For such a reading, see the references in Wildberger, *Jesaja*, p. 234, under 13b.

17. For a careful reexamination of the evidence, see Carlston, *Parables*, pp. 97-109.

18. I have been unable to locate a citation to this precise phrase, which has become the standard way to refer to Tillich's designation of God. The phrase "ground of being," to designate God, is found in his *Systematic Theology*, Vol. I (Chicago: University of Chicago Press, 1951), p. 156; the phrase "the ground of everything that is" is found in his *Systematic Theology*, Vol. II (Chicago: University of Chicago Press, 1957), p. 8.

19. On this matter see Brevard S. Childs, *Isaiah and the Assyrian Crisis*, Studies in Biblical Theology 2nd Series, 3 (Naperville, IL: Allenson, 1967), pp. 73-103.

20. In "The Martyrdom of Isaiah"; see R.H. Charles, *The Apocrypha and Pseudepigrapha of the Old Testament* (Oxford: Oxford University Press, 1913), II, pp. 155-62, and Eissfeldt, *The Old Testament, An Introduction*, p. 609.

Chapter III

1. For the whole image of the cosmic lawcourt, see B. Gemser, "The *Rîb*- or Controversy-Pattern in Hebrew Mentality," *Supplements to Vetus Testamentum* 3 (Leiden: Brill, 1960), pp. 120-37, especially 128-33.

2. This point of view is that of H.H. Rowley, "The Meaning of Sacrifice in the Old Testament," *Bulletin of the John Rylands Library* 33 (1950), pp. 74-110, reprinted in his *From Moses to Qumran: Studies in the Old Testament* (London: Lutterworth, 1963), pp. 67-107—see especially pp. 84-90, and the note and bibliography there. See also his *The Unity of the Bible* (London: Carey Kingsgate, 1953), pp. 30-39, and compare T.H. Gaster, "Sacrifices," *Interpreter's Dictionary of the Bible* 4, p. 157.

3. John MacDonald, in *Journal of Near Eastern Studies*, 1976, pp. 147-70.

4. Compare Roland de Vaux, *Ancient Israel, Its Life and Institutions* (London: Darton, Longman & Todd, 1961), pp. 69-72.

5. So Kaiser, *Isaiah 1-12*, and so the *Jerusalem Bible* and the *New English Bible*.

6. See my *Jeremiah: Spokesman*, pp. 110-13, regarding Jer.

30:5-7 + 10-11, and 12-15 + 16-17.

7. W.W. Hallo, "Isaiah 28:9-13 and the Ugaritic Abecedaries," *Journal of Biblical Literature*, 1958, pp. 337-38.

8. So Kaiser, *Isaiah 1-12*, p. 60.

9. See, for example, Cyrus H. Gordon, *Ugaritic Textbook* (Rome: Pontifical Biblical Institute, 1965), p. 183, text 77, lines 22-23; for a convenient translation of these lines, see G.R. Driver, *Canaanite Myths and Legends* (Edinburgh: T. & T. Clark, 1956), p. 125, "Nikkal and the Kathirat," lines 22-23.

10. Compare the discussion of this verb in Walther Zimmerli, *Man and his Hope in the Old Testament*, Studies in Biblical Theology 2nd Series, 20 (London: SCM Press, 1971), p. 97.

11. *The Book of Isaiah* (London: Isaac Pitman & Sons, 1908), p. 41.

12. *Die Heilige Schrift des Alten und Neuen Testaments*, *Zürcher Bibel* (Zürich: Verlag der Zwingli-Bibel, 1954).

Chapter IV

1. A.M. Honeyman has suggested that Pekah took over the name, perhaps the throne-name of his predecessor, when he took over the throne; see Honeyman in *Journal of Biblical Literature*, 1948, p. 24, and see Bright, *History of Israel*, p. 270, note 5.

2. The name, as we know from Assyrian sources, was *Razion*, which in its Aramaic form would mean "agreeable." "Rezin" in Aramaic might mean "[people] who are crushed"; for the suggestion of a parody here, which is that of Johannes Lindblom, see Kaiser, *Isaiah 1-12*, p. 88, note c.

3. See the good discussion in Kaiser, *Isaiah 1-12*, pp. 98-99.

4. For this suggestion of ambiguity, see Good, *Irony*, p. 123 and note 19.

5. See Johannes Lindblom, *A Study on the Immanuel Section in Isaiah 7.1-9.6*, Studier utgiv. av Kungl. Humanistiska Vetenskapssamfundet i Lund, 1957-58 (Lund: Gleerup), 4, pp. 36ff, especially p. 41.

6. Compare J.M. Ward, "Isaiah," *Interpreter's Dictionary of the Bible, Supplementary Volume* (New York: Abingdon, 1976), p. 458.

7. Other suggestions: that curds and honey represent the basic foods of nomads; or that they represent rich food for the Messiah. The alternatives are discussed in Wildberger, *Jesaja*, pp. 295-96.

8. Some commentators have doubted the authenticity of the

whole of vs. 17, but I take this material as authentic except for the final gloss.

9. The ashes are now in a canister which has been in the possession of Weigle's successor as committee chairman, Professor Herbert Gordon May.

10. See Luther A. Weigle, "English Versions Since 1611," *The Cambridge History of the Bible*, III (Cambridge: Cambridge University Press, 1963), p. 361.

11. For the background of this section of the chapter I am particularly dependent on Bright, *History of Israel*, chapter 7, especially pp. 277-84.

12. The translation is somewhat free; I have omitted the parentheses around certain supplied words in the source, which is Pritchard, *Ancient Near Eastern Texts*, p. 285; it forms lines 72-76 of the so-called Display Inscription for the fifth year of Sargon. The translation is that of D.D. Luckenbill, *Ancient Records of Assyria and Babylonia* (Chicago: University of Chicago Press, 1926-27), II, sect. 8.

13. The fall of Samaria occurred within Ahaz's reign if current views of chronology are sound, that is, the view of W.F. Albright and John Bright, for which see Bright, *History of Israel*, p. 274, and note 21 there. The book of 2 Kings itself puts the event early in Hezekiah's reign (2 Kings 18:9). For a full discussion of the problem, see John Gray, *I & II Kings*, pp. 60-62.

14. For a reproduction of the picture, see Pritchard, *The Ancient Near East in Pictures*, p. 124, No. 358.

15. I take the *mēm* suffix on "hand" as an "enclitic" *mēm*, present for assonance with *yedammeh* in vs. 7. For instances of the enclitic *mēm* in construct chains, see the instances in the Psalms in Mitchell Dahood, *Psalms III*, Anchor Bible 17A (Garden City, NY: Doubleday, 1970), pp. 382-83. The literature on this phenomenon is growing; for two more examples in Isaiah, see Dahood, *Psalms I*, Anchor Bible 16 (Garden City, NY: Doubleday, 1966), pp. 109-10, on Isa. 30:20 and 37:25.

16. Many commentators try to explain away the meaning "woe" here, I think wrongly; R.B.Y. Scott, in *Interpreter's Bible* 5, p. 240, and Good, *Irony*, p. 118, note 6, are correct, I believe.

17. *Isaiah 1-12*, pp. 141-42.

18. Wildberger, *Jesaja*, and Kaiser, *Isaiah 1-12*, both take vss. 16-19 to be later additions.

19. Good, *Irony*, pp. 120-21.

20. Otto Kaiser, *Isaiah 13-39* (Philadelphia: Westminster, 1974), pp. 248-57, believes these lines to be an unauthentic addition from much later times, but I disagree. The imagery of these lines seems thoroughly Isaianic, and the occurrence of the word *qaw* "line" in vs. 17, identical in form with the mysterious *qaw* in vss. 10 and 23 (see the discussion in Chapter III), suggests

that there is a linkage of key words here, suggesting in turn the early placement of the totality of vss. 14-22 after vss. 1-13. For the idea of key words see Chapter I.

21. So Scott, *Interpreter's Bible* 5. But I reject as unlikely the suggestion of Scott, followed by Victor Gold in his notes in the *Oxford Annotated Bible, Revised Standard Version* (New York: Oxford University Press, 1962, to emend "beast" to "in the heat."

22. So Kaiser, *Isaiah 13-39*.

23. For this and other suggestions, see Kaiser, *Isaiah 13-39*, p. 287, note f.

24. This passage "simply bristles with problems," notes Childs, *Isaiah and the Assyrian Crisis*, p. 54. My own approach is simply to seek some kind of reasonable synthesis of recent opinion, adding some observations that may not have been made heretofore.

25. For a thorough discussion of the meaning of the name, see C.R. North, "Ariel," 2, in *Interpreter's Dictionary of the Bible*, 2 p. 218; see also Kaiser, *Isaiah 13-39*, pp. 266-67.

26. The distribution of consonants is quite different in vss. 1-6 and in vss. 7-8, and this distribution depends not on the repetition of specific words or roots but is quite generally distributed in the vocabulary of the two sections. Specifically, the normal distribution of each of the two consonants ṣ and p is roughly 1.6 percent in a consonantal text; but vss. 1-6 offer 3.1 percent for ṣ and 3.5 percent for p, while vss. 7-8 offer 5.2 percent for ṣ and 1.1 percent for p. This contrast is quite perceptible when the passage is read aloud in Hebrew.

27. The text is in Pritchard, *Ancient Near Eastern Texts*, p. 288. One of several inscriptions containing the text is to be found at the Oriental Institute of the University of Chicago.

28. See the reproductions in Pritchard, *The Ancient Near East in Pictures*, pp. 129-32, Nos. 371-374; clearer reproductions are to be found in Yigael Yadin, *The Art of Warfare in Biblical Lands* (New York: McGraw-Hill, 1963), pp. 430-35, and there is a superb color reconstruction of the scene on pp. 436-37, the best single picture of Assyrian warfare of which I am aware.

29. For a discussion see John Gray, *I & II Kings*, p. 694.

30. So Bright, *History of Israel*, pp. 296-308, with careful weighing of the evidence. For a rejection of this view on form-critical grounds, see Childs, *Isaiah and the Assyrian Crisis*.

Chapter V

1. Among those scholars who take vs. 18b as irony: Scott, *Interpreter's Bible* 5; Good, *Irony*, pp. 153-54; B. Davie Napier,

Song of the Vineyard (New York: Harper, 1962), p. 225. Wildberger, *Jesaja*, understands vs. 18b to offer questions addressed by God to Israel, and so does the *Zürcher Bibel* in German.

2. In Greek *prosthen* meant both "in front" and "formerly," and *opisthen* meant both "behind" and "hereafter."

3. For a general discussion of this matter, see Thorleif Boman, *Hebrew Thought Compared with Greek* (Philadelphia: Westminster, 1960), pp. 123-85, especially 149-50, though Boman does not deal with the parallel Greek imagery; and see H.W. Wolff, *Anthropology of the Old Testament* (Philadelphia: Fortress, 1974), pp. 83-92.

4. For the text, see Pritchard, *Ancient Near Eastern Texts*, p. 284, Sargon's Display Inscription (for the first year), lines 10-17.

5. W.F. Albright, "An Ostracon from Calah and North-Israelite Diaspora," *Bulletin of the American Schools of Oriental Research* 149 (Feb. 1958), pp. 33-36.

6. Conceivably all four verses could come from the same hand (so Wildberger, *Jesaja*, and Kaiser, *Isaiah 1-12*), but it seems more plausible to me to understand them from two hands (so Scott, *Interpreter's Bible* 5).

7. The question whether Isaiah really believed in the inviolability of Jerusalem is greatly controverted. For a thoughtful discussion which doubts that this item was part of Isaiah's theology, see Th. C. Vriezen, "Essentials of the Theology of Isaiah," in B.W. Anderson and W. Harrelson (eds.), *Israel's Prophetic Heritage* (New York: Harper, 1962), pp. 138-41. For a summary of the data, see John Hayes, "The Tradition of Zion's Inviolability," *Journal of Biblical Literature*, 1963, pp. 419-26. Hayes is convinced of the genuineness of this item of Isaiah's faith, as is Childs, *Isaiah and the Assyrian Crisis*, pp. 66-68. I agree.

8. For a good description of the outlook of the Egyptians on the function of the temple, see Henri Frankfort *et al.*, *Before Philosophy* (Baltimore: Penguin, 1949), pp. 30-31; and of the outlook of the Assyrians and Babylonians, pp. 201-207 there.

9. So most authorities; see in particular Richard J. Clifford, *The Cosmic Mountain in Canaan and in the Old Testament* (Cambridge, MA: Harvard University Press, 1972), p. 39 and elsewhere. Clifford's whole work is a massive review of the motif of the cosmic mountain in the ancient Near East.

10. So now Frank M. Cross, Jr., *Canaanite Myth and Hebrew Epic*, pp. 26-28, citing new evidence.

11. For geographical descriptions of both mountains see Denis Baly and A.D. Tushingham, *Atlas of the Biblical World* (New York: World, 1971), p. 86.

12. On the joining of the two see Hayes, "The Tradition of Zion's Inviolability," pp. 421-22.

13. See Jub. 8:19 in the Old Testament Pseudepigrapha; for the English see Charles, *Apocrypha and Pseudepigrapha*, II, p. 26.

14. For a clear analysis of these attitudes, see Bright, *History of Israel*, pp. 182-85.

15. See the thorough discussion in Wildberger, *Jesaja*, pp. 368-70. His conclusion: for vss. 1-4 (English 2-5) at least, the vocabulary has so much in common with that of Isaiah that the burden of proof is on the doubters.

16. This view is argued in detail in Albrecht Alt, "Jesaja 8,23-9,6. Befreiungsnacht und Krönungstag," *Festschrift Alfred Bertholet zum 80. Geburtstag gewidmet* (Tübingen, Germany: J.C.B. Mohr, 1950), pp. 29-49, reprinted in Albrecht Alt, *Kleine Schriften zur Geschichte des Volkes Israel* (Munich: C.H. Beck, 1953), II, pp. 206-25; it is adopted by Gerhard von Rad, *Old Testament Theology* II (New York: Harper, 1965), pp. 171-75, and Walter Harrelson, "Nonroyal Motifs in the Royal Eschatology," in B. Anderson and W. Harrelson (eds.), *Israel's Prophetic Heritage*, pp. 149-53.

17. For a thorough discussion of this matter see Ivan Engnell, *Studies in Divine Kingship in the Ancient Near East* (Oxford: Blackwell, 1967), e.g. pp. 4-5 for Egyptian phrases, pp. 16-17 for Mesopotamian phrases, pp. 78-80 for Canaanite phrases.

18. This is the common judgment of scholars; see, for example, William R. Taylor in his exegesis of Psalm 2 in *The Interpreter's Bible* 4 (New York: Abingdon, 1955), p. 23.

19. Compare Scott, *Interpreter's Bible* 5, pp. 231-32; Kaiser, *Isaiah 1-12*, p. 128.

20. Quoted in Wildberger, *Jesaja*, p. 381.

21. So Wildberger, *Jesaja*; Kaiser, *Isaiah 1-12*.

22. Wildberger, *Jesaja*, struggles with the question, pp. 382-83, and attempts to argue from Egyptian throne-names. But in Egypt the king *was* a god, so that divine titles were appropriate to a king in Egypt; the same would not hold for Israel.

23. The *New Jewish Version* solves the problem of the phrase "mighty God" by making a sentence of the first two throne-names: "The Mighty God is planning grace. . . ."

24. Compare the discussion in Scott, *Interpreter's Bible* 5, p. 232.

25. For example, the First Apology of Justin Martyr (about A.D. 155), sect. 35.

26. So G.B. Gray, *The Book of Isaiah*, pp. 213-15.

27. For a listing of major scholars taking each of these three

positions, see Wildberger, *Jesaja*, p. 442.

28. Pritchard, *Ancient Near Eastern Texts*, p. 38; the quotation is lines 15-16 of the myth.

29. For this suggestion I am indebted to my former student Haroutioun Avakian of Utrecht, the Netherlands.

30. The two words for "lion" are different, but they are synonymous.

31. See the discussion in Scott, *Interpreter's Bible* 5, pp. 247-48.

Chapter VI

1. *The Holy Bible, A Translation from the Latin Vulgate in the Light of the Hebrew and Greek Originals,* translated by Ronald Knox (New York: Sheed & Ward, 1956).

2. According to the chronology of most scholars, in spite of the statement in 2 Kings 21:1. See H.B. MacLean, "Manasseh," *Interpreter's Dictionary of the Bible,* 3, p. 254; and Bright, *History of Israel,* p. 310.

3. For the details, see Bright, *History of Israel,* pp. 310-45.

4. See Bright, *History of Israel,* p. 346.

5. For a helpful review of the theological mood of Israel after the exile, see James Muilenburg, "The History of the Religion of Israel," *The Interpreter's Bible* 1 (New York: Abingdon-Cokesbury, 1952), pp. 330-33.

6. The most helpful presentation of the poetic effects of Second Isaiah is that of James Muilenburg in *The Interpreter's Bible* 5, pp. 386-93.

7. For a discussion of this matter, with literature, see Muilenburg, *The Interpreter's Bible* 5, p. 422.

8. Gen. 50:21b has the same parallelism, and there the translation in the *Revised Standard Version* is "reassured." P.A.H. de Boer translates the phrase in Isa. 40:2 "speak convincingly to Jerusalem," *Second Isaiah's Message,* Oudtestamentische Studiën XI (Leiden: Brill, 1956), pp. 3, 40.

9. For this point see Claus Westermann, *Isaiah 40-66* (Philadelphia: Westminster, 1969), p. 39.

10. See, for example, Samuel Terrien in *The Interpreter's Bible* 3 (New York: Abingdon, 1954), pp. 884-88.

11. See Muilenburg, *The Interpreter's Bible* 1, p. 331.

12. Karl Elliger, *Jesaja II*, Biblischer Kommentar, Altes Testament (Neukirchen-Vluyn, Germany: Neukirchener Verlag, 1970-), pp. 104-05.

13. Westermann, *Isaiah 40-66*, p. 63; see this portion of his commentary for background on the court scene.

14. See the discussion in Elliger, *Jesaja II*, p. 149.
15. So Elliger, *Jesaja II*.
16. So Muilenburg, *The Interpreter's Bible* 5.
17. So Muilenburg, *The Interpreter's Bible* 5; Westermann, *Isaiah 40-66*.
18. So Elliger, *Jesaja II*.

Chapter VII

1. But Jer. 10:1-16 is usually considered a later addition to Jeremiah.
2. For illustrations see Pritchard, *The Ancient Near East in Pictures*, p. 162, No. 469.
3. Robert Koldewey, *The Excavations at Babylon* (London: Macmillan, 1914), pp. 184, 204.
4. For an illustration see Pritchard, *The Ancient Near East in Pictures*, p. 212, No. 646.
5. A. Leo Oppenheim, "Assyria and Babylonia," *Interpreter's Dictionary of the Bible*, 1, pp. 298-99.
6. A. Leo Oppenheim, *Ancient Mesopotamia, Portrait of a Dead Civilization* (Chicago: University of Chicago Press, 1964), p. 185.
7. See Cyrus's inscription quoted in Pritchard, *Ancient Near Eastern Texts*, p. 316: for the detail, see the material toward the end of that inscription. For the policy of the Assyrians toward captured images, see John McKay, *Religion in Judah under the Assyrians*, Studies in Biblical Theology 2nd Series, 26 (Naperville, IL: Allenson, 1973), pp. 60-61, and the references cited there on p. 119, note 3.
8. See, for example, the quotations from the *Baltimore Catechism* and the related *Catechism of Christian Doctrine* in Stanley I. Stuber, *Primer of Roman Catholicism for Protestants* (New York: Association Press, 1953), p. 52.
9. R.M. French, *The Eastern Orthodox Church* (London: Hutchinson House, 1951), p. 131.
10. Oppenheim, in *Interpreter's Dictionary of the Bible*, 1, p. 298.
11. Oppenheim, in *Interpreter's Dictionary of the Bible*, 1, p. 299.
12. For a sketch of the relation between temple and palace see Oppenheim, *Ancient Mesopotamia*, pp. 95-109; and for an acute description of the way the gods sponsored the nation-state, see Thorkild Jacobsen, "Mesopotamia," in Henri Frankfort *et al.*, *Before Philosophy*, pp. 207-13.

13. Westermann, *Isaiah 40-66*, p. 63 (so above, Chapter VI, note 13).

14. For a classic description of the contrast between the pagan deities and the God of Israel, see G. Ernest Wright, *The Old Testament Against its Environment*, Studies in Biblical Theology 2 (London: S.C.M. Press, 1950); see also G. Ernest Wright, *God Who Acts, Biblical Theology as Recital*, Studies in Biblical Theology 8 (Chicago: Regnery, 1952).

15. So Muilenburg, *Interpreter's Bible* 5, and Westermann, *Isaiah 40-66*.

16. Compare the discussion in Westermann, *Isaiah 40-66*.

17. So A.S. Herbert, *The Book of the Prophet Isaiah 40-66*, The Cambridge Bible Commentary on the New English Bible (Cambridge: Cambridge University Press, 1975), p. 3.

18. The interested reader concerned for Yehuda Radday's computer work on the book of Isaiah should refer to Chapter I, note 19, on Radday's contrasting grouping of the material in chapters 40-66.

19. The most important literature is cited in the bibliography offered in Eissfeldt, *The Old Testament, An Introduction*, pp. 330-32; probably the most inclusive work in English on the matter is C.R. North, *The Suffering Servant in Deutero-Isaiah* (Oxford: Oxford University Press, 1956).

20. So Westermann, *Isaiah 40-66*.

21. The data are carefully set forth in J. Jeremias, "Pais theou," G. Kittel (ed.), *Theological Dictionary of the New Testament* (Grand Rapids, MI: Eerdmans, 1964-76), V, pp. 705-07; and see the thoughtful analysis in Reginald H. Fuller, *The Mission and Achievement of Jesus*, Studies in Biblical Theology, 12 (Naperville, IL: Allenson, 1954), pp. 55-64.

22. So Westermann, *Isaiah 40-66*.

23. So Westermann, *Isaiah 40-66*.

24. On the identity of the speaker, see Westermann, *Isaiah 40-66*.

25. On the details, see Westermann, *Isaiah 40-66*, pp. 266-67.

Chapter VIII

1. I am indebted to David E. Roberts, *The Grandeur and Misery of Man* (Oxford: Oxford University Press, 1955), for the turn of phrase I have adopted for the title of this chapter. For the basic orientation of the chapter, for many details and even for a few phrases I am deeply indebted to Paul D. Hanson, *The Dawn of Apocalyptic* (Philadelphia: Fortress, 1975), pp. 32-308. My in-

debtedness to Hanson's study is so pervasive that I shall not acknowledge each use in a separate note.

2. See Pritchard, *Ancient Near Eastern Texts,* p. 316 (Cyrus Cylinder, lines 30-32).

3. The large number of colonists listed in Ezra 2:64, repeated in Neh. 7:66, evidently refers to the situation at a later period; on this tangled matter see Bright, *History of Israel,* pp. 363, 378.

4. The records of this period are in such confusion that even this uncle/nephew relationship is insecure. Some scholars have thought Sheshbazzar and Zerubbabel to be the same person, but the relation given here is probably correct. For the argumentation, see B.T. Dahlberg, "Sheshbazzar," *Interpreter's Dictionary of the Bible,* 4, p. 326. For the existence of a second expedition under Zerubbabel, see conveniently Bright, *History of Israel,* pp. 366-67.

5. Hanson, *Dawn of Apocalyptic,* p. 198.

6. For a brief discussion of some of the difficulties, see Muilenburg, *Interpreter's Bible* 5, pp. 666-67.

7. Hanson, *Dawn of Apocalyptic,* pp. 92-98.

8. R.W. Corney, "Zadok the Priest," *Interpreter's Dictionary of the Bible,* 4, pp. 928-29.

9. The whole story is quite complex; see R. Abba, "Priests and Levites," *Interpreter's Dictionary of the Bible,* 3, pp. 880-89.

10. This is the theory of Gerhard von Rad; see his "Deuteronomy," *Interpreter's Dictionary of the Bible,* 1, p. 836, and in more detail his *Studies in Deuteronomy,* Studies in Biblical Theology 9 (London: SCM Press, 1953), pp. 66-67. This theory has been challenged more recently; see N. Lohfink, "Deuteronomy," *Interpreter's Dictionary of the Bible, Supplementary Volume,* pp. 229-30.

11. Compare Westermann, *Isaiah 40-66,* p. 366.

12. Compare my discussion of the same word in Jer. 11:20 in *Jeremiah: Spokesman,* p. 91. For the basic study, see George E. Mendenhall, *The Tenth Generation* (Baltimore: Johns Hopkins University Press, 1973), pp. 69-104.

13. That is, the Hebrew *'am haqqōdesh.*

14. Hanson, *Dawn of Apocalyptic,* p. 147.

Chapter IX

1. See W.F. Albright, in a review in *Journal of Biblical Literature,* 1942, p. 119; and see my discussion in *Jeremiah: Spokesman,* p. 123.

2. For the division of opinion, see the reference above in Chapter I, note 20.

3. See Eissfeldt, *The Old Testament, An Introduction*, p. 317, for the suggestion of its authenticity.

4. For the idea of a liturgy here, see Johannes Lindblom, *Die Jesaja-Apokalypse, Jes. 24-27*, Lunds Universitets Årsskrift, N.F. I, 34, 3 (Lund and Leipzig, 1938).

5. Scott, in *Interpreter's Bible* 5, p. 298, insists on "the land" through the whole passage.

6. Scott, *Interpreter's Bible* 5, p. 300.

7. For this idea see the intertestamental work (Eth.) En. 18:14, 86:1, 2; for the English text see Charles, *Apocrypha and Pseudepigrapha*, II, pp. 200, 250.

8. A striking example in the Old Testament is Psalm 29, which was originally a Canaanite psalm to Baal; the Israelites took this psalm over and substituted "Yahweh" for "Baal." See Aloysius Fitzgerald, "A Note on Psalm 29," *Bulletin of the American Schools of Oriental Research* 215 (Oct. 1974), pp. 61-63.

9. For such a Ugaritic text see Gordon, *Ugaritic Textbook*, p. 197, text 137, lines 20-21, and for an English translation see Driver, *Canaanite Myths and Legends*, p. 79, Baal III* B 18-19.

10. So, evidently, the missing end of Gordon, *Ugaritic Textbook*, p. 169, text 49, col. VI, lines 35ff; see also Driver, *Canaanite Myths and Legends*, p. 115, Baal III vi lines 35ff.

11. So in the intertestamental work 2 Bar. ([Syr.] Apocal. Bar.) 29:4; see Charles, *Apocrypha and Pseudepigrapha*, II, p. 497.

12. See the Qumran document 1QSa II 17-21; the most convenient English translation is Geza Vermes, *The Dead Sea Scrolls in English* (Baltimore: Penguin, 1968), p. 121.

13. The literature on this subject is of course vast; see conveniently M.H. Shepherd, Jr., "Last Supper," *Interpreter's Dictionary of the Bible*, 3, pp. 74-75.

14. Commentators who favor "be born" for *npl* cannot cite this meaning for any other occurrence of this verb in the *qal*; and then they must explain who the "inhabitants of the world" are here, as against the meaning in vs. 9; the interpretation "children," i.e., of Jews (so Delitzsch and many others), seems thoroughly forced. See G.B. Gray, *The Book of Isaiah*, pp. 445-46.

15. Kaiser's view, *Isaiah 13-39*, that vs. 19 does not belong with the previous verses, is implausible; the poetic motifs are too closely tied with what has come before.

16. For older literature on the matter, see G.B. Gray, *The Book of Isaiah*, p. 447. For recent discussion, including parallels

from the ancient Near East and Ugarit, see Kaiser, *Isaiah 13-39*, pp. 217-18.

17. For a good recent study on the matter, see Gene M. Schramm, "Poetic Patterning in Biblical Hebrew," Louis L. Orlin (ed.), *Michigan Oriental Studies in Honor of George G. Cameron* (Ann Arbor, MI: University of Michigan Press, 1976), pp. 167-91.

18. See T.H. Gaster, "Resurrection," in *Interpreter's Dictionary of the Bible*, 4, pp. 41-43, and G.W.E. Nickelsburg, Jr., "Future Life in Intertestamental Literature," *Interpreter's Dictionary of the Bible, Supplementary Volume*, pp. 348-51.

19. Notably by Wildberger, *Jesaja*, p. 542, who refers to earlier studies as well.

20. Scholars suggest that the word "Lord" here was added later. See the discussion in Wildberger, *Jesaja*, pp. 541-42.

21. See Good, *Irony*, pp. 163-67; he offers many other striking suggestions for understanding the poem.

22. The myth may be related to, and the same as, the narrative known to us in which Baal's throne is temporarily vacant, and it is proposed that his son Athtar take his place; but "he sat on the seat of the victor Baal; his feet reached not to the stool, his head reached not to its top. And the terrible Athtar answered, 'I cannot be king in the recesses of the north.' The terrible Athtar came down, came down from the seat of the victor Baal and became king of the earth, god of it all." The translation is from Driver, *Canaanite Myths and Legends*, p. 111; the citation there is Baal III i 26-37; the numeration of Gordon, *Ugaritic Textbook*, is text 49 I 26-37.

23. The *King James Version*, following the Latin Vulgate, translates the word for "Day Star" as "Lucifer." There was a Jewish belief in intertestamental times that Satan had been cast down from heaven; compare 2 Enoch (=Book of the Secrets of Enoch) 29:4-5, and Books of Adam and Eve xii—see Charles, *Apocrypha and Pseudepigrapha*, II, pp. 447, 137. The identification of these two traditions, that of Isa. 14:12, and the myth of Satan's fall from heaven, resulted in the use of the name "Lucifer" for Satan from the time of the church fathers onward.

24. So Wildberger, *Jesaja*.

25. See note 20 above.

Chapter X

1. For the occurrences of this phrase, see Chapter I, note 17.

2. The occurrences in Ps. 71:22 and 78:41 would seem to be later.

3. For this judgment see Paul D. Hanson, "Apocalypticism,"

Interpreter's Dictionary of the Bible, Supplementary Volume, p. 33.

4. See again Hanson, *Interpreter's Dictionary of the Bible, Supplementary Volume*, p. 33.

5. For an edition and English translation of this Aramaic rendering, see Stenning, *Targum of Isaiah* (compare Chapter II above, note 2); for a date for its origin, see Paul E. Kahle, *The Cairo Geniza* (Oxford: Blackwell, 1959), p. 196, and Pierre Grelot, "L'Exégèse Messianique d'Isaie," *Revue Biblique*, 1963, pp. 371-80, especially p. 379.

6. For the most accessible English rendering of some of this material, see Vermes, *The Dead Sea Scrolls in English*, pp. 226-29. For the Hebrew text and English translation of the Cave 4 material, see John M. Allegro, "Further Messianic References in Qumran Literature," *Journal of Biblical Literature*, 1956, pp. 177-82 ("Document III"), and his "More Isaiah Commentaries from Qumran's Fourth Cave," *Journal of Biblical Literature*, 1958, pp. 215-21. For the material from both Caves 3 and 4 in French translation and with detailed notes, see "Interprétation d'Isaïe," J. Carmignac and P. Guilbert, *Les Textes de Qumran* II (Paris: LeTouzey et Ané, 1963), pp. 65-76.

7. A convenient survey is Erwin I.J. Rosenthal, "The Study of the Bible in Medieval Judaism," *Cambridge History of the Bible*, II (Cambridge: Cambridge University Press, 1969), pp. 252-79.

8. Hebrew term: *miqre'ôt gedôlôt*.

9. In this section the following works have proved helpful: Willem J. de Wilde, *De Messiaansche Opvattingen der Middeleeuwsche Exegeten Rasji, Aben Ezra en Kimchi, Vooral volgens hun Commentaren op Jesaja* (Wageningen, Netherlands: Veendam, 1929); S.R. Driver and Ad. Neubauer, *The Fifty-Third Chapter of Isaiah according to the Jewish Interpreters*, II, Translations (Oxford, 1877); M. Friedländer, *The Commentary of Ibn Ezra on Isaiah* (London, 1873). I have used available translations but have occasionally altered them by reference to the Hebrew texts.

10. For example, Rabbi Naphtali ben Asher Altschuler, a Talmudic scholar in Russia and Poland, whose exegetical work was published in 1593-95. Compare Driver and Neubauer, *The Fifth-Third Chapter*, pp. 318-23.

11. Compare on this De Wilde, *De Messiaansche Opvattingen*, pp. 93-94.

12. For example, I.W. Slotki, *Isaiah* (London: Soncino, 1949).

13. Heschel, *The Prophets*, p. 155. We have already referred to Heschel in our discussion of the meaning of 6:9-13 in Chapter II.

14. Unless we include the text of selection 49, which is from

1 Cor. 15:54, but that verse is a quotation from Isa. 25:8.

15. Out of 150 Psalms, 101 are represented by 309 quotations or reminiscences.

16. For a brief account of Bible commentaries by Christians from the earliest period to the present (though with a bias toward the Western church) see D.R. Jones, Appendix II in *Cambridge History of the Bible*, III, pp. 531-35.

17. *Eusebius Werke*, Vol. 9, *Der Jesaja-kommentar*, ed. by J. Ziegler (Berlin: Akademie Verlag, 1975).

18. *Corpus Christianorum, Series Latina*, 73: *S. Hieronymi Presbyteri Opera, Pars I, Opera Exegetica*, 2-2A (Turnhout, Belgium: Brepols, 1963).

19. For an assessment of Jerome as a commentator, see H.F.D. Sparks, "Jerome as Biblical Scholar," *Cambridge History of the Bible*, I, pp. 510-41, especially pp. 535-41.

20. *Commentaire d'Išo'dad de Merv sur l'Ancien Testament: IV, Isaïe et les Douze*, ed. by C. van den Eynde, *Corpus Scriptorum Christianorum Orientalium, Scriptores Syri*, 128 text, 129 French translation (Louvain, 1969).

21. For a citation of this commentary, see Puzant Yeghiayan, *The Separation of the Armenian Catholic and Protestant Denominations in the XIX Century* (Antelias, Lebanon: Armenian Press, 1971), p. 542. This volume is mostly in Armenian, but the reference is to an English portion. The commentary of Mekhitar Kosh remains untranslated so far as I am aware, nor am I aware of a published edition of the Armenian text.

22. John Calvin, *Commentary on the Book of the Prophet Isaiah* (Edinburgh: Constable, 4 vols., 1850-54).

23. On Calvin as commentator see briefly Basil Hall, in *Cambridge History of the Bible*, III, pp. 87-90, and, more extensively, J. Haroutunian, in *Calvin: Commentaries*, Library of Christian Classics 23 (Philadelphia: Westminster, 1958), pp. 15-50; P.T. Fuhrmann, "Calvin the Expositor of Scripture," *Interpretation*, 1952, pp. 188-209, with bibliography, and recently Hans-Joachim Kraus, "Calvin's Exegetical Principles," *Interpretation*, 1977, pp. 8-18.

Index of Passages

This index includes all scripture citations in the body of the text and in the notes, both Old and New Testament, Old Testament Pseudepigrapha, Apostolic Fathers, and Ugaritic and other ancient Near East written material. It was not felt necessary to include citations to the *commentary* material on Isaiah cited in Chapter X (that is, Qumran commentaries, Jerome and the like). Citations within the *titles* of books are not listed (for example, Kaiser, *Isaiah 1-12*). The verse citations are to the English versification, not the Hebrew, where these differ. All references to portions of a verse are ignored (that is, "vs. 5b" is treated as if it were "vs. 5"). The more inclusive citations are listed before the less inclusive ones (that is, the following order is observed: Isa. 1:21-27, 1:21-26, 1:21-23, 1:21). Substantive discussions are found on *italicized* pages.

Genesis		6:6	135	23:14	48
1-2	128	7:1	35	23:16	62
1:2	149, 196	10:1	39	24:1-8	47
1:14-16	198-99	14:24	193	32:32	192
1:26	34, 128	15:1-18	176	33:20	26
9:4-6	196	15:3	107		
9:16	196	15:11	106-07	*Leviticus*	
10:11-12	98	15:15	176	1-7	177
12:1	52	15:16	176	4:3	137
12:2-3	208	19:4	129	5:1-19	155
16:5	63	20:1	144	6:20	179
18:5	94	20:2	144	13:45-46	152
19:24-25	6	20:4-5	143	13:45	33
20:7	35	20:5	157	19:14	32
22:1	69	21-23	48, 65	19:31	182
22:13	94	21:12-14	48	21:17-23	164, 173
22:17	99	21:20-21	48	22:4	33
29:31	50	21:28-29	48		
31:1	31	22:16-17	48	*Numbers*	
39:6	152	23:1	48	11:29	224
50:21	252	23:2	48	35:33	195-96
		23:4	48		
Exodus		23:7	155	*Deuteronomy*	
2:1	173	23:9	48	4:19	198

5:9	205
18:18	35
21:15	50
21:18-21	40, 46
28:57	29
32:10-11	130
32:21	140
32:38	140

Joshua
10:9-14	83

Judges
5:15	105
5:30	96
6:1-8:17	105
8:9	107
8:22-23	27
8:23	104
18:5	172
18:7-13	172

1-2 Samuel 243

1 Samuel
1:22	222
6:20	30
9:9	94
10:5	35
16:3	179
16:18	152
24:6	137
25:1	243

2 Samuel
5:9	102
5:20	83
6	102
6:2	30
7:8-16	104
7:14	106, 107
11:1-12:23	28
12:1-23	35
15:24-37	172
17:12	204
19:5	200
19:21-22	27

1 Kings
2:35	172

6:2	29
8:54	144
11:26	108
18	35
18:17-46	102
19:16	179
21	35
22:1-28	38-39
22:19-23	38

2 Kings 248
10:7	96
11:12	109
15:1-3	25
15:1-2	244
15:25	68
15:29	105
15:37	67
16:2	67
16:5	67
16:7-8	73
16:10-18	76
17:1-6	76
17:3-5	58
17:6	29, 59, 98
18-19	44
18:2	76
18:9	248
18:13-20:19	14
18:13-19:7	87-90
18:13	87
18:14	87-88
18:15-16	88
18:16	222
18:18	88
18:19-25	88
18:26-27	88-89
18:28-35	89
18:34-35	80
19:2-7	110
19:3	89
19:6	89
19:7	89
19:22	243
19:30-34	100-01
19:34	103
19:35	89
21:1	252
21:2-9	120
23:4	41

24:18-25:30	14

1 Chronicles
23:2-5	172
23:2	172

2 Chronicles
26:6-15	25

Ezra
1:1-7	165
1:4	166
1:5	172
1:6	166
1:8-11	165
2:64	255
3:2-3	167
3:2	166
3:12-13	167
4:24	166
6:1-12	166
6:15	167
7:1-6	218

Nehemiah
7:66	255

Job
2:9	205
12:12	52
14:7-19	205
14:8	111
38-41	128

Psalms
1	201
1:6	201
2	106, 109, 226, 251
2:6	102
2:7	106
20	104
20:2	104
22:6	152
22:7	132
24:8-10	27
29	256
37:25	205
45	109
46:1	82
46:4, 5	102

48:2	102	1:2	6, 39, *51*, 61	2:14	8
71:22	243, 257	1:3	6, 9, *51*	2:15	28
72	109	1:4-9	7	2:16	28
72:1	106	1:4	6, *51*, 61, 243	2:17	28
78:41	243, 257	1:5-6	*51*, 153	2:19	15
87:4	84	1:5	92	2:20	140
88	153	1:7-8	*51*	3:1-15	8-9, *51-52*
89:3-4	215	1:7	65, 195, 199	3:1-8	*51-53*
89:9-10	84	1:8	6, 9, 58, 84, 101,	3:1	7, 8, 10, *51*
89:18	215, 243		147	3:2-3	*51-52*, 195
91:7	84	1:9	6, *51*, 228, 235	3:2	7
93:1	27	1:10-17	7, *49-51*	3:3	7, 106, 107
104	128	1:10	6, *49*, 191	3:4-5	52
104:15	54	1:11	*49, 50*	3:4	52
105:15	137-38	1:12-15	177	3:5	52
113:4	28	1:13-14	*49*	3:6	*53*, 65
137	121	1:15-16	7	3:7	53
137:4	122	1:15	*49*, 181	3:8	58
139:16	192	1:16-17	*49*	3:12	8, *54*
143:3-4	150	1:16	*49*	3:13-15	9, *54-55*
143:9-10	145	1:17	7, 163, 164	3:13-14	53
145:1	199	1:18-20	7, 92, 97	3:14-15	53
		1:18	7, 249	3:14	9
Proverbs		1:19-20	37	3:15	9
6:13	174	1:19	99	3:16-17 + 24	*53-54*
16:23	32	1:21-27	216	3:16-17	9
26:8	31	1:21-26	8	3:16	9, 58
29:8	81	1:21-23	*51*, 164	3:17	53
29:15	157	1:21	7, 101, 103,	3:18-23	9
			163, 224	3:24	9, *53-54*
Ecclesiastes		1:23	7, 165	3:25-26	9
12:12	241	1:24	101	4:1	9
		1:25	103	4:2-6	9, 19, 103,
Song of Songs		1:26	7, 10, 101,		*192-93*
2:15	62		106, 224	4:2	*192*
6:8	70	1:27-2:22	10	4:3-6	*192-93*
8:11-12	62	1:27-28	8	4:3	*192*
		1:28	8	4:4	9, *192-93*
Isaiah		1:29-31	8	4:5	*193*
1-39	14, 15, 17, 19,	1:31	8	4:6	199
	91, 92, 103, 117,	2:2-4	8, 19, 92,	5	220
	189, 239, 240, 243		*191-92*, 193	5:1-7	9, 38, *62-64*,
1-35	16, 244	2:2	8, 15, *191-92*		129, 201, 206
1-27	240	2:5-22	8, 28	5:1-2	219
1-12	19, 20, 239	2:8	140	5:1	62, 220
1	220	2:11	17, 28, 151	5:2	*62-63*, 64
1:1	16, 43	2:12	8, 17, 151, 216	5:3-4	63
1:2-5:7	14	2:13-16	195	5:4	64
1:2-4	34	2:13-14	28	5:5-6	63
1:2-3	6, 7, 44-45,	2:13	8	5:7	9, 62, *63-64*, 220
	46-49				

5:8-30	10, 14, 176	6:11	12, 36, 38, 40	9:1	105
5:8-23	10	6:12	98	9:2-7	103, *105-11*,
5:8-10	54	6:13	*40-41*, 91		150, 216, 232, 235
5:8	9, *54*	7:1-8:4	67-72	9:2-6	226, 228
5:9	9, 12, *54*	7	216, 228, 234	9:2-5	*105*, 109, 251
5:10	10, *54*	7:1-17	73	9:2	92-93, 236
5:11-13	54-55	7:1-9	12, 43	9:3-5	236
5:11	9, *54*, 231	7:1	*67-68*	9:4	*105*, 107
5:12	54	7:2	*68*, 69	9:5	105
5:13	*54-55*	7:3-4	110	9:6-7	222
5:14-17	10, *55*, 210	7:3	12, 19, 44, 71,	9:6	vi, 12, 100,
5:14	200		77, 95, *97-99*		*106-09*, 202, 236
5:15-16	55	7:4	*68*, 69	9:7	105, *109*, 111,
5:17	*55*, 65, 111	7:5	*68-69*		222
5:18-19	55	7:6	68	9:8-10:4	10, 14
5:18	9, *55*	7:8	68	9:8-10	35
5:19	243	7:9	*68-69*	9:8	10
5:20-23	*55-56*	7:10-17	12, 43, 72	9:12	5, 10, 11
5:20	9, 12, 32, *56*	7:10	69	9:14	68
5:21	9, *56*	7:11	69	9:17	5, 10, 11
5:22	9, *56*	7:12	69	9:19	11
5:23	56	7:14-17	*69-71*	9:20-21	11
5:24-29	10	7:14-16	52	9:21	5, 8, 10, 11
5:24-25	viii, 10, 11	7:14	12, 16, 67,	10	220
5:24	243		*69-71*, *73-74*, 92,	10:1-4	10, 11, *56-57*
5:25-30	10		95, 105, 150, 226,	10:1-2	11
5:25-29	86		228, 234	10:3-4	11, 65
5:25	5, 10, 195	7:17	19, *71*, 247-48	10:4	viii, 5, 10
5:26-30	5, 11	7:18-25	19	10:5-17	14
5:26-29	78-79	7:19	*71*	10:5-15	11, *79-81*,
5:26	12	7:20	*71*		86, 217
5:27	78-79	7:22	*71-72*	10:5-11	6, 11, 137
5:28	79	7:25	*71-72*	10:5	11, 79, 80, 81
5:29	79, 84, 111, 112	8:1-4	43, 72	10:6	79
5:30	10, 12, 78	8:1-3	77	10:7	79, 137, 248
6:1-9:7	10, 11, 14,	8:1	12, 72, 95, *96-97*	10:9	79, 195
	100	8:2	71	10:10	79
6:1	11, 15, 17, *25-29*,	8:3	12, 44, 71, 72,	10:11	*79-80*
	31, 43, 67, 94,		95, *96-97*	10:12-15	11
	151, 170, 216, 219	8:4	72, 95	10:12-14	28
6:2	29	8:5-8	70, 72-73	10:12	*80*
6:3	*29-31*	8:5	72	10:13	*80*
6:4	15, *31-32*	8:6-8	72, 84	10:14	*80*, 87
6:5-8	237	8:7	58	10:15	13, *80-81*
6:5	*32-33*, 37	8:8	12, 70, 71, 72	10:16-27	13, 19
6:6	32, 33	8:10	12	10:16-19	*81*, 248
6:7	32, *33-34*	8:11-22	12	10:19	99
6:8	*34*	8:16	18, 37, 44, 149	10:20-23	19, 99
6:9-13	*35-43*, 258	8:22	12	10:20-21	99
6:9-10	*35-40*, 41, 58	9	228	10:20	243
6:9	35	9:1-7	12, 16	10:21	107
6:10	39, *98-99*	9:1-2	12	10:22-23	99

10:22	228, 235	15:1-16:14	5, 190	24:12	*196*
10:27-32	13	15:1	32	24:13	194, 195,
10:27	13	15:28-32	5		*196-97*
10:33-34	13	16	190	24:14-16	13
11	220	16:13	190	24:14-15	194
11:1-9	103, 105,	17:1-14	5	24:14	*197*
	111-13, 150, 216,	17:1-6	69, 189	24:15	*197*
	223, 231, 235	17:4	69	24:16	*197-98*
11:1-5	111	17:6	69, 197	24:17-23	194
11:1-4	221	17:7	243	24:17	*198*
11:1	13, 92-93, 105,	17:12-14	189	24:18	*198*
	111	18:1-20:6	5, 77-78	24:20	*198*
11:2	133	18:1-6	189	24:21-23	194, *198-99*
11:3-5	112	18:2	77	24:21	*198*, 229
11:4	105	18:3	77	24:23	*198-99*, 216
11:6-9	*111-12*, 183	18:4	77	25:1-5	*199*
11:6-8	*111-12*	19:1-5	189	25:2	*199*
11:6-7	195	19:2	77	25:4	*199*
11:6	109, 112	19:11-15	77	25:5	*199*
11:10-16	19	19:19-25	208	25:6-8	*199-200*
11:10	13, 230, 234	19:25	239	25:6	*199*
12	5, 13, 19	20:1-6	77, 189	25:7	*200*
12:6	243	21:1-10	5, 190	25:8	*200*, 259
13-39	20, 239	21:5	179	25:9-10	*199-201*
13-23	5, 13, 20, 189	21:9	15	25:10-12	*201*
13:1-22	5, 190	21:11-12	5	25:10	*199, 201*
13:1	5, 15	21:13-17	5	26:20-27:1	*206*
13:19	15	22:1-25	5	26	*201*
14:1-23	5	22:24	31	26:1-6	*201*, 216
14:4-20	129, 190,	23:1-18	5	26:1	*201*
	208-11, 228, 234	24-27	13, 14,	26:6	*201*
14:4-8	*210*		*193-208*, 216	26:7-19	*201-06*
14:4-5	*209*	24	*194-99*	26:7	*201*, 202
14:4	15, *209*, 210	24:1-13	13, *194-95*	26:8-9	*201-02*
14:5	211	24:1-12	194	26:8	*201*, 202
14:7	*209-10*	24:1-3	xi, 20, *195*,	26:9	*201-02*, 204
14:8	*209-10*		197	26:10	*202*
14:9-11	*210*	24:1	*194-95*	26:11	*202*
14:10	*210*	24:2	*195*	26:12	*202*
14:11	*210*	24:3	*195*	26:13	*202*
14:12-15	*210*	24:4-13	197	26:14	*202-03*, 204,
14:12	*210*, 257	24:4-12	196		205, 211
14:13-14	*210*	24:4	*195*, 196	26:15	*203*
14:15	*210*	24:5	*195-96*, 206,	26:16-18	*203-04*
14:16-17	*210-11*		207	26:16	*203*
14:17	*210-11*	24:6	194, *196*	26:17-18	*203-04*
14:18-20	*211*	24:7-9	*196*	26:17	*203*
14:18	*211*	24:7	*196*	26:18	*203-04*, 205
14:19	*211*	24:8	*196*	26:19	*204-06*
14:20	*211*	24:9	*196*	27	*206*
14:22	15	24:10	*196*	27:2-6	*206*
14:24-27	5	24:11	*196*	27:7-11	*206*

27:12-13	*206*	29:9-10	38	35:2	31	
28-39	240	29:19	243	36-39	14, 44	
28:1-31:9	14, 20	30	220	36:1-37:7	87	
28:1-13	249	30:1-7	*83-84*, 87	37:1	15	
28:1-4	*58-59*	30:1	13	37:14	15	
28:1	13, 58, 59	30:3	*83*	37:23	243	
28:2	58	30:4	*83*	37:25	248	
28:3	13, 58	30:5	*83*	38:20	15	
28:4	13, 58, 59	30:6	*83*	38:22	15	
28:5-6	*58-59*	30:7	*83-84*, 136,	39	15	
28:5	13		147, 206	39:8	222	
28:7-13	58, *59-61*	30:8-14	*61-62*	40-66	15, 16, 17, 18,	
28:7-8	59	30:9	*61*		221, 230, 239,	
28:7	13, 59, 60	30:10	*61*, 221		240, 254	
28:8	193	30:11	*61*, 243	40-55	ix, 15, 18, 20,	
28:9-13	*60-61*	30:12	243		113, 117, 119,	
28:9-10	60	30:13-14	*61-62*		136, 163, 164,	
28:9	60, 61	30:15-18	221		167, 215, 243, 244	
28:10	*60-61*, 248	30:15-17	83, *84*, 87	40-48	147, 244	
28:11-13	65	30:15	103, 243	40	117, 122, 123,	
28:11	60, 61	30:18-26	*208*		*124-30*, 133, 228,	
28:12	61	30:19	*208*		243	
28:13	61	30:20	248	40:1-11	226, 228	
28:14-22	*81-84*, 86,	30:26	198, *208*	40:1-2	118	
	249	31:1-3	83, *84*, 85,	40:1	15, 123, *124*,	
28:14	*81-82*		87, 100		126, 156, 226	
28:15	82	31:1	13, 84, 174,	40:2	*124*, 125, 157,	
28:16-17	82		243		252	
28:16	83, 103	31:2	35	40:3-5	118, 126	
28:17	82, 248	31:3	85	40:3-4	*125*	
28:18	82, 100	31:4-5	85, 87, 100,	40:3	*125*, 126	
28:19-22	*82-83*		176	40:4	132	
28:19	82	31:4	85, 111	40:5	119, 123, 125,	
28:20	*82-83*	31:5	86, 100, 103		*126*, 130, 170,	
28:21	38, *83*, 170	31:6-7	84		174, 178, 227, 238	
28:22	83	31:8-9	*84-85*, 87,	40:6-8	118, *126*	
28:23-29	*61*		100	40:6-7	122	
28:23	248	31:8	85	40:6	123, 125, 126,	
29:1-8	*85-86*	31:9	100		130, 150	
29:1-6	86, 87, 100,	32-35	14, 20	40:7	125, *126*	
	249	32-33	14	40:8	*126*, 129	
29:1	13, 85	32:1	14	40:9-11	118	
29:2	85	33	*208*	40:9	123, *126-27*, 180	
29:3	85	33:1	14	40:10	*127*, 130,	
29:4	85	33:7	14		145, 149	
29:5-8	189	33:17-24	*208*	40:11	*127*	
29:5	86	33:17	*208*	40:12-17	118	
29:6	86	33:19	*208*	40:12	122, *127-29*	
29:7-8	86, 87, 100,	33:24	*208*	40:13-14	*127*	
	249	34	14, *208*	40:17	122	
29:7	85, 86	34:5	14	40:18-20	118-19, 139	
29:8	86	35	14, 20			

40:18	122, 127, 128, 144, 152	42:1	133, 148, 155	44:21	*146*, 148, 149
40:21-26	119, 122	42:2-4	*134*	44:23	149
40:21	123, 129	42:2	*134*, 148, 154	44:28	15, 131, 137
40:22-23	129	42:3	*134*	45:1-7	136, *137-38*
40:22	17, 122, 123	42:4	*134*	45:1	131, 134,
40:23-24	130	42:5-9	*134*		*137-38*, 179, 216
40:23	122, 126, *129*, 151, 211	42:6	134	45:4	137, 148
		42:7	134	45:8	163
40:24	111, 122, 129, 131	42:8	134	45:9-10	136
		42:10-13	*134-35*	45:11	243
40:26	124	42:10	135	45:12	145
40:27-31	118, 119	42:13	176	45:16	139
40:27	*129*, 132	42:14-17	*135*	45:20-25	136
40:28	123, 129	42:14	135, 136	46:1	15, 139, *144*
40:29-31	129	42:15	135	46:2	*144*
40:29	130	42:16	*135*	46:4	*144*
40:30	179	42:17	139	46:5-7	139, *144-45*
40:31	*129-30*, 132, 136	42:18	*135*	46:6	*145*
		42:19	*135*, 148	46:7	*145*
41	130, 133	42:22	*135*	46:11	134
41:1	119, *130-31*, 134, 148, 197	42:23	*135*	47:1-15	147
		42:24-25	*135*	47:1	15, *147*
41:2-4	*131-32*	43:1-7	*135-36*	47:2-3	*147*
41:2	119, *131*, 132, 137, 170	43:1	136	47:4	243
		43:2	136, 147	48	148
41:4	130, *131-32*	43:3-4	*136*	48:14	15, 137
41:5	*132*	43:3	243	48:15	134
41:6-7	*132*, 139	43:5-7	178	48:17	243
41:7	119, *132*	43:5	*136*	48:20	15
41:8-10	119	43:6	*136*	49-66	244
41:8	*132*, 133, 148, 149, 156	43:7	*136*	49-57	244
		43:8-15	136	49-55	147, 244
41:9	*132*	43:14	15, 136, 243	49	244
41:10	*132*	43:16-19	136	49:1-6	*148-49*
41:11	145	43:18-19	158	49:1	*148*, 149
41:14	*132*, 243	43:18	218	49:2	152, 156, 224
41:15	*132*, 133	44:1	148, 149	49:3	*148-49*, 151
41:16	132, 243	44:2	148	49:4	*149*
41:17-20	119	44:6-8	136, 145	49:5	*149*
41:18	135, 236	44:8	*146*, 239	49:6	*149*, 225
41:20	243	44:9-20	139, *145-46*	49:7	243
41:21-24	131	44:9-11	*145*	49:9	158
41:21-23	133	44:10	146	49:10	145
41:21	119	44:11	145	49:12	235
41:24	133	44:12	*145*	49:14-15	137, 184
41:25-29	133	44:13	145	49:23	178
41:25	119, 137	44:14	145	49:26	178
41:27	180	44:15	*145*	50:2	175
41:29	119, 133	44:16-17	*145-46*	50:4-9	148, *149-50*, 156
42	133	44:19	*146*		
42:1-4	147	44:20	*146*	50:4	148, *149-50*
		44:21-22	145	50:6	*150*

50:7-9	*150*	54:11	220-21	59	173, *175-77*	
51	136	55	18	59:1-8	*175-76*	
51:3	123	55:3-5	216	59:1-2	*175*	
51:4	174, 176	55:5	243	59:3	*175*	
51:5	163-64, 243	55:10-11	35	59:4-8	*175*	
51:6	183	55:12-13	18, 167	59:4	*175*	
51:9-11	136	55:12	160	59:5	*175*	
51:9-10	206	55:13	183, 184, 236	59:6	*175*	
51:9	136	56-66	ix, 15, 18, 163,	59:9-15	*176*	
51:10	136		167, 215, 243, 244	59:9	*176*	
51:12	123	56-57	244	59:10	*176*	
51:17	178	56	18, 163, 167	59:11	*176*	
51:19	123	56:1-2	18, *163-64*	59:15-20	*176-77*	
52:1	178	56:1	*163-64*, 168	59:16	*176*	
52:7	180, 216	56:2	*164*, 168	59:17	*176*	
52:12	174, 223	56:3-8	18, *164*	59:18	*176-77*	
52:13-53:12	16, 148,	56:3-7	168	60-62	177-81	
	150-58, 223-24, 233	56:4	*164*	60	177-79, 228, 232	
52:13	17, 148, 151,	56:5	*164*	60:1-3	226, 228	
	155, 216, 223	56:6	*164*	60:1	*177-78*	
52:14	*151*, 152	56:7	18, *164*	60:4	*178*	
52:15	27, 150, *151*	56:9-57:13	171	60:8-14	18	
53	220, 228	56:9-12	*165*, 168	60:9	243	
53:1-6	*151-54*, 155	56:9	*165*	60:10	*178*	
53:1	*151-52*	56:10	*165*	60:14	178-79, 243	
53:2	151, *152*, 156,	56:12	*165*	60:16	178, 179	
	159	57-66	244	60:17	*179*	
53:3-8	226, 228	57:1-13	*168-69*	60:18	*179*	
53:3-7	150	57:1-2	*168*	61	*179-80*	
53:3	150, *152*, 159,	57:1	*168*	61:1-4	18	
	220	57:3-5	*168*	61:1-3	*179*, 180	
53:4-5	157	57:3	*168*	61:1-2	233	
53:4	150, *152-53*,	57:5-9	182	61:1	177-78, *179*,	
	154	57:6-13	178		216, 231-32	
53:5	*153*, 155	57:6	*168*	61:2	*180*	
53:6	150, *154*	57:7-8	*168*	61:3	*180*	
53:7-9	*154*	57:8	*168-69*	61:5-7	*180*	
53:7-8	150	57:11	*169*	61:5	*180*	
53:7	*154*, 156	57:13	168, *169*	61:6	*180*	
53:8	*154*, 220	57:15	216	61:8-9	*180*	
53:9	*154*	58-66	244	61:10-11	180	
53:10-11	*154-55*	58	173	62	*180-81*	
53:10	150, *154-55*,	58:1-12	*174-75*	62:4-5	*181*	
	159, 223	58:2	*174*	62:5	*181*	
53:11-12	154	58:3	*174*	62:12	*181*	
53:11	150, *154-55*	58:5	*174*	63	171	
53:12	150, *155-56*,	58:6	*174*	63:4-64:12	*169-73*	
	159, 223	58:7	*174*	63:7-9	*169*	
54-55	160	58:8	*174*	63:10	*169*	
54	220	58:9-12	*174*	63:11-13	*169*	
54:1	160, 181, 223	58:9-10	*174*	63:11	*171*, 173	
54:5	243	58:9	*174*	63:12	*171*, 173	

63:15-64:12	*170*	23:22	124	*Joel*		
63:15	*170*	27:2	77	3:10	191	
63:16	*171, 173,* 184	28:8-9	91	3:28	52	
63:17	*173*	28:10	77			
64	*170-71*	30:5-7	246-47	*Amos*		
64:1-2	*170*	30:10-11	247	1:2	85, 101	
64:3	*170*	30:12-15	247	3:7	94	
64:8	*171, 173,* 184	30:16-17	247	3:12	84, 112	
65	*181-84*	31:29-30	205	5:3	97	
65:1	*181*	32:18	107	5:15	97-98	
65:2	*181*	40:5-6	166	5:21-24	51	
65:3	*181-82*	41:5	172			
65:4	*182*	48	190	*Obadiah*		
65:5	*182,* 192	51:5	243	8-14	166	
65:6-7	*182*	52	14			
65:8-12	*182-83*			*Micah*		
65:13-15	*182-83*	*Lamentations*		1:2	46	
65:17-25	*183-84,* 193	4:22	124	1:5-9	101	
65:17	*183*			3:10	81	
65:18-19	*183*	*Ezekiel*		3:12	81, 101	
65:20	112, *183*	1:28	26, 42	4:1-4	8, 19, 191	
65:21-22	*183*	16	181	6:1-2	46	
65:25	112, *183-84*	16:44	82	6:2	70	
66:1-6	*177*	18	205	6:4	171	
66:1	*177*	20:32	140			
66:3-4	*177*	23	181	*Haggai*		
66:3	*177,* 182	29:3	84	1:2-11	175	
66:13	184-85	38-39	222	1:2-3	167	
66:15-16	14	38:12	102	1:4-6	166	
		40-42	179	1:7-11	167	
Jeremiah		40:46	172	1:12	167	
1:5	148, 225	43:18-27	177	2:2	166	
1:6-7	52	44:11	179	2:20-23	166	
1:6	34	45:11	54			
2-3	181	48:11	172	*Zechariah*		
2:4	149			8:20-23	191-92	
2:12	46	*Daniel*				
2:16	168	10:12-13	198	*Matthew*		
2:25	168	12:1-2	205	1:23	70, 73-75	
2:27	140			4:1-11	159	
3	216	*Hosea*		5:9	110	
4:23-26	129	1-3	181	8:11	235	
5:6	112	1	77	8:17	150	
6:18-19	46	1:4	96	9:36	159	
10:1-16	140, 253	1:6	96	10:6	159	
11:19	154	1:9	96	10:29-31	137	
11:20	255	3:4	104	11:22	228	
14:2-6	195	4:1	70	12:18-21	133	
14:3-4	200	4:9	195	13:13	36, 41	
15:1	171	8:4	104	16:1-3	61	
17:6	152	12:2	70	21:3-5	110	
23:10	196	13:10-11	104	23:23	51	

23:29-39	40	15:51-57	228	**Books of Adam**	
23:37	40	15:54-55	200	**and Eve**	
		15:54	259	xii	257
Mark					
4:12	36, 41	**Galatians**		**Apostolic Fathers:**	
7:14-23	33	6:16	236		
8:31	150				
9:12	150	**Philippians**		**Justin Martyr,**	
9:31	150	2:9-10	110	**First Apology**	
10:45	150			§35	251
Luke		**Hebrews**			
1:32-33	110	1:1-2	238	**Ugaritic Texts**	
1:46-55	135	1:1	21	**(Gordon's**	
1:51-53	135	11:37	44	**Numeration)**	
2	228			§49 I 26-37	257
4:16-21	x, 4	**James**		VI 35ff	256
4:16-20	178	5:12	33	§77 22-23	247
4:18-19	233			§137 20-21	256
4:18	232				
6:20-26	182-83	**Revelation**		**Qumran Texts**	
8:10	36, 41	5:12-13	226	1QSa II 17-21	256
10:15	228	8:10-11	228		
10:29-37	164				
11:11-13	137			**Other Ancient Near**	
13:29	200	**Old Testament**		**Eastern Texts:**	
14:15-24	200	**Pseudepigrapha:**			
18:1-6	50			**Wen Amun**	
		(Ethiopian) Enoch		35-41	245
John		18:14	256		
17:5	231	86:1-2	256	**Sargon, Display**	
				Inscription, Year 1	
Acts		**2 Enoch**		10-17	250
2:44-47	113	29:4-5	257		
8:27-35	150			**Sargon, Display**	
23:6-8	206	**Jubilees**		**Inscription, Year 5**	
		8:19	251	72-76	76, 248
Romans					
9:27	228, 235	**2 Baruch ([Syriac]**		**Sennacherib**	
9:29	228, 235	**Apocalypse of Baruch**		**Inscription**	
11:17-24	236	29:4	256		88, 249
15:21	150				
		Martyrdom of Isaiah		**Cyrus Cylinder**	
1 Corinthians			246	30-32	255
8	140